HIDDEN VALUE

HOW TO REVEAL THE IMPACT OF ORGANIZATIONAL LEARNING

DR. KEITH KEATING

ISBN: 979-8-89079-282-2 (hardcover)
ISBN: 979-8-89079-279-2 (paperback)
ISBN: 979-8-89079-280-8 (ebook)

Jetlaunch Publishing
Illustrations by Jake Tobin

TABLE OF CONTENTS

INTRODUCTION

*"What we think, we become. What we feel, we attract.
What we imagine, we create."*

—Buddha

"What do you do here?"

As the story goes, President John F. Kennedy posed this question as he stood in NASA's luminous hallway, face-to-face with a janitor gripping his broom. It was the 1960s, and Kennedy's moonshot vision was taking shape in the surrounding buildings. The President, known for engaging everyone around him with equal respect, looked at the man before him with genuine interest.

The middle-aged janitor, with a warm smile and a gleam of pride in his eyes, didn't hesitate. Standing taller, he met the President's gaze and answered with quiet conviction: "Mr. President, I'm helping put a man on the moon."

Whether fact or parable, this story has been widely shared as a testament to the purpose and value of employees in an organization. The janitor could have described his daily tasks—sweeping floors, emptying bins, maintaining cleanliness. Instead, he saw beyond the mundane to recognize his role in one of humanity's greatest achievements. He understood something profound:

*Excellence isn't built by lone geniuses but by
an ecosystem of contributors.*

The President, they say, was speechless.

And why wouldn't he be? Would you or I have made the connection between our work and greater purpose so readily? Most of us might have described the tasks: sweeping, cleaning, and maintenance.

> EXCELLENCE ISN'T BUILT BY LONE GENIUSES BUT BY AN ECOSYSTEM OF CONTRIBUTORS.

Even the President, with his grand vision of space exploration, might have seen *just* a janitor doing his job. However, this janitor saw deeper. He understood his daily work, however mundane it might appear, was intrinsically linked to NASA's mission. Most remarkably, he didn't downplay his role or wait for others to recognize his value. He knew it himself and spoke it with quiet confidence.

Therein lies the challenge for learning and development (L&D) practitioners. Every day, you face the same question: What do you do here? Too often, the response includes the list of tasks: scheduling training, designing modules, and managing platforms. However, your true impact, like the janitor's, extends far beyond your daily activities. You're not *just* delivering programs but architecting transformations that ripple through entire organizations. And like the janitor, *you create conditions where excellence becomes possible.*

This powerful anecdote illuminates a fundamental truth: achieving excellence depends on an ecosystem of hidden enablers. Just as NASA's achievements required astronauts and janitors, organizational success relies on visible leaders and vital catalysts behind the scenes. You are one of the hidden enablers, creating environments where innovation thrives, careers transform, and organizations grow.

THE POWER OF THE UNSEEN

Consider the humble honeybee. On a single spring day, a bee might visit thousands of flowers, leaving behind no trace except perhaps a fallen petal. Now, imagine a world without bees—crops failing, food chains collapsing, and ecosystems unraveling. It sounds apocalyptic, yet few notice these tiny architects of life until they're gone. Their silent work pollinates one-third of the world's food supply, generating $9 billion annually for the U.S. economy alone. Still, most see them as nothing more than insects that sting.

Your impact mirrors this similar pattern. Like the bee transforming one flower's scattered pollen into an ecosystem's sustenance, you transform individual learning moments into organizational capabilities. Yet, this vital contribution often becomes apparent only in absence: when skills gaps widen, change initiatives falter, and talent leaves for better development opportunities.

While stakeholders might focus on surface metrics—completion rates, smile sheets, training hours, program costs—the true transformation unfolds beneath: culture shifts, emerging capabilities, and tomorrow's competitive advantage taking root.

So, what do *you* do here?

Before you answer, consider this:

YOU ARE A CATALYST FOR
TRANSFORMATION, A
CHAMPION OF GROWTH,
AND AN ARCHITECT OF
POTENTIAL.

When a customer service representative applies your conflict resolution training to defuse a volatile situation—that's your impact.

When a manager uses the leadership skills you taught to transform a toxic team into a high-performing unit—that's your fingerprint.

When an organization successfully navigates change using the adaptability frameworks you implemented—that's your legacy.

You are a catalyst for transformation, a champion of growth, and an architect of potential.

However, here's the reality: Most people don't see it—yet.

Learning is the lifeblood of innovation and progress; you are its steward. Without your efforts to nurture, enable, and advocate for learning, individuals might struggle to adapt, teams could lose their edge, and organizations would stagnate in the face of change. Your work doesn't just support the organization; it propels it forward, equipping people with the tools and confidence they need to meet today's challenges and seize tomorrow's opportunities.

FROM HIDDEN TO INDISPENSABLE

In today's rapidly evolving business landscape, learning agility isn't just advantageous; it's existential. Organizations that fail to nurture learning face extinction. The business world is littered with examples of companies that once led their industries but faltered when they failed to embrace a learning culture. Nokia, a pioneer in mobile technology, couldn't adapt to the rapid rise of smartphones, losing its competitive edge by clinging to outdated strengths rather than equipping its workforce to innovate. For over a century, Sears, a retail giant, relied too heavily on legacy business models instead of learning to anticipate and respond to shifting consumer expectations. Toys

"R" Us followed a similar path, outsourcing innovation instead of fostering internal learning, and ultimately collapsed in the face of e-commerce disruptors.

On the other hand, organizations that prioritize learning agility not only survive but also thrive. Microsoft, under CEO Satya Nadella, offers a powerful example of what happens when learning becomes a cultural cornerstone. By shifting to a "learn-it-all" mindset, Microsoft reinvigorated its workforce, embracing cloud computing and artificial intelligence to reclaim its place as a global technology leader. Similarly, Amazon has embedded learning into its DNA, cultivating a culture of curiosity and adaptation. Its "day one thinking" philosophy empowers employees at every level to embrace change, acquire new skills, and innovate continuously, enabling Amazon to evolve from an online bookstore to a global powerhouse in e-commerce, logistics, and cloud computing.

The pandemic further underscored the critical nature of learning agility. Companies that rapidly retrained their workforce on new technologies or adapted their business models—such as healthcare providers pivoting to telemedicine or manufacturers shifting production to personal protective equipment—demonstrated resilience and remained competitive. Meanwhile, those who lacked a culture of learning found themselves struggling to navigate the crisis.

The lesson is clear: *Organizational learning is no longer optional; it's the cornerstone of survival and growth in today's volatile business landscape.* Learning is no longer *just* a support function; it's a strategic imperative. Organizations must embrace a learning culture and embed it into their DNA, ensuring every individual—from the frontline worker to the executive—has the tools and mindset to adapt to whatever challenges the future holds.

Yet paradoxically, while the importance of learning has never been greater, its value often remains unrealized and inadequately measured. Too many organizations still view learning as a "nice-to-have" rather than an indispensable driver of performance and resilience. This misalignment leaves untapped potential on the table and creates blind spots that can jeopardize long-term success.

Just as the NASA janitor understood his role was more than his tasks, and as bees sustain life through their daily work, *you drive evolution throughout your organization*. Your role transcends the tactical to become strategic, the visible to influence the hidden, and the immediate to shape the future. By connecting people to purpose and empowering them with knowledge, you create conditions for individuals, teams, and entire organizations to flourish.

In my earlier work, I emphasized the importance of moving beyond a reactive, order-taking role to become a trusted learning advisor—a strategic partner aligned with business priorities. The key takeaway was clear: Trust and influence are built when your work directly connects to organizational goals and speaks to what stakeholders value most.

This book builds on that foundation. While trust is essential, it's just the beginning. To thrive in today's competitive environment, you must make your value unmistakable. This book equips you with practical frameworks, proven strategies, and actionable tools to identify, create, measure, and amplify your impact, ensuring your value is visible, understood, and recognized.

Your journey begins by uncovering the **Hidden Network**—an intricate web where learning powers every aspect of organizational success, often in ways we never see. This revelation leads you to discover **The Diamond's Secret**, where you'll master the art of understanding value and recognizing what others routinely overlook.

Armed with a **Treasure Hunter's Guide**, you'll develop an eye for spotting hidden opportunities, transforming you into a true **Value Architect** who creates an impact that resonates throughout your organization. Like an explorer uncovering **Ancient Tracks**, you'll learn to measure what truly matters, translating your discoveries into compelling evidence through **The Untold Well**, where raw data transforms into stories that captivate stakeholders.

As your influence grows, you'll harness **The Purple Cow Effect**, ensuring your impact stands out and leaves a lasting impression. This distinctive presence catalyzes a **Breakfast Revolution**, where learning becomes as essential to your organization's daily rhythm as the morning meal. When challenges arise—and they will—the

Bridge Builder's Handbook equips you with practical strategies to transform obstacles into opportunities.

Each chapter flows into the next, taking you from understanding the hidden power of your work to making its value clear and compelling at every level of your organization. Like an expert **Water Bearer**, you'll learn to channel learning's life-giving force through your organization, making the hidden not just visible but indispensable.

This isn't just a journey of discovery; it's an opportunity to illuminate your true value. By the end, you'll be equipped to help others recognize the vital force you bring to your organization, revealing what has always been there.

You stand at a pivotal moment in organizational history. The accelerating pace of technological advancements, shifting workforce dynamics, and global disruptions have created an unprecedented level of uncertainty. Yet, where others see disruption and risk, you see opportunity—the chance to redefine how organizations grow, adapt, and thrive in this new era.

This moment is critical because the stakes have never been higher. Organizations that fail to make learning a core capability risk irrelevance, while those that embed it into their DNA unlock an unrivaled competitive edge. You are uniquely positioned to lead this transformation. This book's tools, frameworks, and strategies will help you create a measurable impact and establish learning as a driving force behind innovation, resilience, and success.

Your impact ripples far beyond training rooms and learning platforms; it transforms careers, elevates teams, and propels entire organizations forward. You are not just responding to change; you are shaping the future.

It's time to bring your hidden value into the light. The story of revealing your true impact begins now. Turn the page.

1

HIDDEN NETWORK: HOW LEARNING POWERS EVERYTHING

"The more that you read, the more things you will know.
The more that you learn, the more places you'll go."

—Dr. Seuss

THE FOREST BENEATH THE SURFACE

Deep in the Amazon rainforest stands the Kapok Tree, its massive trunk and sprawling canopy dominating the landscape. At first glance, the Kapok appears as the rainforest's hero—a vital centerpiece in the ecosystem, providing visible shelter for monkeys, birds, and countless other species. However, the Kapok's strength comes from two hidden systems: its extensive root network that anchors and nourishes it and an even more remarkable hidden world that connects the entire forest.

If you were to dig beneath the surface, you'd discover the mycelium network—a vast web of underground fungi that links not just the Kapok's roots but nearly every tree in the forest. This hidden network cycles nutrients, facilitates communication, and ensures the entire ecosystem thrives. The quiet force fuels life, fosters resilience, and allows giants like the Kapok to flourish.

Scientists call this network the "wood-wide web" because of its remarkable ability to sustain and strengthen the forest. Like the internet connecting computers across the globe, this unseen network links trees in an intricate dance of survival and growth.

If the mycelium disappeared, the forest wouldn't immediately collapse, but over time, it would falter. The majestic trees would wither without its support, and the ecosystem around them would unravel. Though hidden from most eyes, the network is critical to the forest's survival.

Ecosystems thrive because of their interconnectedness. Every element, whether above or below the surface, plays a role in sustaining the whole. Like these natural networks, learning creates both visible achievements and hidden foundations that make those achievements possible. While we can see learning's impact through changed behaviors and improved performance, the deeper processes of growth, connection, and development often remain hidden beneath the surface, quietly powering everything we do.

THE TRANSFORMATIVE POWER OF LEARNING

The forest's hidden network and learning share a common power: operating through invisible processes that enable remarkable transformations. Perhaps no example illustrates this better than nature's master of metamorphosis: the caterpillar. At first glance, it appears unremarkable: a creature that inches along the ground, focused only on survival, its world confined to leaves and earth. Yet within this modest being lies the blueprint for an extraordinary change.

LEARNING IS OUR CHRYSALIS.

The caterpillar undergoes one of nature's most remarkable processes within its chrysalis. It doesn't simply grow wings; it completely breaks down its existing structure, dissolving and rebuilding itself cell by cell. This hidden metamorphosis transforms the creature entirely, turning a ground-bound caterpillar into a soaring butterfly. When it emerges, it experiences the world from an entirely new perspective, discovering capabilities its former self never could have imagined.

Learning is our chrysalis.

Like the caterpillar's transformation, learning empowers us to break free from perceived limitations and rebuild ourselves. The process may not be visible—as it's happening beneath the surface—but its impact reshapes what we can do and who we become.

THE DROPOUT PROPHECY

At fifteen, I walked away from high school, carrying the weight of others' judgments with each step.

The contradictions haunted me. Some teachers saw potential, urging me to skip grades, while others branded me with a learning disability—a label that clung to me like a shadow. "You'll never amount to much," they said, their words sharp with certainty. "Fast food work will be your ceiling"—as if serving others was somehow beneath dignity and honest work could diminish human worth.

The cruelest part was I believed them.

With their verdict echoing in my mind, I took a job in fast food. I worked hard and found pride in small tasks but felt trapped in a narrative I didn't know how to rewrite. My world felt small, confined like a caterpillar to the ground. I wanted more but didn't know what "more" looked like or how to get there.

I thought the problem was me—that I wasn't smart enough or disciplined enough to succeed. I couldn't see that my potential wasn't limited; it was just waiting to be unleashed. I simply hadn't found my chrysalis yet.

THE TURNING POINT

The exact moment my life began to change wasn't in a classroom or through some grand epiphany; it was on a quiet Sunday afternoon as I flipped through the classified ads in the local paper. Among the columns of job postings, one headline caught my eye: "Microsoft Office Trainer."

At seventeen, I was still working in fast food and carrying the weight of others' judgments. However, something about that ad sparked curiosity—and something more. *I use Microsoft Office,* I thought. *How hard could it be to teach it?*

I applied without qualifications, without experience, with nothing but the raw conviction that I could figure it out. Surprisingly, I got the job—not for any expertise (I had none) but because I had car insurance and no criminal record. Just like that, I was responsible for teaching government employees how to use Microsoft Office 2000.

Reality hit hard on day one. Standing in front of a room of adults who expected guidance through Excel formulas and PowerPoint presentations, the weight of what I'd taken on nearly crushed me. I didn't know how to teach. I barely knew the content. My first few classes were disasters—awkward silences, blank stares, and a deep sense of inadequacy that kept me awake at night.

However, instead of giving up, I made a decision:

I would learn.

LEARNING TO LEARN

Before I could teach others, I had to become a student. Each night after work, I immersed myself in Microsoft Office's world. I pored over user manuals until my eyes burned, tested every function I could find, and deliberately broke things just to understand how to fix them. More than desperation drove me, I discovered a hunger to understand the how and why behind each tool, task, and function.

Little by little, something remarkable happened. I began to see patterns—not just in the software but in my mind. Complex features that once seemed overwhelming could be broken down into smaller pieces, like puzzle parts waiting to be connected. I realized I wasn't just learning Microsoft Office; I was discovering how my mind worked and how I learned best. For the first time in my life, I wasn't fighting against my way of learning; I was working with it.

> TELLING ISN'T TEACHING.

Through this process, I stumbled upon a truth that would change everything:

Telling isn't teaching.

Standing in front of a room reciting instructions wasn't enough. Real teaching meant taking what I'd learned and transforming it into something others could grasp, something that mattered to them. Each class became an experiment, and each student's reaction was a lesson on what worked and what didn't. Slowly and steadily, I began to find my way.

THE MOMENT OF DISCOVERY

About six months into the role, something remarkable happened. I was guiding a group through Excel formulas—a task that had once intimidated me. As we worked through the problem together, breaking down the logic step by step, something magical happened; the lightbulb moment appeared.

A woman in the back of the room looked up, her eyes bright with sudden understanding. In that instant, I saw myself reflected in her expression—that same rush of discovery and thrill of mastery. I realized the true power of what I was doing: I wasn't just teaching Excel but unlocking potential.

That moment transformed me.

I was no longer the high school dropout carrying the weight of a "learning disability" label. I was someone who could make a difference and help others break through their own barriers. Each class became an opportunity to prove that limiting narratives—mine and others'—could be rewritten.

> LEARNING SAVED MY LIFE.

The job became my mission. I pushed myself to master new topics so I could teach them, each challenge building my confidence, each success expanding my horizons. There was a beautiful irony in it all: The kid who'd been told he'd never amount to much was now teaching government professionals, helping them excel in their careers.

Learning saved my life.

It gave me the tools to rewrite my story and adapt to challenges I once thought were insurmountable. Each small victory—mastering formulas in Excel, guiding a student to a breakthrough, or finally understanding how I learned best—built something more profound than just skills. It built belief in myself.

Psychologist Albert Bandura describes this as *self-efficacy*—the confidence that comes from mastering challenging tasks, which then fuels your ability to tackle future obstacles. Each success rewrote the narrative I'd carried for years, transforming "I'm not good enough" into "I can figure this out." It wasn't just about Microsoft Office; it was about reclaiming my potential, breaking through the boundaries others had placed around me, and discovering the power of learning to unlock entirely new possibilities.

THE RIPPLE EFFECT

In the same way the mycelium network nourishes an entire forest, learning's influence permeates every level of human experience, creating connections that transform lives, organizations, and societies. Learning transforms the world in three ways: First, *learning unlocks human potential.* Second, *learning fuels organizational evolution.* Finally, *learning shapes entire societies.* Each dimension reveals a different facet of learning's extraordinary power to create change.

1. LEARNING UNLOCKS HUMAN POTENTIAL

Imagine standing in front of a locked door, unsure of what lies beyond. In your hand is a key, but you've never been shown how to use it. That's what untapped potential feels like—a store of energy waiting to be released. Learning isn't just the key that turns the lock; it's the force that transforms potential energy into kinetic energy, setting progress into motion and unlocking what's possible.

Take James, for example. He worked as a customer service representative at a mid-sized insurance company. By all accounts, James was excellent at his job and known for his empathy and professionalism. However, behind his polite demeanor, he felt stuck and unsure about how to move forward.

When his company introduced a professional development program, everything changed. Courses on communication, problem-solving, and conflict resolution gave James the tools he needed, and the encouragement of his manager gave him the confidence to dive in. Slowly, James began to see himself differently—not *just* as a customer service representative but as a leader in the making.

> LEARNING DOESN'T JUST PROVIDE SKILLS; IT UNLOCKS POTENTIAL.

A year later, James wasn't just thriving in his role; he was promoted to a team lead position. However, the impact didn't stop there. The confidence James gained at work began to ripple into his personal life. He started mentoring his younger siblings, helping them navigate their education and career paths.

*Learning doesn't just provide skills;
it unlocks potential.*

It transforms how we see ourselves, challenges our internalized limitations, and opens doors we never thought we could walk through.

For me, learning was a lifeline. As a high school dropout, I had accepted the world's harshest judgments about my lack of potential. I believed the voices that told me I wasn't good enough and wouldn't amount to anything. I lived inside the small, confining story those voices had written for me for a long time.

Learning shattered that narrative.

It didn't just give me the tools to survive; it gave me the confidence to grow, the agency to change, and the courage to dream. Learning showed me that the future wasn't fixed; it could be rewritten. It didn't just teach me how to navigate uncertainty; it gave me the power to thrive in it.

This journey took me from being a high school dropout to earning a doctorate in education from an Ivy League university. Learning didn't just change what I could do; it transformed who I believed I could become. It proved that growth is possible, even in the face of doubt and uncertainty, and that we can rewrite the stories we've been told about ourselves.

Think about your organization. Many people are waiting for the same opportunity to rewrite their stories. They need your guidance, support, and belief in their potential to reach new levels of success.

The Seed and the Soil

A seed holds everything it needs to grow into a towering tree but cannot thrive without the right conditions—water, sunlight, and fertile soil. Learning is the catalyst that transforms potential into growth, much like sunlight activates life within the seed.

Think of an employee who hesitates to speak up in meetings, doubting their ability to contribute. They attend a workshop on communication skills and begin to take small steps, sharing ideas here and there. Each moment of bravery builds confidence, and over time, they transform. That same employee might go on to lead a project, mentor others, or drive innovation—all because learning gave them the tools to unlock what was already inside.

The transformation through learning extends beyond individual achievement. When one person's potential is unlocked, they naturally inspire and elevate others, creating ripples of growth across teams, organizations, and communities. Each person who grows through learning becomes a catalyst for others' development.

Think back to the caterpillar, inching its way through the world, unaware of what it's capable of becoming. Inside, it carries all the ingredients for transformation, but it takes the right process—its chrysalis phase—to reorganize and reimagine itself into a butterfly.

Learning is our chrysalis; it reveals, reorganizes, and activates what's already there. It helps us see the possibilities within ourselves and gives us the confidence to take flight.

2. LEARNING FUELS ORGANIZATIONAL EVOLUTION

Picture a world where the rules of business are rewritten daily—where industries rise and fall, established practices become obsolete, and market opportunities emerge and vanish rapidly. In this professional landscape, organizations wake each morning facing unprecedented uncertainty. The foundation of tried-and-true business methods shifts like sand, and ambiguity pervades every decision. Traditional approaches and legacy skills that once guaranteed success now cloud our ability to navigate this constantly changing terrain. The urgency to adapt and evolve has replaced the comfort of established business knowledge and proven expertise.

> "FOR AN ORGANIZATION TO SURVIVE, ITS RATE OF LEARNING MUST BE AT LEAST EQUAL TO THE RATE OF CHANGE IN ITS EXTERNAL ENVIRONMENT."

Now, imagine stepping into your workplace in this world. The energy is electric, but it's tinged with an undercurrent of anxiety. Your colleagues are hustling to keep up, learning new skills on the fly, and pivoting strategies to stay relevant. It's exhilarating and exhausting all at once. You can't help but wonder: *Is this what the future holds?*

The truth is that this isn't a hypothetical future. It's the reality organizations face in today's world—a relentless acceleration of change that reshapes industries, upends business models, and redefines the skills required to succeed. Technology evolves at breakneck speed, markets demand constant reinvention, and employee expectations are in perpetual flux. In this environment, survival isn't about keeping pace; it's about staying ahead.

Professor Reginald Revans—a pioneer in action learning—articulated this reality in what's known as Revans' Law:

> *"For an organization to survive, its rate of learning*
> *must be at least equal to the rate of change*
> *in its external environment."*

Think about that for a moment. If change is exponential—and by every measure, it is—the ability to learn must also grow exponentially. Without continuous learning, an organization risks becoming irrelevant and overtaken by competitors who are faster to adapt. In many ways, *learning is the engine of survival and success.* It is the bridge between where an organization is today and where it needs to be tomorrow.

The Culture of Learning

Organizations that embrace learning as a core value become more agile, innovative, and resilient. They aren't just reacting to change; they're anticipating it, equipping their people with the skills and mindset to navigate uncharted waters. In a learning culture, employees aren't paralyzed by disruption; they're energized by it. They see change not as a threat but as an opportunity.

Think about an employee confronted with a new challenge, like transitioning to a technology-heavy role or managing a team for the first time. Without learning, they may falter, struggling to find their footing in unfamiliar territory. However, with access to continuous development—whether through coaching, workshops, or self-directed learning—they can adapt, thrive, and even lead through uncertainty.

Learning doesn't just unlock individual potential; *learning amplifies the collective potential of teams and organizations.* The ripple effect drives long-term success when people are equipped to solve complex problems, take calculated risks, and innovate.

Satya Nadella and Microsoft: A Case Study in Organizational Learning

When Nadella joined Microsoft in 1992 as an engineer, the company was synonymous with software dominance. Yet even in a company filled with brilliant minds, Nadella stood out—not because he knew more than his peers but because of his unrelenting commitment to learning. He understood that leadership required more than technical expertise; it demanded strategic insight, emotional intelligence, and a growth mindset.

While working full-time at Microsoft, Nadella pursued a part-time MBA at the University of Chicago, bridging the gap between his technical background and the broader business acumen needed to lead. His deliberate approach to learning prepared him for pivotal roles, including his leadership of Microsoft's Server and Tools division in 2011. At the time, the company was struggling to keep pace with competitors like Amazon Web Services in the rapidly evolving cloud technology space. Nadella immersed himself in learning everything about the cloud, both technically and strategically, and spearheaded the transformation of Microsoft Azure into one of the world's leading cloud platforms.

By the time Nadella became CEO in 2014, Microsoft faced existential questions. It had missed major trends like mobile computing and social media and was often viewed as a legacy tech company. Nadella's first act as CEO wasn't to launch a flashy new product or restructure the company but to change its mindset.

His philosophy was simple but profound:

"Don't be a know-it-all; be a learn-it-all."

Nadella infused this ethos into Microsoft's culture, encouraging leaders and employees to embrace curiosity, continuous growth, and a willingness to adapt. The result? A revitalized Microsoft that not only caught up but also often led the way in innovation. Under his leadership, Microsoft's stock price surged by over 900 percent, its valuation surpassed $3 trillion, and the company became a leader in cloud computing and artificial intelligence through its Azure platform. In contrast, during the previous "know-it-all" era under Steve Ballmer, Microsoft's stock performance stagnated, reflecting a company that struggled to innovate and adapt. Nadella's "learn-it-all" philosophy didn't just shift Microsoft's mindset; it drove exponential growth and redefined its relevance in the modern tech landscape.

> "DON'T BE A KNOW-IT-ALL; BE A LEARN-IT-ALL."

The Exponential Demand for Learning

Microsoft's story highlights a larger truth: Learning is no longer optional; it's essential. As industries are transformed overnight and the skills of today become obsolete tomorrow, the ability to learn, unlearn, and relearn becomes the most critical competency for any organization.

Consider jobs that didn't exist a decade ago: data scientists, UX designers, and AI trainers. Each of these roles emerged in response to technological advances and shifting market demands. Now, think about the jobs of the next decade, many of which we can't yet imagine. Think about that for a moment. How do you prepare for a role that hasn't been invented yet? The answer lies not in what you know but in your capacity to learn. Organizations that foster a culture of continuous learning will be the ones to pivot, thrive, and lead in this new reality.

In this volatile environment, learning isn't just a skill; learning is the foundation of organizational agility. It's what allows teams to reimagine their approaches, innovate at scale, and stay ahead of disruption. Without learning, organizations risk stagnation and irrelevance.

3. LEARNING SHAPES SOCIETIES

It starts with a single drop.

Picture yourself standing at the edge of a calm, glassy pond. The surface is so still it mirrors the sky above. You pick up a small pebble and toss it in. The splash seems insignificant for a moment—barely noticeable in the vast expanse of water. Then, something remarkable happens: Ripples begin to form. They grow wider, stretching outward, touching parts of the pond far beyond where the pebble landed.

Learning is that pebble. It starts small—a new skill, a moment of understanding, a flash of inspiration—but its ripples extend far beyond the individual. Those ripples flow into families, communities, and entire societies, creating waves of change that can reshape the world.

A FORCE FOR EQUITY AND EMPOWERMENT

Learning is more than personal growth; it's a force for equity, empowerment, and societal advancement. Learning bridges divides, breaks cycles of poverty, and empowers individuals to rewrite their narratives. When people gain access to learning, they unlock their potential and, with it, the ability to contribute to the collective good.

Take the story of Project Shakti, an initiative launched by Hindustan Unilever Limited in 2001 to address systemic challenges in rural India. The project aimed to empower women by offering them the opportunity to become micro-entrepreneurs. These women, known as "Shakti Ammas," learned business and sales skills to sell Unilever products in their local communities.

By the end of 2020, over 136,000 women across eighteen states had joined as Shakti Ammas, earned sustainable incomes, and gained first-time access to formal banking systems. However, the impact of Project Shakti went far beyond economic empowerment. These women became role models in their communities, fostering a culture of self-reliance and confidence. The program tackled systemic gender inequality by giving women tools to succeed, transforming not just their lives but the lives of their families and neighbors.

This ripple effect—starting with learning and extending to entire communities—illustrates the profound societal power of learning. It's not just about skills; it's about creating environments where equity and opportunity thrive.

The Power of Access: The Story of Khan Academy

Another example of learning's transformative power on societies is reflected in Khan Academy, a platform that has redefined access to education globally. When Sal Khan began tutoring his cousin in math, he could never have imagined the ripples his efforts would create. His simple, self-made videos became the foundation for a global movement to democratize learning.

Since its founding, Khan Academy has reached over 145 million users in 190 countries, offering free, world-class education to anyone with an internet connection. Its resources, translated into more than fifty languages, have opened doors for students who might otherwise have been left behind.

In Colombia, for example, rural schools with limited resources adopted Khan Academy to supplement their curricula. Students who had once struggled with basic math began excelling, outperforming expectations on national tests. Teachers used the platform to "flip" their classrooms, assigning videos for homework and using class time for interactive discussions. The results were transformative—not just in academic outcomes but in the confidence and aspirations of the students themselves.

Sal Khan's commitment to learning didn't stop there. In 2023, he launched Khanmigo, an AI-powered tutor and teaching assistant designed to personalize learning experiences for students. Leveraging advanced AI, Khanmigo helps guide learners through subjects like math, science, and coding, fostering critical thinking and problem-solving skills. Unlike traditional AI tools, Khanmigo emphasizes helping students discover answers themselves, deepening their understanding and engagement. Beyond benefiting students, it also supports educators by assisting with lesson planning and providing immediate feedback, making teaching more impactful and efficient.

Khan Academy and Khanmigo exemplify how accessible learning and continual innovation can break down barriers of privilege, geography, and cost, creating opportunities for societal uplift. It's a powerful reminder that education is not a zero-sum game; its benefits multiply, touching lives far beyond the individual learner.

LEARNING'S TRANSFORMATIVE IMPACT ON SOCIETY

Leading global institutions have extensively documented learning's profound societal impact. Economic mobility emerges as a critical outcome, with the Brookings Institution showing how higher education levels consistently correlate with increased earnings and improved employment prospects. This isn't just about individual success; it's about breaking cycles of economic limitation and opening doors of opportunity that span generations.

The impact on gender equality proves equally striking. UNESCO's research reveals a powerful correlation: Each additional year of girls' schooling can boost their future earnings by up to 20 percent. Moreover, countries that invest in female education see cascading benefits: lower child mortality rates, better maternal health outcomes, and stronger economic growth. This demonstrates how learning acts as a catalyst for broader societal advancement.

The World Bank's research reveals learning's role in building stable, equitable societies. Education stands as one of our most powerful tools for reducing poverty, improving health outcomes, advancing gender equality, and fostering peace and stability. It delivers consistent returns in income and creates more inclusive, equitable communities.

Perhaps most striking is learning's impact on global poverty. UNESCO's research points to a revolutionary possibility: World poverty could be cut by more than half if all adults completed secondary education. This startling finding underscores learning's potential to break intergenerational cycles of poverty and create lasting social change.

These findings reinforce what we've seen in programs like Project Shakti, where learning catalyzes both individual and community transformation. When women gain business skills and knowledge, they don't just improve their lives; they lift entire communities. Similarly, platforms like Khan Academy, reaching over 145 million users across 190 countries, demonstrate how digital learning can democratize access to knowledge and create opportunities at an unprecedented scale.

The evidence is clear: Learning doesn't *just* change lives; learning transforms societies. It acts as a fundamental driver of progress, breaking down barriers, opening opportunities, and creating ripples of positive change that extend far beyond the individual learner. Just as societies thrive when they prioritize education, innovation, and shared growth, organizations succeed when they embed learning into their culture. In many ways, organizations mirror societies; they are ecosystems of people, ideas, and relationships shaped by a shared vision and collective effort. Every investment in learning—whether in education systems, workplace training, or community programs—contributes to individual development and the larger story of organizational and societal transformation.

A COMMITMENT TO HUMANITY

The societal impact of learning isn't abstract; it's deeply human. It's a mother breaking the cycle of poverty for her children. It's a community leader inspiring others to pursue education. It's a workforce equipped to adapt to the challenges ahead.

When we invest in learning, we invest in humanity.

We build a world better equipped to face challenges, embrace change, and create a brighter, more equitable future.

These three dimensions of learning's impact—individual transformation, organizational evolution, and societal change—demonstrate its fundamental role in human progress. Yet despite this profound influence, learning's power often operates unnoticed. This subtle nature presents a unique challenge for those of us tasked with nurturing and sustaining learning in organizations. As L&D practitioners, we are the stewards of this hidden force, but our impact is often hidden.

> WHEN WE INVEST IN LEARNING, WE INVEST IN HUMANITY.

THE ESSENTIAL ROLE OF THE L&D FUNCTION

In a thriving organization, success radiates from every corner. Teams collaborate seamlessly, innovation flows naturally, and leaders drive the company toward ambitious goals. While it's easy to point to the "kapoks" of the organization—the bold leaders, game-changing products, and celebrated wins—beneath this success lies another force that is quiet yet powerful, hidden yet essential: the L&D function.

Just as the mycelium sustains the rainforest, L&D forms the living network of organizational growth. You don't just support success; you make it possible. You create the conditions where potential blooms into achievement, uncertainty transforms into opportunity, and individual growth becomes collective triumph.

ARCHITECTS OF POSSIBILITY

As L&D practitioners, we are architects of transformation. Every program we design, resource we create, and environment we cultivate carries the seeds of possibility. We don't just teach skills or transfer knowledge; we unlock potential and inspire discovery. Like the butterfly emerging from its chrysalis, each person we touch has the potential to soar beyond their perceived limitations.

THE POWER TO SHAPE TOMORROW

Here lies the beautiful paradox of our work: While learning drives organizational transformation, its impact often goes unnoticed. When companies celebrate breakthrough innovations or record-breaking achievements, few recognize the quiet force that made it all possible. Think of Satya Nadella's transformation of Microsoft, where a shift in learning culture revolutionized an entire organization. Consider Project Shakti, where learning lifted not just individuals but entire communities.

WE BUILD FUTURES.

We are the hidden architects of organizational growth, much like the mycelium network, nourishing mighty forests from below and creating conditions where excellence can flourish. Learning serves as the invisible force, preparing people for today's challenges and tomorrow's possibilities.

We build futures.

Learning changed my life. It's changed all our lives in some way. In this chapter, I want you to see the bigger picture—the hidden impact of learning on individuals, organizations, and society. Because when we create learning opportunities, we create opportunities for transformation.

A CALL TO ACTION

As L&D practitioners, we stand at a remarkable intersection—where individual aspiration meets organizational potential. In a world of constant change, you don't just help organizations adapt; you help them lead. When learning thrives, everything flourishes. The butterfly takes flight. The forest grows stronger. The organization thrives.

WE DEVELOP TOMORROW.

This is your moment to shine a light on L&D's transformative power and claim your place as an essential architect of organizational success. Because in the end, we don't just develop talent—

We develop tomorrow.

🔑 KEY LEARNINGS

- **Authors of Our Destinies:** Like a blank page awaiting its story, learning empowers us to break free from prescribed narratives. Just as master writers craft their unique tales, we become the authors of our transformation through learning, writing new chapters of possibility and potential.

- **The Dance of Adaptation:** As nature's creatures must evolve to thrive in changing environments, organizations engage in a perpetual dance with change. Those who match or exceed their environment's learning tempo lead the dance into tomorrow's possibilities.

- **Ripples of Transformation:** Like a stone cast into still waters, learning's impact extends far beyond its initial point of contact. Everyone's growth creates expanding circles of change, transforming families, organizations, and entire communities in their quest for equity and advancement.

- **Architects of Growth:** Like masterful guides who illuminate hidden paths, you create the essential conditions where potential flourishes. Through thoughtful design and careful cultivation, you build the foundations where individuals and organizations discover their fullest capabilities.

2

THE DIAMOND'S BRILLIANCE:
THE ART OF VALUE

"Price is what you pay. Value is what you get."

—*Warren Buffett*

THE HIDDEN SPECTRUM OF VALUE

In a jewelry store your gaze locks onto a diamond under the glass, its brilliance mesmerizing, its allure undeniable. "That's valuable," you think.

But is it? Is its value as simple as what meets the eye?

A gemologist sees beyond surface brilliance to understand the intricate qualities that create value. Through careful analysis of the Four Cs—clarity, cut, carat weight, and color—they reveal dimensions of worth that others might miss. Each characteristic tells a story of value, speaking to different audiences in different ways.

Two people could examine the same diamond and assign it completely different levels of value. One might focus on its imperfections, another on its potential. One might see an investment; another might see a priceless symbol of love. The diamond itself remains unchanged, but the eye of the beholder shapes its worth.

At its core, value represents the fundamental worth, importance, or utility something provides. In L&D, like a diamond, this value manifests in multiple dimensions—some immediately apparent, others requiring careful examination to appreciate fully. Yet, as with a diamond, much of its brilliance can remain hidden if viewed without care. Stakeholders often focus on visible outcomes, like financial gains or immediate productivity improvements, while overlooking the nuanced processes that create those results and the enduring ripple effects that transform organizations over time.

Like the mycelium network we explored in Chapter 1, value often remains hidden beneath the surface, sustaining and connecting seemingly disparate elements. This invisible web nourishes entire forests through complex, interconnected pathways. Similarly, the true worth of L&D initiatives is often found in unseen impacts—the subtle shifts in culture, gradual building of capabilities, and strengthening of organizational resilience. Understanding this value requires the same careful observation that reveals a diamond's hidden facets, where every surface contributes to its true brilliance and worth.

A JOURNEY TO UNDERSTANDING VALUE

The concept of value in L&D is as complex as it is critical. For decades, practitioners have argued for the importance of training and its role in shaping organizational success. Yet, despite its transformative potential, the value of L&D often remains misunderstood or undervalued—both within organizations and by the very leaders who control its resources.

This journey to understand value is not mine alone; it's a collective challenge that has persisted throughout the L&D industry for decades. From boardrooms to breakrooms, practitioners have wrestled with questions of worth, striving to balance the needs of learners with the priorities of leaders. It's a challenge that has sparked countless debates, prompted new frameworks, and driven professionals to question whether their efforts are truly *seen*. For me, this struggle wasn't just a professional frustration; it became a central theme of my career, manifesting in three pivotal moments:

- When a promising leadership development program was canceled despite strong participant feedback
- When a successful L&D initiative that generated $3 million in combined cost savings and revenue was deliberately kept hidden from finance
- During budget discussions where L&D investments were consistently labeled as "nice to have"
- These experiences drove me to make this challenge the focus of my doctoral research.

I sought to understand how financial decision-makers, particularly chief financial officers (CFOs), perceive the value of organizational learning. These gatekeepers of budgets and resources hold the power to determine the fate of L&D initiatives, yet their metrics, priorities, and definitions of value often stand in stark contrast to ours. Through in-depth interviews with CFOs across diverse industries, my research set out to bridge this critical gap, uncovering ways we, as L&D practitioners, can better align our narrative and build stronger partnerships with business leaders.

What I discovered was both enlightening and humbling. The research revealed four fundamental disconnects:

1. **The Perception Gap:** While CFOs readily acknowledge that employees are an organization's most important asset and recognize the potential benefits of training, they struggle to see concrete evidence of its impact. As one CFO put it, "I believe in the power of development, but I need more than faith to justify these investments."

2. **The Measurement Challenge:** CFOs cited the lack of clear, standardized metrics and meaningful reporting as a major barrier. However, surprisingly, many expressed skepticism about traditional ROI calculations, viewing them as "manufactured" or disconnected from business realities. One participant noted, "Don't give me complex formulas—show me how this moves our strategic needles."

3. **The Story-Data Balance:** While L&D often relies heavily on quantitative data and spreadsheets, CFOs expressed a desire for richer qualitative evidence. They want to understand the human impact through stories that illuminate how learning initiatives transform individuals and the organization. As one CFO shared, "Numbers tell part of the story, but show me the real transformation happening in our teams."

4. **The Partnership Void:** Perhaps most surprisingly, CFOs strongly desire a deeper partnership with L&D, but they expect L&D to take the initiative in building this relationship. They want to understand and support learning initiatives but need L&D leaders to actively bridge the gap and create opportunities for meaningful collaboration.

This disconnect isn't merely about metrics but bridging fundamentally different worldviews and building stronger partnerships. While CFOs often focus on quantifiable outcomes to validate investments, we are acutely aware of our work's deeply transformative but harder-to-measure aspects. One CFO candidly said, "The stories of individual transformation are powerful, but I need to see how these individual successes translate to organizational performance."

Why does this gap persist? Part of the problem lies in our traditional approach to demonstrating value. We often rely on internal models, such as Kirkpatrick's Four Levels of Evaluation or Phillips's ROI methodology, to justify our contributions. While these tools are valuable within the L&D community, they often fail to resonate with executives driven by a broader understanding of organizational value. Instead, CFOs consistently emphasized their desire for:

- Clear alignment between learning initiatives and strategic priorities
- Evidence of impact on key business metrics
- Compelling narratives that connect individual growth to organizational success
- Regular, simplified reporting that speaks their language

This disconnect raises fundamental questions for our profession. If we cannot effectively communicate the value of what we do in terms that resonate with stakeholders, does the value exist? It's like the age-old philosophical question: If a tree falls in the woods and no one hears it, does it make a sound? If employees are an organization's most important asset, why are training budgets seemingly the first cut during economic downturns?

The answers to these questions are crucial for defending L&D's role and ensuring its future relevance. My research revealed that the key lies in understanding and articulating value in three key dimensions—economic, personal, and societal. It's about moving beyond isolated metrics to tell a compelling, multifaceted story that aligns with the priorities of financial leaders while reflecting learning's broader impact.

This journey to understand value isn't just theoretical; it's practical and urgent. As organizations face unprecedented change and complexity, L&D's ability to articulate and deliver value becomes increasingly critical. The insights from my research with CFOs reveal a crucial gap between how we communicate value and how key stakeholders perceive it. Bridging this gap requires both a deeper understanding of value's dimensions and practical tools for making that value visible.

In this chapter, we'll explore the multifaceted nature of value, beginning with the three core dimensions—economic, personal, and societal—that shape L&D's impact. We'll then examine the dynamic interplay between abstract and concrete value before diving into how different contexts—organizational, industry, market, and cultural—influence how value is perceived and realized. By understanding these elements, you'll be better equipped to uncover and communicate the full brilliance of your L&D initiatives.

FACETS OF VALUE: UNDERSTANDING THE DIMENSIONS OF IMPACT

Just as light reveals a diamond's brilliance through different angles, examining L&D's value through multiple perspectives uncovers its true worth. Each facet illuminates a different aspect of impact, from immediate financial returns to long-term cultural transformation. Understanding these dimensions is essential for designing initiatives that deliver comprehensive value. Like a master jeweler who knows precisely how to position a diamond to showcase its finest qualities, you must learn to present your initiatives in ways that highlight their full spectrum of value.

THE THREE DIMENSIONS OF VALUE: A PRACTICAL FRAMEWORK

Value in L&D shines through three essential dimensions, each contributing to our initiatives' full impact:

1. **Economic Value:** Measurable business impact
2. **Personal Value:** Individual growth and transformation
3. **Societal Value:** Broader community and cultural impact

Each dimension requires different approaches to design, measurement, and communication. More importantly, they often reinforce each other, creating a multiplier effect that enhances overall impact.

ECONOMIC VALUE: THE BOTTOM LINE

Economic value represents the quantifiable business impact of L&D initiatives. While it's often the most scrutinized dimension, particularly by financial stakeholders, it manifests across two distinct timeframes: immediate and long-term.

Immediate Economic Value:
- Cost reduction through improved efficiency
- Revenue increases from enhanced skills
- Error reduction and quality improvements
- Time savings through optimized processes

Long-term Economic Value:

- Market expansion capabilities
- Innovation potential
- Competitive advantage
- Organizational agility

Organizations prioritize initiatives that deliver measurable financial outcomes, and learning is no exception.

Stakeholders often ask: How does learning impact the bottom line? Can it drive revenue, reduce costs, or enhance efficiency? These are critical questions, and answering them is essential to gaining buy-in and securing resources.

Consider how this plays out in practice. When a sales team undergoes negotiation training, stakeholders naturally focus on immediate metrics like close rates and revenue. These numbers matter; they speak directly to business performance and justify the investment. However, the true economic value often extends far beyond these initial metrics. As sales professionals apply their enhanced skills over time, they may uncover new market opportunities, build stronger client relationships, and contribute to the organization's competitive positioning. The immediate gains in sales performance evolve into sustained business advantages.

Similarly, leadership development programs illustrate the patience required to realize full economic value. While participants might immediately apply new skills to improve team efficiency or decision-making, the profound economic impact often emerges gradually. As these leaders grow into their roles, they shape strategy, drive innovation, and build organizational capabilities that create lasting economic value. This delayed gratification can make articulating economic value in traditional return on investment (ROI) terms challenging, but it doesn't diminish its importance to organizational success.

Understanding economic value requires you to think beyond simple cost-benefit calculations. It demands that you connect learning initiatives to operational excellence and strategic advantage. When you demonstrate how your programs drive business results—both immediate and long-term—you speak the language of your stakeholders and position L&D as a strategic investment rather than a discretionary expense.

Yet economic value doesn't exist in isolation. As we'll explore in the following sections, it intertwines with personal and societal values to create a comprehensive picture of L&D's impact. By understanding how these dimensions reinforce each other, you can design initiatives that deliver multiple forms of value.

PERSONAL VALUE: THE HUMAN CONNECTION

While economic value speaks to the organization, personal value speaks to the individual. It's the clarity of our diamond—the moment when someone realizes their untapped potential and takes ownership of their growth. This is the deeply human side of learning, where transformation happens in skills and self-belief.

Take, for example, a single mother named Elena who felt trapped in a cycle of low-paying jobs. With little time or resources to pursue formal education, her dreams of providing a better life for her children seemed out of reach. When her employer offered access to a flexible online learning program, Elena hesitated—unsure if she could balance work, parenting, and studying. After thinking of her kids, however, she took the leap. Over time, she gained new skills in data analysis and earned a certification. A year later, she was promoted to an analyst role, increasing her income and self-worth and inspiring her children to see education as a pathway to opportunity.

The personal value of learning extends beyond the workplace. It transforms how people see themselves and their futures. For Elena, it wasn't just about getting a better job; it was about breaking barriers, rewriting her story, and showing her children what resilience looks like. Personal value is about unlocking potential and igniting a sense of purpose that can ripple through families and communities.

At its core, personal value is deeply subjective, tied to fulfillment, meaning, and empowerment. Psychologist Abraham Maslow's hierarchy of needs, a well-known framework for understanding human motivation, provides a helpful lens to explore this idea. Maslow proposed that humans have five levels of needs, ranging from basic physiological needs like food and safety to higher-order needs like esteem and self-actualization. Personal value connects most strongly to these higher levels. Esteem represents the desire for recognition, confidence, and a sense of accomplishment, while self-actualization reflects the pursuit of realizing one's potential, personal growth, and the desire to achieve meaning in life.

It's the light in someone's eyes when they realize they are capable of more than they ever imagined. It's the quiet confidence of an employee who finally feels seen and supported. It's the pride of a team member stepping into a leadership role for the first time, embodying the profound sense of purpose and achievement that fuels human motivation at its highest levels.

These transformations may not always appear in metrics, but they are no less vital. They are the moments that define careers, rebuild lives, and set people on a course toward greater contributions to their organizations and society. While personal value is harder to measure than economic value, it carries a power that shapes the very fabric of our workplaces and world. This is the heart and soul of what we do.

Mapping Personal Value: The Growth Impact Framework

The journey of personal development isn't linear; it's a dynamic interplay of growth across multiple dimensions. The Growth Impact Framework illuminates four interconnected paths that, when developed thoughtfully, create lasting personal value through learning. Each path reinforces and amplifies the others, creating a powerful foundation for transformation.

Growth Impact Framework

Connection Development

Capability Enhancement

Career Advancement

Confidence Building

The Four Paths of Growth

Capability Enhancement

- Development of technical skills and professional expertise
- Growth in leadership abilities and strategic thinking
- Mastery of tools and methodologies in your domain
- Enhanced problem-solving and decision-making abilities

Confidence Building

- Greater self-awareness and belief in your abilities
- Comfort with ambiguity and complex decisions
- Development of your authentic voice and perspective
- Resilience in facing challenges and setbacks

Career Advancement

- Expanded roles and responsibilities
- Clearer career trajectory and professional identity

- Increased impact and influence in your organization
- Recognition as a subject matter expert

Connection Development

- Strong relationships with mentors and advisors
- Robust peer network for collaboration and support
- Cross-functional relationships that expand influence
- Professional connections beyond the immediate team

These dimensions of personal growth don't exist in isolation; they reinforce and amplify each other. When capability enhancement meets strong professional connections, new opportunities emerge. As confidence grows, career advancement becomes not just possible but natural. The framework helps us recognize these synergies and intentionally design learning experiences that tap into multiple dimensions of growth.

While individual achievements matter, the true power of the Growth Impact Framework lies in its holistic nature. When organizations embrace this comprehensive view of personal value, they create environments where individual transformation becomes possible. These individual transformations, multiplied across teams and departments, lay the foundation for broader impact—turning personal growth into a catalyst for organizational and societal change.

SOCIETAL VALUE: THE BROADER HORIZON

Societal value represents L&D's radiant impact on communities, industries, and society at large. Like light dispersing through a diamond to illuminate an entire room, this dimension extends far beyond its source, transforming not just individuals or organizations but entire communities, as we discussed in Chapter 1. This dimension often emerges from the cumulative effect of economic and personal value creation, but it can also be intentionally designed into programs from the start. Understanding societal value helps us:

- Align initiatives with broader organizational purpose
- Create sustainable, long-term impact
- Build stronger stakeholder relationships
- Address systemic challenges through learning
- Foster innovation that benefits entire industries

The key is recognizing that societal value isn't just a byproduct; it's an achievable outcome that can be planned for and measured.

Consider the story of Generation, a global nonprofit focused on equipping underserved populations with the skills needed to secure meaningful employment. Through targeted training programs, Generation has helped individuals break out of cycles of poverty and contributed to broader economic revitalization. For example, their initiative in Kenya trains young people for careers in healthcare, IT, and customer service, fields with high demand but low accessibility for marginalized communities. Over 80 percent of participants secure employment within three months of completing the program, and many report increased financial stability for their families. By focusing on skills development and job placement, Generation creates waves of change that strengthen communities and reshape industries.

This societal impact is not just about economic growth but addressing deep-rooted inequities. Programs like Generation's improve the lives of individual participants and challenge the structures that perpetuate inequality. Learning creates access to opportunities that were previously out of reach and builds a foundation for generational change.

> EDUCATION AND OPPORTUNITY MUST STAND NOT AS PRIVILEGES FOR THE FEW BUT AS FUNDAMENTAL RIGHTS FOR ALL.

Societal value also shows up in corporate efforts to integrate learning into their broader social responsibility strategies. For instance, Microsoft's global skills initiative, launched in response to the COVID-19 pandemic, aimed to reskill 25 million people worldwide for a digital economy. The program enhanced individual employability by offering free access to online learning platforms and certification opportunities. It addressed a looming global skills gap, enabling economies to rebuild with resilience and adaptability.

The essence of societal value is the power of learning to address collective challenges, empower marginalized groups, and drive progress that transcends organizational boundaries.

Education and opportunity must stand not as privileges for the few but as fundamental rights for all.

While societal value can feel abstract or difficult to measure, its significance is profound. The impact of empowering one individual can transform families, neighborhoods, and even nations. When we invest with societal impact in mind, we are not just funding training; we are investing in the future—building a world where progress is shared, equity is prioritized, and the transformative power of learning reaches everyone.

⚡ YOUR TURN: VALUE DIMENSIONS IN ACTION

Take fifteen minutes to reflect on a recent or current learning initiative through the lens of these three dimensions.

1. Choose one of your recent or planned L&D initiatives.
2. For each dimension, identify at least one way your initiative creates value:
   - **Economic Value:** What measurable business impact does it deliver? (Consider both immediate and long-term.)
   - **Personal Value:** How does it transform individual participants? (Think across the Growth Impact Framework.)
   - **Societal Value:** What broader ripple effects might it create beyond your organization?

---

3. Circle the dimension where you see the greatest opportunity to expand impact.

4. Write down one specific action you could take to strengthen that dimension.

This quick exercise helps you:

- Practice seeing value through multiple lenses

- Identify missed opportunities

- Begin thinking more holistically about your L&D initiatives

📌 **Remember:** The most powerful L&D initiatives often create value across all three dimensions. How might you design future programs with this in mind?

Connecting the Dimensions: The Full Spectrum of Value

Like a masterfully cut diamond, the true brilliance of L&D emerges when all three dimensions of value align and reinforce each other:

- Economic value provides the foundation, ensuring learning initiatives contribute meaningfully to organizational success.

- Personal value creates transformative experiences that change lives and unlock human potential.

- Societal value extends this impact beyond organizational boundaries, creating lasting change in communities and industries.

The brilliance of these dimensions lies in their interplay. Economic success enables greater investment in personal development, which in turn creates the foundation for broader societal impact. When we design programs with all three in mind, we create initiatives that deliver results, transform lives, strengthen organizations, and build a better world. This is the power of understanding value in all its facets; it enables us to create learning experiences that shine with purpose, impact, and lasting significance.

Why does this matter? Recognizing and articulating these dimensions is the first step in making our hidden value visible. The value of learning must be illuminated, understood, and communicated in the same way a diamond's brilliance

_____

VALUE IS NEVER ABSOLUTE.

_____

is revealed through careful appraisal. When we unveil all the facets, we don't just highlight the significance of our work; we ensure it is valued, championed, and prioritized.

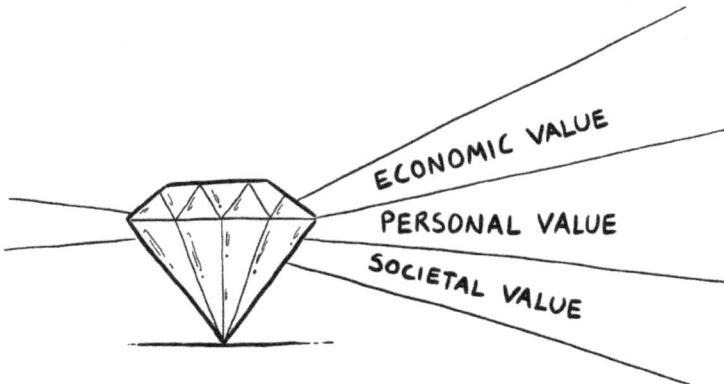

VALUE IS FLUID, SUBJECTIVE, AND CONTEXTUAL

If the facets of a diamond reveal its brilliance, the conditions under which it is viewed determine how the brilliance is perceived. Under harsh fluorescent light, a diamond might lose its luster, but under a jeweler's spotlight, its beauty becomes undeniable. The same is true for value in L&D; it is shaped by perspective, context, and timing.

Value is never absolute.

Value is fluid, shifting with circumstances and evolving needs; subjective, influenced by the unique priorities and perceptions of stakeholders; and contextual, defined by the environment in which it exists.

Understanding this dynamic nature of value is critical. It helps you design initiatives that resonate with diverse stakeholders, align with organizational priorities, and adapt to ever-changing landscapes. Value reveals itself most clearly through two distinct forms: the abstract and the concrete.

ABSTRACT AND CONCRETE VALUE

You sit in a concert hall as a breathtaking symphony unfolds. The conductor, musicians, and intricate interplay of instruments create an experience that stirs the soul. You leave the concert hall feeling inspired, moved, and connected. But how do you measure the value of that performance? Is it in ticket sales, the technical precision of the musicians, or the emotional resonance you carry home?

This tension mirrors the dual lens through which value in L&D must be understood: abstract and concrete. Abstract value encompasses the impact's intangible, qualitative aspects—emotional resonance, personal growth, and cultural shifts that shape an organization's identity. For instance, fostering a growth mindset within an organization might lead to stronger collaboration, heightened morale, and a sense of purpose—outcomes that are challenging to quantify but still transformative.

Concrete value, on the other hand, provides the measurable outcomes stakeholders often seek to justify investments. These are hard numbers: revenue gains, efficiency improvements, or reductions in errors—the economic value. Examples include a compliance training initiative that results in a measurable reduction of regulatory fines or a customer service program that increases net promoter scores (NPS) by 20 percent. Similarly, a technical skills training program might directly correlate with faster project completion times or a measurable decrease in production errors.

Yet these two forms of value are not opposites; they are deeply intertwined. A culture of continuous learning (abstract) often leads to measurable improvements in employee productivity and retention (concrete). Conversely, without tangible results, abstract benefits risk being dismissed as "nice-to-haves."

Both forms of value are essential, yet they align differently with stakeholders. Abstract value inspires people; it speaks to their hearts, builds long-term connections, and, in some cases, lays the foundation for concrete value to emerge. Concrete value satisfies the need for accountability; it provides evidence of impact and justifies investment. Together, they illuminate the full spectrum of L&D's contributions, showing that the most meaningful outcomes often emerge from the interplay of what can—and cannot—be easily quantified.

As L&D practitioners, recognizing and balancing these dimensions is critical. A program that delivers concrete results without fostering an emotional connection risks being viewed as transactional. Conversely, initiatives that focus solely on abstract value may struggle to secure buy-in from stakeholders who demand measurable outcomes. By integrating both, we can reveal the full brilliance of L&D's impact—just as a symphony's magic lies in both its technical precision and emotional resonance.

> 📌 **Remember:** The most impactful L&D initiatives balance concrete and abstract value, just as a diamond's worth comes from its measurable qualities and emotional appeal.

THE ESSENCE OF ABSTRACT VALUE

Abstract value encompasses the intangible, qualitative aspects of impact. It's the emotional satisfaction, personal fulfillment, and cultural resonance, which can't easily be captured in a spreadsheet but often hold profound importance.

Consider these examples:

- **Brand Loyalty:** Employees who feel deeply connected to their company's mission after attending a transformational leadership workshop
- **Social Responsibility:** L&D initiatives that address diversity, equity, and inclusion, aligning the organization's values with societal progress
- **Reputation:** A well-trained workforce that enhances the company's standing as an industry leader and employer of choice

One CFO I interviewed put it succinctly: "I believe in the power of learning, but when you try to assign a dollar value to things like teamwork or morale, it doesn't resonate. Show me a story instead. Help me feel the impact."

This insight highlights a critical truth: Abstract value often drives the motivation, loyalty, and engagement that fuel long-term success, even if it's challenging to measure.

THE CLARITY OF CONCRETE VALUE

Concrete value, in contrast, is rooted in measurable, actionable outcomes. These are the hard numbers that stakeholders often seek to justify investments in L&D initiatives.

Examples include:

- **Profitability:** Sales training that results in measurable increases in revenue
- **Operational Efficiency:** Process improvement courses that save time or reduce errors
- **Customer Satisfaction:** Enhanced net promoter scores (NPS) following customer service training

Concrete value provides the tangible evidence stakeholders rely on to make decisions. As one CFO shared during my research, "If you're telling me this training reduced errors by 15 percent, I can take that to my board. That's a win."

> WHETHER CONCRETE OR ABSTRACT, VALUE IS ULTIMATELY DETERMINED BY THE PERSPECTIVE OF THOSE WHO EXPERIENCE IT.

Yet my research revealed an unexpected insight: While concrete metrics matter, they tell only part of the story. Even CFOs—traditionally seen as the guardians of measurable returns—expressed a deeper appreciation for the human element of learning. "Numbers get attention," one executive explained, "but stories create understanding." This recognition that value transcends pure metrics leads us to a fundamental truth:

Whether concrete or abstract, value is ultimately determined by the perspective of those who experience it.

VALUE IS IN THE EYE OF THE BEHOLDER

You hand someone a bottle of water, and they offer to pay you. But how much? In a grocery store, it's worth $1. At a concert, it might be $10. However, to someone lost in a desert, it's priceless. The water hasn't changed; the context and needs of the individual determine its value.

The same is true for learning. A leadership workshop might be invaluable to a new manager struggling with team dynamics but holds little immediate relevance for an experienced executive. A technical certification program might be a lifeline for an IT department racing to adopt new technologies, but it may seem disconnected from the priorities of the sales team.

Much like a diamond whose value is influenced by factors such as its rarity, clarity, and the context in which it's appreciated, learning's value is determined by the context and needs of the stakeholder. A CEO might prioritize learning initiatives that drive innovation and long-term growth, while a department manager might focus on immediate performance improvements. On the other hand, employees often value learning for its personal and professional development opportunities.

Consider these differing perspectives:

- **For Executives:** Learning is a strategic tool for driving competitive advantage. It's about aligning talent development with the company's vision and ensuring the workforce is future-ready.

- **For Managers:** Learning is about solving immediate problems—improving team productivity, reducing errors, or addressing skill gaps that hinder day-to-day operations.

- **For Employees:** Learning represents empowerment. It's the opportunity to grow, advance, and find fulfillment in their roles.

These perspectives aren't in competition; *they are interconnected.* However, the subjective nature of value means it's up to you to uncover the context of value for each stakeholder. Understanding their unique priorities and pressures ensures your initiatives align across the spectrum, bridging individual aspirations with organizational goals.

Value is subjective because it is deeply tied to personal and organizational priorities. For L&D, this means one size never fits all. Your work must be tailored to meet the unique needs and aspirations of our learners, as well as the strategic objectives of your organization.

✄ **Remember:** Different stakeholders see value through different lenses. Success requires speaking the language of value that resonates with each audience.

CONTEXTUAL PERSPECTIVES: HOW VALUE CHANGES ACROSS ENVIRONMENTS

As L&D practitioners, we often look at what others are doing—their programs, strategies, and metrics—and think, *I should be doing it that way*. It's an easy trap to fall into, especially when we see shining examples from high-profile organizations or celebrated peers in the field. However, everything we do in L&D is contextualized. What works in one organization, industry, or culture doesn't necessarily translate to another.

I've experienced this firsthand throughout my career. What succeeded at General Motors didn't work at Archwell. What's thriving at BDO Canada wouldn't have worked at HSBC. Each organization operates within its unique ecosystem, with its own challenges, priorities, and cultures. You can look at others for inspiration or ideas, but ultimately, *the value you deliver must be tailored to your world*—your stakeholders, goals, and variables.

THE CONTEXT FRAMEWORK: FOUR ESSENTIAL LENSES

To effectively create and communicate value that drives meaningful impact, your strategy should account for four key contextual dimensions:

1. **Organizational Context:** Internal dynamics and priorities
2. **Industry Context:** Sector-specific needs and trends

3. **Market Context:** Competitive pressures and opportunities
4. **Cultural Context:** Values, norms, and expectations

1. ORGANIZATIONAL CONTEXT

Organizational context shapes how L&D value is perceived and delivered at two distinct levels: between different organizations and within individual organizations. Understanding these variations helps you tailor your approach to maximize impact wherever you operate.

Different Priorities Across Organizations: Each organization operates within its unique ecosystem, shaped by its industry, culture, leadership, and strategic goals. For example:

- A tech company might view L&D as a means to drive innovation, focusing on upskilling in emerging technologies and fostering a culture of experimentation.

- A financial institution may prioritize compliance and risk management, where mandatory training ensures adherence to regulatory standards.

- A nonprofit organization might emphasize community impact, offering training that enhances employee engagement and mission alignment.

The key is to understand these organizational priorities and align your initiatives accordingly.

Diverse Priorities Within Organizations: Even within a single organization, different business units and departments often view L&D value through distinct lenses:

- Sales teams may prioritize programs that enhance negotiation skills, improve client relationships, and drive revenue growth.

- IT departments often value technical certifications, cyberse-curity training, and programs that address rapid technological advancements.

- Leadership teams typically focus on initiatives that build emotional intelligence, strategic thinking, and succession planning to ensure organizational resilience.

Success requires understanding and addressing both levels of organizational context. By recognizing these nuances, you can create initiatives that resonate across different organizations while meeting the diverse needs of departments within each organization.

2. INDUSTRY CONTEXT

Industries operate within unique environments that profoundly shape how they define the value of L&D. For example, priorities in healthcare can differ vastly from those in technology or retail, and understanding these distinctions is essential for creating relevant and impactful programs. While the core principles of L&D may remain consistent, the way value is perceived and measured varies based on industry-specific drivers and challenges.

Navigating Industry-Specific Priorities

Understanding these drivers goes beyond designing programs; it's about aligning L&D with the broader strategic objectives of the industry. For example:

- **In financial services**, where risk management and compliance are paramount, L&D might focus on regulatory training to avoid costly fines or reputational damage. At the same time, leadership programs could address the need for decision-making in high-pressure environments.

- **In manufacturing**, L&D often centers on safety training, operational efficiency, and workforce upskilling to adapt to advancements like robotics and automation.

Shifts in Industry Contexts

Industries are not static; they evolve based on technological advancements, market conditions, and global trends. L&D must stay agile to respond to these shifts. For example:

- **In hospitality**, the post-pandemic landscape has led to an increased focus on health protocols and hybrid service delivery models. L&D programs now need to address both in-person and virtual customer interactions.

- **In automotive**, transitioning to electric vehicles requires retraining workers on new technologies, processes, and sustainability practices.

Anticipating Industry Trends

When you proactively address emerging industry trends, you position your organizations to stay ahead of the curve, ensuring relevance and resilience. For instance, the rise of telehealth in healthcare during the pandemic underscored the need for rapid training on virtual patient care technologies. L&D teams that anticipated this shift could quickly roll out programs that equipped healthcare workers with the skills needed to adapt seamlessly, avoiding disruptions in patient care.

By tailoring your approach to the specific needs of your industry, you can create programs that address current demands and position your organization to thrive in a dynamic, competitive landscape. Industry context is more than a backdrop; it's the framework within which L&D delivers value.

3. MARKET CONTEXT

The competitive landscape in which an organization operates greatly influences what is considered valuable in L&D. Industries, sectors, and even specific market conditions can shape the priorities of stakeholders and redefine what success looks like for L&D initiatives. While some organizations focus on speed and scalability, others prioritize precision, specialization, or brand alignment. Recognizing these nuances allows L&D practitioners to design programs that meet organizational goals and give companies a competitive edge.

For example:

- **Rapid Growth and Competition:** In fast-paced, competitive markets, such as technology startups or fintech, agility often takes precedence. Here, L&D initiatives might focus on accelerated learning programs that enable employees to quickly acquire new skills and adapt to evolving demands. For instance, a startup entering a crowded market may value microlearning modules and cross-functional training to ensure its workforce can scale rapidly and innovate faster than competitors.

- **Specialized Markets:** In niche industries, such as luxury retail or aerospace, L&D may prioritize specialized knowledge and expertise. A luxury brand, for example, might invest heavily in customer service training to ensure every client interaction reflects the brand's high-end image. In aerospace, the focus might be on rigorous technical certifications and compliance training to meet exacting regulatory and safety standards.

- **Regulated Industries:** For markets with stringent regulations—like healthcare or financial services—L&D initiatives often center on compliance and risk management. Training programs in these industries must ensure employees meet mandatory standards and contribute to a culture of accountability and trust. A pharmaceutical company, for example, might prioritize L&D programs designed to align with FDA regulations while fostering innovation in product development.

- **Evolving Consumer Expectations:** In markets driven by consumer demand, such as e-commerce or hospitality, L&D often emphasizes customer experience. For instance, an e-commerce company facing intense competition might invest in training programs to enhance user interface design and optimize supply chain efficiency. Meanwhile, a hotel chain may prioritize employee cultural sensitivity training to create exceptional guest experiences across global locations.

Market Contexts Within the Same Industry

Even organizations operating in the same industry can experience different market contexts based on their unique strategies, customer bases, and competitive pressures:

- A high-growth online retailer may focus on L&D programs that optimize warehouse efficiency and logistics to keep up with demand spikes. In contrast, an established brick-and-mortar retailer might prioritize upskilling employees in digital transformation to compete with e-commerce giants.

- Two healthcare organizations in different regions may face distinct challenges—one focusing on telehealth training to meet patient expectations for virtual care, while another prioritizes in-person care models for underserved rural communities.

4. CULTURAL CONTEXT

Cultural intelligence is a critical competency for L&D practitioners working in multinational organizations. It involves understanding and respecting the nuances of national, regional, and organizational cultures to design programs that resonate deeply. For example:

- **National Culture:** In Western cultures, continuous learning is often tied to individual achievement and career progression. Employees may value programs that help them stand out and climb the corporate ladder. In contrast, Eastern cultures often emphasize collective success, viewing L&D as a tool for strengthening team cohesion and organizational alignment.

- **Organizational Microcultures:** Even within the same company, departments or regions can develop unique cultural identities. A European office may prioritize work-life balance, while a South American division may emphasize community-driven, in-person learning experiences. Recognizing these subtleties ensures learning programs feel relevant and impactful to every audience.

Recognizing and respecting these layers of cultural diversity allows L&D practitioners to design programs that connect meaningfully with the audience. Success in one region or department does not guarantee success elsewhere. Instead, aligning initiatives with local values and priorities ensures effective learning is embraced by those it serves.

Making Context Actionable

To understand and deliver meaningful value in L&D, you must embrace the diversity of contexts—organizational, industry, market, and cultural—that shape perceptions of value. This requires active listening, engagement with stakeholders, and continuous adaptation. Whether aligning with organizational goals, anticipating industry trends, responding to market shifts, or respecting cultural nuances, the key is to remain flexible and contextually attuned. By doing so, you create programs that inspire action and position learning as a cornerstone of organizational success.

When you view value through these interconnected lenses, you can create solutions that meet immediate needs and drive long-term growth, innovation, and resilience. The more contextually attuned your strategies are, the more indispensable your contributions become.

⚡ YOUR TURN: MAP YOUR CONTEXT

Take thirty minutes to create your contextual map using these four lenses. This exercise will help you understand where you operate and how to deliver value more effectively.

1. **Assess Your Current State**

   o Draw four quadrants on a page, one for each contextual lens.

   o In each quadrant, answer these key questions:

      ▪ **Organizational Context:** What are the top priorities for your organization overall? How do these priorities differ across the departments you support?

      ▪ **Industry Context:** What are the major trends and challenges shaping your industry right now?

      ▪ **Market Context:** What competitive pressures is your organization facing? How do these impact learning needs?

      ▪ **Cultural Context:** What cultural factors (organizational, regional, or national) influence how learning is perceived and valued?

2. **Identify Gaps and Opportunities**

   o Review your answers and mark areas where:

      ▪ You need more information.

      ▪ You see potential misalignment between current L&D initiatives and context.

      ▪ You spot opportunities to create greater value.

3. **Take Action**

   o Choose the two most critical insights from your analysis.

   o Schedule conversations with key stakeholders to validate your understanding.

   o Use these insights to adjust your strategy or upcoming initiatives.

✎ **Remember:** This map isn't static. Plan to revisit and update it annually as your context evolves. The more deeply you understand your context, the more effectively you can create and communicate value.

BRINGING CONTEXT INTO FOCUS

As L&D practitioners, we often face the challenge of delivering value to diverse stakeholders with varying perspectives. What a CEO values in an L&D program—such as its alignment with strategic goals—might differ from what an employee values, like career advancement opportunities. Understanding these different viewpoints is crucial for positioning L&D as a vital, responsive partner within the organization.

This context-driven approach emphasizes the importance of asking the right questions:

- Who is evaluating the value?
- What are their priorities?
- How does their context influence what they see as valuable?

Understanding value extends beyond identifying stakeholder needs; it requires recognizing how different contexts interact and shape the forms value takes. In an organizational context, the concrete value might appear as cost savings or productivity gains, while in a cultural context, the abstract value might manifest as enhanced trust or employee engagement. These interplays demonstrate how value exists on a spectrum from the abstract to the concrete.

The key to mastering this complexity lies in both understanding today's context and preparing for tomorrow's changes. Value isn't static; it evolves with changing circumstances, priorities, and needs. By maintaining this dual focus on the current context and future adaptability, you position yourself as a true driver of transformation within your organization.

> ✒ **Remember: The Power of Context**
> What works brilliantly in one organization may fail in another. Success in L&D requires understanding your unique ecosystem.

EMBRACING THE DYNAMIC NATURE OF VALUE

Understanding the concept of value is both an art and a science. Like a master jeweler examining a precious stone, it demands that you look beyond the surface to recognize the hidden brilliance—the empowerment of individuals, the growth of organizations, and the progress of society. Value is not static; it is dynamic, shifting with time, context, and perspective, much like how a diamond's brilliance changes as it catches different angles of light. When you recognize the value as dynamic, you can:

- Design initiatives that align with both immediate needs and long-term goals
- Communicate the relevance of your work to diverse stakeholders
- Adapt to changing landscapes, ensuring your contributions remain indispensable

As we've explored, value is multifaceted. It is abstract and concrete, subjective and measurable, immediate and long-term. The key to unlocking its full potential lies in acknowledging this complexity and designing initiatives that address these diverse dimensions. For L&D practitioners, this means tailoring our efforts to align with the priorities of our stakeholders, fostering emotional connections while delivering tangible results.

> ✒ **Remember:** Value is never one-dimensional.

Value is a living, breathing concept, and it's your job to bring it to life and reveal its brilliance from every angle.

However, understanding the concept of value is only the beginning. The real challenge lies in seeking it—intentionally, strategically, and systematically. Like a skilled treasure hunter, you must develop the ability to spot opportunities where others see obstacles. How do you cultivate the mindset to uncover hidden potential? How do you develop the skills to recognize value that others might miss?

These questions set the stage for the next chapter, where we'll explore the art of value-seeking. By mastering the skills of observation, investigation, and discovery, you can transform from a passive observer into an active value seeker. Imagine approaching every challenge with the eye of a curator, an explorer's curiosity, and a strategist's insight—seeing beyond the surface to uncover the true potential within. That's the promise of value seeking, and it begins with learning to look deeper, think broader, and envision possibilities that others might overlook.

🔑 KEY LEARNINGS

- **The Diamond's Hidden Brilliance:** Like a master jeweler revealing a diamond's true worth by carefully examining each facet, L&D's value shines differently under various lights. What appears invaluable to one stakeholder may remain hidden to another without proper illumination and perspective.

- **The Triple Crown of Value Creation:** Just as a tree's strength flows from roots to crown to ecosystem, learning's impact radiates through three vital dimensions: economic foundations that fuel business growth, personal transformations that reshape individual journeys, and societal ripples that elevate entire communities.

- **The Symphony of Impact:** Like an orchestra weaving technical precision with emotional resonance, meaningful L&D initiatives blend concrete metrics with abstract human impact masterfully. True value emerges when quantifiable results harmonize with deeper transformational outcomes.

- **The Four Windows of Context:** Much as light passing through different prisms reveals distinct spectrums, value flows through four essential contextual lenses: organizational, industry, market, and cultural. Each lens shapes how learning's impact is perceived, measured, and realized.

- **From Cost Center to Value Creator:** Just as a skilled translator bridges different languages while preserving meaning, L&D must speak the distinct dialects of value that resonate with each stakeholder while remaining true to learning's transformative essence. This translation transforms perception from expense to investment.

3

TREASURE HUNTER'S GUIDE: *SEEKING VALUE*

"Not all treasure is silver and gold."

—*Captain Jack Sparrow*

THE ART OF SEEKING VALUE: THE AEROSMITH VAN STORY

On a seemingly ordinary day in rural Chesterfield, Massachusetts, a discovery was waiting to be made. Hidden in an unassuming garage sat a 1964 International Harvester Metro van, its surface marked by rust and peeling paint. To most passing by, it was just another abandoned vehicle destined for the scrapyard. However, for Mike Wolfe and Frank Fritz of *American Pickers*, something about this particular relic caught their attention. After all, years of experience had taught them a crucial lesson: True value often lurks beneath the most weathered surfaces.

The two pickers moved methodically through the cluttered garage, their practiced eyes scanning decades of accumulated artifacts. They almost dismissed the van as another lost cause; its tires were flat, its windows clouded with grime, and patches of rust had eaten through the metal like decay. However, just as they were about to move on, a shaft of sunlight caught the vehicle's side at just the right angle, illuminating what appeared to be carefully painted lettering beneath years of dust and neglect. Mike stepped closer, his heart quickening as he wiped away a small section with his sleeve. He caught a glimpse of something beneath the grime—a faint, hand-painted word on the side of the van: "Aerosmith."

That single word sparked a cascade of possibilities. Mike and Frank felt the weight of potential history in their hands. In the 1970s, Aerosmith had risen from the streets of Boston to become one of rock's most iconic bands. Could this rusted shell have been part of that journey? Standing in the dim garage, they could almost hear the echoes of power chords and smell the lingering traces of backstage dreams. If this truly was the band's van, it wasn't just a vehicle they'd discovered; it was a time capsule from rock and roll history, holding untold stories of late-night drives, breakthrough performances, and the raw determination of a band on the verge of greatness.

Their burning curiosity led them to track down Ray Tabano, one of Aerosmith's founding members. When they showed him photos of the van, his face lit up with instant recognition. He didn't just confirm its authenticity; he brought its history roaring back to life. Through Ray's eyes, they saw five young musicians crammed inside, traveling from gig to gig in the early 1970s before they made it big. For Aerosmith, this van had been more than a vehicle. It had been their lifeline—a rolling home that carried them through the struggles and triumphs of their early days.

The van's discovery sparked something larger than a typical restoration project. Each layer of rust they stripped away revealed another piece of rock and roll history. What others had dismissed as junk was transformed through their curiosity and expertise into a valuable artifact—a tangible piece of Aerosmith's journey from Boston's club scene to international stardom.

This is the essence of value seeking: the ability to see value beneath the surface and let curiosity guide you when others would walk away. Mike and Frank didn't just find a van on that ordinary day in Chesterfield. They uncovered a piece of history that had been hiding in plain sight, waiting for someone with the right combination of experience, instinct, and curiosity to recognize its true value.

⚡ **YOUR TURN: DISCOVER HIDDEN VALUE**

Think about a time when you discovered hidden value in something others had overlooked. What initial clues sparked your curiosity? How did you transform that initial spark into something of real worth?

THE L&D VALUE SEEKER'S MISSION

Your role is to enable people to become their best selves, and in doing so, you unlock untapped value that benefits individuals and the organization. You help employees discover their worth, identify their strengths, and cultivate the skills they need to succeed in an ever-changing world. This is the heart of value creation in L&D: helping others grow so they can contribute their best to the world around them.

As an L&D practitioner, you have a distinctive vantage point. Through your work with teams across functions and levels, you see connections and opportunities that others might miss—patterns that can unlock hidden value throughout your organization. Just as Mike and Frank see potential in forgotten artifacts, you must develop a keen eye for potential across multiple dimensions:

- **People:** You can spot the leadership spark in a quiet individual, recognize transferable skills others overlook, or identify mentoring relationships that could transform careers and strengthen teams.

- **Programs:** You see how existing courses could be repurposed to serve new needs, how forgotten initiatives could solve current challenges, or how combining resources could multiply their impact.

- **Processes:** Where others accept inefficiency, you envision streamlined workflows. In outdated systems, you see opportunities for innovation.

- **Partnerships:** You recognize how unexpected collaborations could create new value and how existing relationships could deepen to benefit everyone involved.

Like valuable artifacts waiting to be discovered, the greatest opportunities often lie hidden within your organization. They're waiting for someone with your perspective to recognize their worth and unleash their potential.

> BEFORE CREATING VALUE, YOU MUST DEVELOP THE ABILITY TO SEEK IT, OFTEN IN PLACES OTHERS OVERLOOK.

The difference between good and great often lies not in what you see but how you see it. This skill—the ability to uncover hidden opportunities—separates reactive problem-solvers from proactive value creators.

Before creating value, you must develop the ability to seek it, often in places others overlook.

To move from reactive to proactive, you must evolve beyond traditional L&D roles to become:

- **Value Hunters:** You actively seek hidden potential that others walk past, using your unique perspective to spot opportunities for growth and transformation.

- **Transformation Architects:** You design clear pathways to turn that potential into measurable impact, building bridges between current reality and future possibility.

- **Impact Amplifiers:** You find creative ways to maximize returns on learning investments, ensuring every initiative creates ripples of positive change throughout the organization.

At its core, seeking value is a deliberate practice—a combination of mindset and methodology that transforms potential into measurable impact. As we saw with the Aerosmith van discovery, value often lies hidden in plain sight, waiting for someone with the right perspective to recognize it. However, recognizing value is just the beginning. Through the story of a struggling family who transformed an overlooked grapevine into their lifeline during the Great Depression, we'll explore the essential framework of the Four Cs (curiosity, connection, context, and courage). These tools will help you develop the behaviors and mindsets needed to spot opportunities and turn them into meaningful contributions that resonate throughout your organization.

THE FOUR Cs FRAMEWORK: A SYSTEMATIC APPROACH TO VALUE SEEKING

Against the stark backdrop of the Great Depression, a struggling family in Michigan faced bleak days and long, hungry nights. With little money and few prospects, their survival depended on ingenuity and resilience. One afternoon, while surveying their barren property for anything useful, they noticed a tangle of vines creeping along the edge of their land. At first glance, the wiry, unkempt growth seemed worthless, just another reminder of the harshness of their situation. However, something caught their attention: small, dark clusters of fruit hanging amid the leaves.

Driven by curiosity and desperation, they tended to the plant, pruning it and learning how to care for its growth. Over time, their effort bore fruit—literally. The vine was a Concord grapevine, a robust variety capable of thriving in even poor soil. With hard work, the family harvested grapes and turned them into jams and juices, selling their wares in the local community. What began as a scraggly, overlooked vine became a lifeline, sustaining them through the hardest years of their lives and giving them hope and purpose.

This is more than a tale of survival; it's a testament to the power of seeking value where others don't. It teaches us that hidden potential is all around us. Whether it's the unspoken talents of an overlooked employee, the opportunity for innovation within routine processes, or the chance to improve outcomes with a fresh perspective, value often hides in plain sight. We are uniquely positioned to uncover and amplify this value, but it requires a deliberate mindset.

Creating value begins with seeking it intentionally. Like Mike and Frank on *American Pickers*, the act of seeking value requires curiosity and a willingness to dig deeper. The foundation for creating value is built through this discovery phase—identifying needs, aligning with priorities, and exploring untapped potential.

Seeking value is more than just preparation; the proactive exploration transforms L&D from a reactive support function to a strategic driver of impact. By asking insightful questions, connecting with stakeholders, and embedding ourselves within organizational goals, we ensure our efforts don't just address surface needs but resonate deeply with the challenges and aspirations of our stakeholders. To guide this journey of value-seeking, we'll use four powerful catalysts:

Curiosity drives us to explore possibilities, uncover hidden challenges, and ask the questions that matter.

Connection ensures we engage the right people and forge the relationships that unlock potential.

Context grounds our efforts in relevance, aligning our initiatives with organizational and stakeholder needs.

Courage pushes us to act boldly, take risks, and advocate for transformative change.

The process of seeking value, like a master jeweler examining a rough diamond, requires multiple perspectives working in harmony. The Four Cs—curiosity, connection, context, and courage—function as an integrated system for revealing hidden potential. Each builds upon and enhances the others, transforming how we see and create value in our organizations.

UNDERSTANDING THE DYNAMIC INTERPLAY OF THE FOUR Cs

While each of the Four Cs represents a powerful force for seeking value, their true impact emerges when they work together. Think of them not as sequential steps but as interconnected elements that strengthen and inform each other:

Curiosity → Connection

- Curiosity drives you to ask questions that lead to meaningful connections.

- When exploring organizational challenges, your questions naturally lead to conversations across different levels and functions.

- Questions sparked by curiosity create opportunities for deeper relationships.

Connection → Context

- Connections provide the channels through which contextual understanding flows.

- Each relationship offers a unique perspective that enriches your understanding of the organizational landscape.

- Networks of connections reveal patterns that individual viewpoints might miss.

Context → Courage

- Deep contextual understanding builds the confidence needed for courageous action.
- Knowing the full picture helps you advocate for more comprehensive solutions.
- Understanding context helps you anticipate and prepare for challenges.

Courage → Curiosity

- Bold actions often reveal new questions and areas for exploration.
- Courage to challenge assumptions leads to deeper curiosity about alternatives.
- The cycle continues as new discoveries prompt new questions.

This integrated approach transforms you into a practitioner who can spot opportunities and build the coalitions and understanding needed to turn those opportunities into impact.

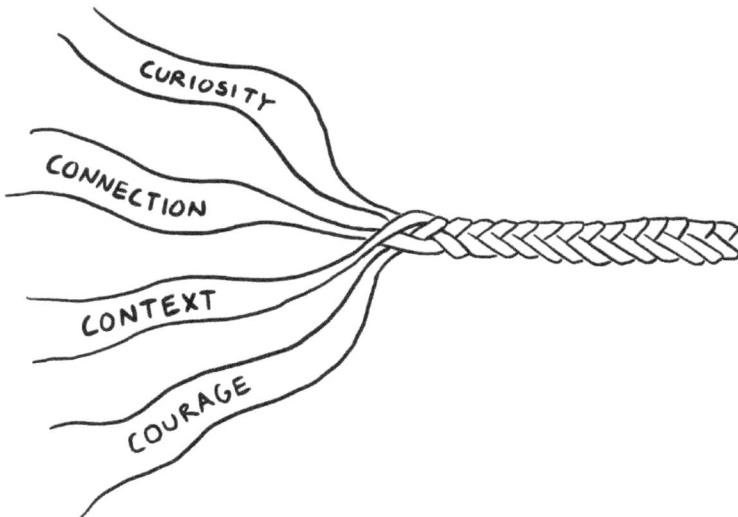

CURIOSITY: DISCOVER HIDDEN OPPORTUNITIES

Picture a master detective entering a room. While others might see just another corporate training request or routine performance issue, the curious L&D practitioner sees the beginning of a story waiting to be uncovered. This investigative mindset—the ability to look beyond surface-level symptoms to underlying opportunities—is where value creation begins.

Consider Sarah, an L&D manager at a global manufacturing firm. The email in her inbox seemed routine: "Need updated safety training ASAP. Incidents up 15 percent this quarter." Many would have immediately pulled the standard compliance deck, updated the dates, and scheduled the sessions. However, Sarah saw a story unfolding beneath the numbers. Her curiosity led her to ask deeper questions: Why were safety incidents increasing in certain departments but not others? What made some teams consistently safer than their peers? This curiosity drove her to the shop floor, where conversations with operators revealed insights no incident report could capture.

Curiosity doesn't operate in isolation. As Sarah's questions opened new doors, she found herself naturally drawn into the next C: connection. Her conversations with operators led to relationships with shift supervisors, safety committees, and eventually senior operations leaders. Each connection added a new perspective, transforming a simple training request into an opportunity for organizational transformation.

Through this lens, curiosity becomes more than just asking questions; it becomes the catalyst that initiates the value-seeking journey. It's the spark that ignites deeper understanding and opens pathways to unprecedented opportunities.

👣 **ACTIONABLE STEPS:**

1. **Challenge Assumptions:** Don't accept surface-level requests. Push deeper with questions that reveal true needs: "Why?" "Why now?" "What happens if we don't do this?" "What would success look like?" "Who else should care about this?" "How will we know it's working?" Each question peels back another layer, revealing the real opportunities for impact.

2. **Explore Hidden Talent:** Use tools like talent inventories, 360-degree feedback, and skill assessments to identify untapped potential within your organization.

3. **Spot Trends:** Dedicate time each month to researching industry shifts, workforce demographics, and technological advances to anticipate needs and position L&D as a strategic driver of success.

Curiosity in action transforms simple requests into opportunities for meaningful change. The following case study demonstrates how one organization's L&D team used deep curiosity to look beyond a straightforward technology request and uncover systemic challenges that, once addressed, created value across multiple dimensions of the business. Their approach exemplifies how asking the right questions can lead to discovering unexpected opportunities for improvement.

Case Study: From Communication Tools to Operational Excellence

Initial Challenge: Avita Home Health and Hospice faced a seemingly straightforward problem: Mobile staff needed better communication tools.

Value Seeking Journey: Instead of simply implementing a new communication platform, the L&D team dug deeper; they:

- Shadowed nurses to understand their daily workflows
- Mapped communication patterns across departments
- Identified bottlenecks in information flow
- Discovered how communication gaps affected patient care

Uncovered Opportunities: This curiosity-driven investigation revealed that communication challenges were symptoms of larger operational inefficiencies. By understanding these connections, the team designed a more comprehensive solution.

Expanded Impact: The implementation of TigerConnect became more than a communication fix:

- Administrative time was reduced by four hours per nurse per week.

- Patient wait times decreased significantly.

- The revenue cycle was shortened by twenty-one days.

- Staff burnout was reduced through streamlined workflows.

Key Value Seeking Insight: By looking beyond the initial request for "better communication tools," the team uncovered and addressed systemic issues that affected operational efficiency, employee satisfaction, and patient care.

CONNECTION: BUILD RELATIONSHIPS THAT UNLOCK POTENTIAL

Think of connection as the mycelium network we explored in Chapter 1—the invisible web that transforms individual insights into organizational impact. Like that living network beneath the forest floor, connections create pathways through which value flows and multiplies throughout an organization.

Sarah's safety investigation could have ended with a few isolated observations. Instead, the connections she built transformed her initial findings into organizational insights. Each conversation created a bridge—between departments, across hierarchies, and through silos that typically kept valuable information contained. These connections revealed patterns that no single perspective could illuminate: how communication gaps between shifts created safety risks, how cultural differences affected procedure adherence, and how informal leadership influenced safety behavior.

Connection transforms the L&D professional from an outside observer into an integral part of the organizational ecosystem. It's through these relationships that we:

- Uncover unspoken needs and hidden opportunities

- Build coalitions for meaningful change

- Access the informal networks where real organizational knowledge resides

- Create the trust necessary for lasting transformation

However, connection isn't just about building a network; it's about activating it purposefully to create value, which leads us naturally to our next C: context.

🐾 ACTIONABLE STEPS:

1. **Foster Collaboration:** Design cross-functional learning initiatives that encourage knowledge-sharing and build networks across departments.

2. **Cultivate Stakeholder Trust:** Engage regularly with stakeholders at all levels, listening to their needs and aligning learning programs with their priorities.

3. **Tailor Learning Experiences:** Create personalized development plans that feel relevant, actionable, and deeply connected to individual and team goals.

The power of connection becomes evident when organizations leverage their existing networks to drive innovation. In the following case study, an L&D team demonstrated how mapping and activating organizational connections could unleash latent potential. Their approach shows how understanding and strengthening the connections between people, ideas, and opportunities can transform an organization's innovation capacity.

Case Study: Innovation Through Value Discovery

Initial Challenge: Alcatel-Lucent sought to increase innovation within its existing workforce.

Value Seeking Journey: The L&D team looked beyond traditional innovation training by:

- Mapping existing pockets of innovation within the company
- Identifying informal networks of creative problem-solvers
- Studying how successful ideas moved from concept to implementation
- Analyzing barriers that prevented good ideas from gaining traction

Uncovered Opportunities: This exploration revealed that innovation potential already existed within the organization; it just needed the right conditions to flourish.

Expanded Impact: The intrapreneurship boot camp became a catalyst for organizational transformation:

- Thirty-two innovative projects launched and developed
- Multiple successful venture spin-offs created
- New revenue streams established
- Entrepreneurial thinking became part of company culture
- Cross-functional collaboration increased

Key Value Seeking Insight: By recognizing that innovation wasn't just about teaching new skills but creating an ecosystem for ideas to thrive, the team unlocked value far beyond the initial program scope.

CONTEXT: ALIGN EFFORTS WITH THE BIGGER PICTURE

While curiosity uncovers opportunities and connection builds networks of understanding, context is what gives meaning to our discoveries. Like a cartographer mapping new territory, context helps us understand where our insights fit within the larger organizational landscape.

Returning to Sarah's safety initiative, her growing network of connections revealed numerous opportunities for improvement. But which ones mattered most? The context provided the lens through which to evaluate these possibilities. She examined:

- How safety performance influenced key strategic goals and business outcomes

- Current industry trends and regulatory changes reshaping safety requirements

- What previous safety initiatives had taught them—both successes and failures

- Whether the organization's culture was ready to embrace significant change

This broader perspective transformed her understanding. What began as a routine training request became a catalyst for organizational change: improving safety metrics, enhancing operational efficiency, strengthening leadership capabilities, and building a more resilient safety culture.

Context doesn't just help us understand where we are; it illuminates the path forward. By placing our discoveries within the larger organizational story, we can better anticipate challenges, identify enablers, and design solutions that resonate with stakeholders at every level.

👣 ACTIONABLE STEPS:

1. **Anchor Initiatives to Organizational Objectives:** Link every program to key business goals, such as increasing market share, enhancing customer satisfaction, or building organizational agility.

2. **Leverage Data:** Analyze performance metrics, employee feedback, and market trends to effectively identify gaps and target solutions.

3. **Adapt for Impact:** Tailor learning initiatives to meet current challenges, whether they involve adapting to remote work, navigating technological disruptions, or meeting regulatory demands.

Understanding context transforms isolated initiatives into catalysts for organizational change. The following case study illustrates how one organization's L&D team used contextual understanding to elevate a standard leadership development request into an opportunity for comprehensive cultural transformation. Their story demonstrates how viewing challenges through the lens of organizational context can reveal deeper opportunities for systemic impact.

Case Study: Leadership Development as Cultural Transformation

Initial Challenge: Otter Tail Corporation needed to strengthen its leadership pipeline.

Value Seeking Journey: The L&D team expanded their investigation to understand:

- What made current leaders successful in their roles
- How leadership affected organizational culture
- Where future leadership challenges might emerge
- What barriers prevented diverse talent from advancing

Uncovered Opportunities: The investigation revealed that leadership development could serve as a vehicle for broader cultural transformation and organizational resilience.

Expanded Impact: Partnership with MDA Leadership delivered multifaceted results:

- Created robust succession planning processes
- Enhanced inclusivity across all leadership levels
- Strengthened cross-functional collaboration
- Improved decision-making at all levels
- Built lasting organizational resilience

Key Value Seeking Insight: By viewing leadership development through a wider lens, the team created a program that didn't just develop individual leaders but transformed the entire organizational ecosystem.

COURAGE: TAKE ACTION TO CREATE IMPACT

While curiosity, connection, and context help you discover and understand opportunities, courage is the catalyst that transforms possibilities into reality. It's the force that moves you from insight to action, from potential to achievement.

Courage manifests in multiple ways throughout the value-seeking journey:

- The courage to ask uncomfortable questions when curiosity leads us to challenging truths
- The courage to build connections across organizational boundaries, even when those connections challenge established hierarchies
- The courage to acknowledge difficult contexts and still move forward with necessary changes

For Sarah, courage meant transforming her insights into bold action. Instead of delivering a standard safety program, she advocated for a comprehensive cultural transformation initiative. This required:

- Challenging executive assumptions about the root causes of safety issues

- Proposing a larger budget than initially allocated

- Committing to measurable outcomes that would put her reputation on the line

- Standing firm when early setbacks led some stakeholders to push for a "simpler" solution

Courage isn't about reckless action. Informed by curiosity, strengthened by connections, and guided by context, courage becomes calculated and strategic. It's the difference between being rash and being bold—between taking blind risks and making informed choices to drive meaningful change.

This is where the Four Cs reveal their true power. Working together, they create a virtuous cycle: Courage informed by context leads to more focused curiosity. Stronger connections provide the support needed for bolder actions. Better context helps us understand where and how to apply courage for maximum impact.

👣 **ACTIONABLE STEPS:**

1. **Pilot Bold Innovations:** Start small by testing new approaches on a limited scale to gather insights and refine ideas before expanding.

2. **Be a Change Advocate:** Use data and storytelling to build compelling cases for initiatives that address organizational challenges and opportunities.

3. **Stay Committed to the Long-Term:** Champion programs that may take time to show results but have the potential to drive transformational change.

Courage in L&D often means challenging conventional approaches to reveal deeper opportunities for transformation. The following case study shows how one organization's L&D team demonstrated the courage to move beyond traditional management training to address fundamental human capabilities. Their story illustrates how informed courage—backed by data and driven by conviction—can lead to programs that create lasting organizational change rather than temporary improvements.

Case Study: Emotional Intelligence as a Performance Multiplier

Initial Challenge: FedEx Express identified a need to improve leadership effectiveness among their managers.

Value Seeking Journey: Rather than implementing standard management training, the L&D team:

- Conducted in-depth interviews with high-performing leaders
- Analyzed patterns in team performance data
- Studied the ripple effects of leadership decisions
- Identified emotional intelligence as a key differentiator

Uncovered Opportunities: The investigation revealed that emotional intelligence was a leadership skill and foundational capability that influenced everything from decision-making to team dynamics.

Expanded Impact: The LEAD1 program evolved into a comprehensive development experience:

- Five-day intensive workshop to build core emotional intelligence capabilities
- Six months of coaching ensured sustained behavior change
- Team engagement metrics improved significantly
- Turnover rates decreased across managed teams
- "People First" philosophy became embedded in daily operations

Key Value Seeking Insight: By exploring the deeper connections between emotional intelligence and organizational performance, the team created a program that transformed both individual leaders and organizational culture.

The Four Cs—curiosity, connection, context, and courage—are not isolated principles; they are the heartbeat of value-seeking. Together, they guide us through an iterative cycle of discovery, alignment, and transformation.

The *American Pickers'* discovery of the Aerosmith van powerfully demonstrates seeking value through curiosity, connection, and context. When Mike Wolfe and Frank Fritz spotted the rusted van, they didn't dismiss it as junk; they asked questions. *Why is it here? What might it have been?* This curiosity led them to discover its hidden potential. However, curiosity alone wasn't enough. Their connection with Ray Tabano, one of Aerosmith's founding members, proved crucial—his firsthand stories transformed the van from a curious artifact into a verified piece of rock history. They fully grasped its significance through context—a deeper understanding of cultural history and its connection to the van's value. Their discovery wasn't just about restoring a vehicle but amplifying its significance by aligning its story with its historical and emotional value.

The Michigan family's experience with the Concord grapevine reveals the power of courage and context in seeking value. Faced with desperation, the family showed courage by taking action—tending to an unassuming vine and transforming it into a lifeline. They didn't stop at what was visible; instead, they saw the vine's potential and contextualized it within their needs, cultivating it into a source of sustenance and hope.

Their perseverance and foresight exemplify key principles of seeking value. Courage enables you to challenge assumptions and take risks, while context ensures your efforts are targeted and meaningful. Like the family, your role is to nurture overlooked opportunities and amplify their impact, even when the outcomes aren't immediately apparent.

These principles are about responding to and anticipating needs. Seeking value shifts our role from reactive problem-solvers to proactive enablers of impact. This intentional focus on seeking value ensures our initiatives are relevant and transformative.

$\stackrel{\star}{\sim}$ **Remember:** Seeking value is the critical first step to creating impact.

A value-seeking mindset ensures our efforts are intentional, informed, and aligned with organizational needs. By embedding the Four Cs into our mindset, we transform value-seeking into an ongoing practice that uncovers opportunities, aligns initiatives with broader goals, and drives lasting impact for people, teams, and organizations.

⚡ YOUR TURN: ACTIVATE THE FOUR Cs

Select a current challenge or opportunity in your organization. Then, complete this value-seeking exercise:

Curiosity Spark:

- Write three questions that challenge your current assumptions about this situation.

- What information are you missing? Where could you look deeper?

Connection Check:

- List two or three unexpected voices you should bring into this conversation.

- Which relationships could you strengthen to better understand this challenge?

Context Compass:

- How does this challenge connect to your organization's bigger picture?

- What similar situations from the past could inform your approach?

Courage Catalyst:

- What bold action could you take that makes you slightly uncomfortable?

- What's the smallest first step you could take toward that action?

Integration: After exploring each C, capture in a single paragraph: What new value do you see now that wasn't visible before? What will you do differently based on these insights?

THE TREASURE YOU HOLD

Like the skilled antique hunters who recognized the value of Aerosmith's historic van beneath years of rust, we have the unique ability to see potential where others see only problems. Through the Four Cs—curiosity, connection, context, and courage—we develop the mindset to uncover opportunities others miss.

Your role goes far beyond delivering programs; you are a value seeker, a transformation architect, and a catalyst for meaningful change. The tools of value-seeking are already in your hands. Now is the time to act with purpose, uncover hidden opportunities, and transform learning into a driver of success for your organization.

Remember, every overlooked detail, unexplored connection, and challenging context contains the potential for transformation. You can unlock value that others might never see by cultivating curiosity, building meaningful connections, understanding broader context, and acting with courage. The journey of value-seeking begins with a single question, conversation, or insight—but it leads to a lasting impact that resonates throughout your organization.

LOOKING AHEAD: FROM SEEKING TO CREATING VALUE

While this chapter has equipped you with the mindset and methods for uncovering hidden opportunities through the Four Cs, seeking value is only the beginning. In Chapter 4, we'll explore how to transform these discoveries into creating measurable impact through the Value Creation Compass. This practical framework will help you navigate from insight to implementation, ensuring the opportunities you uncover translate into tangible results that matter to your stakeholders and organization. As we shift from seeking to creating value, you'll learn how to design, deliver, and measure initiatives that drive lasting transformation.

🔑 KEY LEARNINGS

- **The Value Seeker's Eye:** Like Mike and Frank discovering Aerosmith's forgotten van, transformative value often lies beneath weathered surfaces, waiting for someone with the right perspective to recognize its worth and unleash its potential. When viewed through a skilled seeker's lens, what appears worthless to others can hold untold value.

- **The Power of Integrated Discovery:** The Four Cs—curiosity, connection, context, and courage—function like interwoven strands, each strengthening the others to create a systematic approach to uncovering opportunities. Like the family who transformed an overlooked grapevine into their lifeline, this framework helps us spot and cultivate hidden potential.

- **The Detective's Curiosity:** As Sarah demonstrated with the safety training request, curiosity drives us beyond surface-level problems to uncover deeper truths. We reveal opportunities that others might walk past by asking probing questions and investigating beyond initial symptoms.

- **The Living Network:** Like the mycelium network beneath a forest floor, connection creates vital pathways through which value flows throughout an organization. These connections bridge silos, span hierarchies, and reveal patterns that no single perspective could illuminate.

- **The Strategic Compass:** Context serves as our guide, helping us map where opportunities fit within the larger organizational landscape. This understanding transforms isolated insights into strategically aligned initiatives like a cartographer mapping new territory.

- **The Catalyst of Change:** Courage, fortified by curiosity, connections, and context, becomes the force that transforms insight into impact. Not through reckless action but through calculated boldness—as demonstrated by Sarah's transformation of a routine safety training into an organization-wide cultural initiative.

4

VALUE ARCHITECT: *CREATING WHAT MATTERS*

"Strive not to be a success, but to be of value."

—*Albert Einstein*

FROM CHALLENGE TO TRANSFORMATION: THE DARIEN LIBRARY STORY

I n the early 2000s, the town of Darien, Connecticut, faced a familiar challenge. Its public library, once a bustling hub, had become outdated and underutilized in the age of digital information. With dwindling visitors and declining relevance, the library was seen as a relic—a place for dusty books rather than a vital resource for the community.

When Alan Gray became the library's new director, he saw beyond the challenges to the library's untapped potential. Rather than conceding to obsolescence, he envisioned transforming the library into a driver of community growth and resilience. This vision would require reimagining how a library could serve its community.

Gray began with a fundamental question: "What does our community need to thrive?" His team conducted community surveys, held town halls, and met with local business leaders and educators to find answers. These conversations revealed that residents wanted more than books; they needed a space for skill development, career growth, and community connection. Guided by these insights, they introduced a state-of-the-art makerspace where patrons could learn 3D printing, coding, and design skills. They offered career workshops, partnering with local businesses to help residents build resumes, practice interviews, and develop new job skills. Gray also created programs tailored to local families, such as parenting classes, book clubs, and even teen mental health workshops.

The results were astonishing. Library attendance surged to over one thousand visitors daily—a dramatic increase from previous years. However, raw numbers tell only part of the story. The library evolved into an essential community hub where people came to borrow books and transform their lives through skill development, mutual support, and meaningful connections. Even longtime non-users began to view the library as an indispensable community asset.

Today, Darien Library is celebrated as one of the most innovative libraries in the United States. This success story demonstrates a crucial lesson: Intentional transformation can revolutionize an organization's impact.

CREATING VALUE THROUGH STRATEGIC ALIGNMENT

Alan Gray's transformation of the Darien Library demonstrates how intentional alignment between vision, strategy, and action can meet evolving community needs. His approach exemplified four fundamental principles of organizational value creation that form the foundation of this chapter:

- **Empowering People:** Unlocking and developing human potential
- **Driving Growth:** Expanding organizational impact and reach
- **Building Resilience:** Strengthening adaptive capacity
- **Creating Value:** Exceeding stakeholder expectations

As L&D practitioners, we face a similar challenge: How do we create meaningful impact across our organizations? Like Gray, we must align our initiatives with strategic needs and measurable outcomes. This requires a systematic approach to identifying and activating opportunities for value creation.

The principles that guided the Darien Library's transformation are embedded in the Value Creation Compass, a strategic tool that guides you toward maximum organizational impact. Just as Gray's vision brought clarity and purpose to his efforts, the Compass aligns initiatives with organizational priorities that matter most, turning intent into measurable outcomes.

THE VALUE CREATION COMPASS

Picture yourself as a navigator steering your organization through uncertain waters. As maritime navigators rely on their compass to stay on course through storms and calm seas, the Value Creation Compass offers four cardinal directions to guide your initiatives toward measurable impact and sustainable success.

The Value Creation Compass guides organizations through four fundamental dimensions:

- **True North - Empowering People:** Cultivating potential through targeted skill development, leadership growth, and opportunity creation

- **East - Driving Business Growth:** Catalyzing innovation, optimizing efficiency, and expanding market presence

- **South - Building Organizational Resilience:** Fostering organizational adaptability and ensuring long-term sustainability

- **West - Delivering Customer Value:** Generating measurable impact for stakeholders

The Value Creation Compass serves as your strategic guide by enabling you to:

- Uncover hidden value opportunities and optimize resource allocation for maximum impact
- Align initiatives precisely with stakeholder priorities and organizational objectives
- Transform strategic intent into targeted action through data-driven program development

Each compass direction illuminates pathways to unlock organizational potential, making impact both visible and measurable. Rather than adding complexity, this framework streamlines your approach to value creation by providing a clear strategic focus. The Compass transforms L&D from a support function into a strategic driver of organizational success, directly connecting learning initiatives to business outcomes. Through this lens, you can clearly demonstrate how learning investments fuel innovation, strengthen resilience, and accelerate growth.

Let's explore each direction of the Value Creation Compass in detail, beginning with True North—the foundation of organizational capability.

VALUE CREATION COMPASS

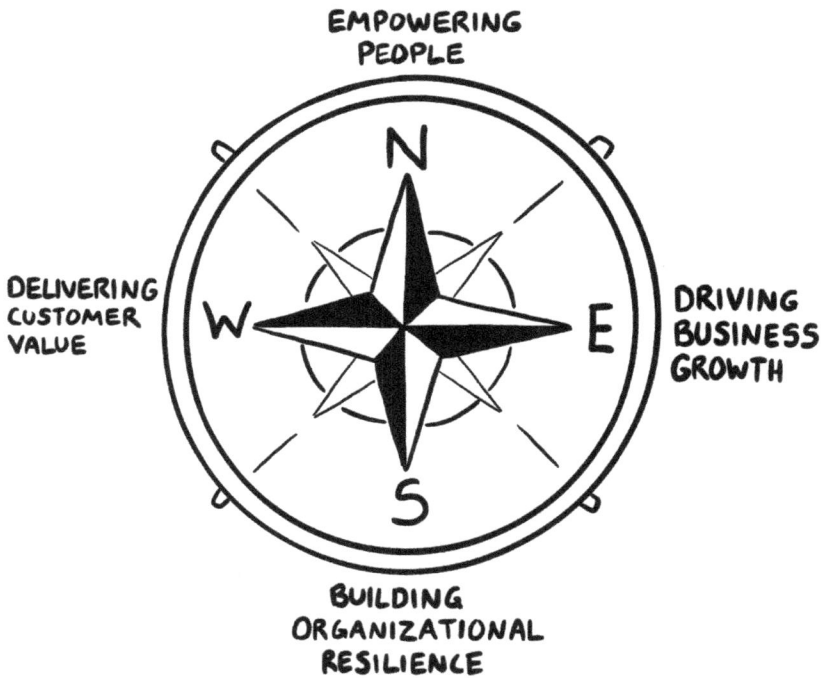

EMPOWERING PEOPLE
DELIVERING CUSTOMER VALUE
DRIVING BUSINESS GROWTH
BUILDING ORGANIZATIONAL RESILIENCE

TRUE NORTH: EMPOWERING PEOPLE

True North focuses on unlocking human potential—the foundational driver of organizational success. This direction transforms individual capability into collective strength by developing three core elements: *strategic skills, leadership capacity, and employee engagement.* You help build the confidence, capacity, and commitment necessary for sustained performance through these elements. Employees drive innovation, enhance collaboration, and strengthen organizational culture when effectively developed.

THREE CORE ELEMENTS OF PEOPLE EMPOWERMENT

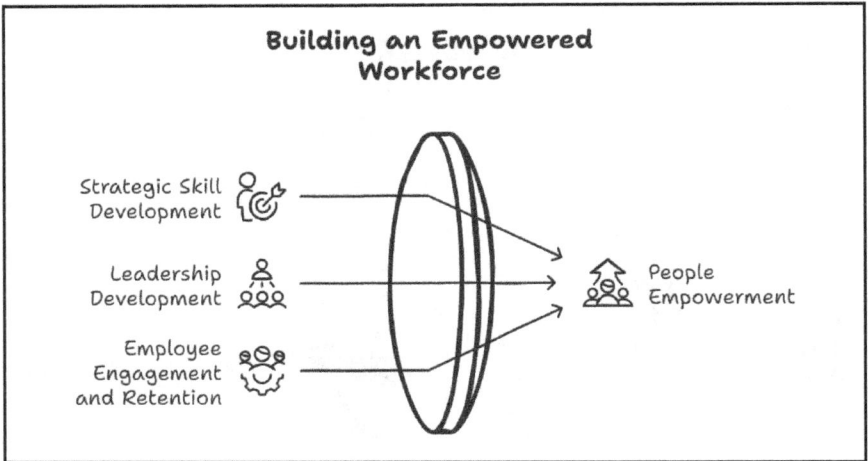

Building an Empowered Workforce

Strategic Skill Development
Leadership Development
Employee Engagement and Retention
People Empowerment

1. Strategic Skill Development

- **What It Is:** Strategic skill development aligns workforce capabilities with organizational objectives, identifying and building the competencies that drive business success. It goes beyond traditional training by focusing on skills that create competitive advantage, enable growth, and prepare the organization for future opportunities. This deliberate approach ensures learning investments directly support business strategy.

- **How L&D Supports:** Through strategic competency mapping and needs assessment, you partner with business leaders to design targeted development programs that combine structured workshops and certification programs with hands-on, experiential learning opportunities. Integrating on-the-job training with continuous feedback mechanisms ensures new skills translate directly into improved performance.

- **The Impact:** Strategic skill development creates a multiplier effect across the organization. As individuals enhance their performance and adaptability, operational efficiency and innovation improve. Employee confidence and job mastery increase, leading to stronger engagement and retention. These individual improvements collectively strengthen organizational capabilities and market competitiveness.

- **Example:** Imagine a manufacturing company embarking on a journey to transform its operations through a data analytics training initiative. In this scenario, the program might begin with foundational data literacy workshops for frontline employees, progress to hands-on training with analytics tools, and culminate in advanced user certification programs. Over six months, such an initiative could result in an 18 percent improvement in operational efficiency by successfully implementing predictive maintenance systems. Additionally, decision-making capabilities across operational levels would improve, while employee engagement in continuous improvement initiatives could rise significantly.

2. Leadership Development

- **What It Is:** Leadership development builds the crucial skills, mindsets, and behaviors needed to guide people, teams, and organizations successfully. It systematically develops leaders at all levels who can execute strategy, drive change, and inspire high performance. This comprehensive approach ensures a strong pipeline of leaders ready to take on greater responsibilities and navigate future challenges.

- **How L&D Supports:** Your role is to design and implement integrated leadership experiences that combine multiple learning approaches and offerings. Start with core skill development in areas like strategic thinking and emotional intelligence, enhanced through personalized coaching and mentorship relationships. Provide practical application through stretch assignments and real-world problem-solving via action learning projects. Regular feedback guides ongoing development and ensures alignment with organizational needs.

- **The Impact:** Effective leadership development strengthens both immediate performance and long-term organizational health. Teams become more engaged and productive under capable leaders. Better succession planning and talent retention create stability, collaboration, and ideation. As leadership capabilities mature across the organization, innovation and collaboration flourish, driving sustainable success.

- **Example:** Consider a global retail chain seeking to transform its leadership pipeline. The company implemented a multi-faceted development program tailored for store managers to achieve this. Monthly leadership workshops laid the foundation for skill-building, while peer mentoring circles fostered collaboration and shared learning. Participants engaged in action learning projects to tackle real business challenges, gaining hands-on experience in problem-solving. Regional leaders provided ongoing coaching, ensuring continuous growth and alignment with organizational goals. Within a year, the company experienced a 20 percent reduction in employee turnover, a 19 percent boost in customer satisfaction, and a 15 percent increase in same-store sales. Additionally, internal promotions for key roles significantly increased, reinforcing the program's long-term impact.

3. Employee Engagement and Retention

- **What It Is:** Employee engagement and retention create a foundation where people commit to your organization's success and choose to build their careers there. It's about creating an environment where employees see their future, understand their value, and actively contribute to organizational goals. When engagement is strong, your organization preserves crucial knowledge, strengthens its culture, and maintains consistent performance.

- **How L&D Supports:** Your role is to develop initiatives that align personal growth with organizational success. Create personalized career pathways that connect individual aspirations with business opportunities. Design skill-building programs that enhance job mastery and cross-functional projects that broaden expertise. Implement recognition programs that celebrate learning achievements and reinforce the link between personal development and organizational impact.

- **The Impact:** Strong engagement and retention deliver both immediate and long-term benefits. Direct financial gains come from reduced recruitment costs and higher productivity from experienced teams. The organization benefits from preserved institutional knowledge, stronger operational capabilities, and enhanced innovation as experienced employees share their expertise. Team cohesion improves, collaboration increases, and the organization builds a sustainable competitive advantage through its people.

- **Example:** A high-growth tech startup grappled with engagement challenges. To address this, the organization launched a dynamic learning initiative designed to foster growth and collaboration. Quarterly learning sprints provided focused skill-building opportunities, while peer mentorship circles encouraged knowledge sharing across teams. To sustain momentum, the company implemented a robust recognition program to celebrate certification milestones and hosted career development workshops to guide employees in planning their growth paths. Over the course of a year, the results were striking: Employee engagement scores climbed by 25 percent, voluntary turnover dropped by 18 percent, internal mobility rose by 30 percent, and employee referrals increased by 16 percent, reflecting a vibrant and motivated workforce.

⚡ **REFLECTION QUESTIONS:**

Consider the following questions when developing your people empowerment strategy:

- How have you mapped the critical skills your organization needs for future success?

- What mechanisms exist to measure and enhance the impact of your development initiatives?

- What steps are you taking to create an environment that encourages continuous learning?

- What processes exist to identify and develop emerging talent?

Empowering People as a Value Multiplier

Empowering people is a fundamental value multiplier, turning individual potential into organizational success. Liz Wiseman's research on *Multipliers* illustrates this vividly: Leaders who act as multipliers don't just manage talent; they amplify it. They unlock the intelligence, creativity, and capability of those around them, fostering an environment where every person's contribution is maximized.

When organizations embrace this multiplier mindset, they ignite a ripple effect that enhances every aspect of performance and possibility. Empowered individuals take ownership, innovate, and collaborate in ways that extend their impact far beyond individual roles, driving personal and organizational growth.

L&D acts as the architect of this empowerment by designing intentional development experiences. Aligning learning initiatives with individual aspirations and organizational objectives creates the conditions for sustainable high performance. This goes beyond building technical skills; it includes fostering confidence, engagement, and the commitment needed to achieve exceptional results.

As we turn to the east direction of our Value Creation Compass, we shift our focus to driving business growth. Empowered people lay the foundation for innovation and progress, enabling organizations to unlock new markets, develop transformative solutions, and expand their impact. Their skills, creativity, and drive fuel the growth strategies that propel organizations toward greater success and resilience in a rapidly evolving world.

East: Driving Business Growth

Driving business growth requires systematically converting organizational potential into measurable market success. This direction focuses on seizing opportunities across four key dimensions: profitability enhancement, market expansion, innovation acceleration, and technology adoption. Success comes through harnessing the combined power of strategic alignment, empowered employees, and a culture of continuous improvement.

We drive growth by aligning development initiatives with organizational goals equipping employees with the skills and attitudes needed to address challenges and unlock opportunities. We serve as a catalyst for sustainable growth through targeted sales training, innovation enablement, and technology adoption.

FOUR KEY DIMENSIONS OF BUSINESS GROWTH

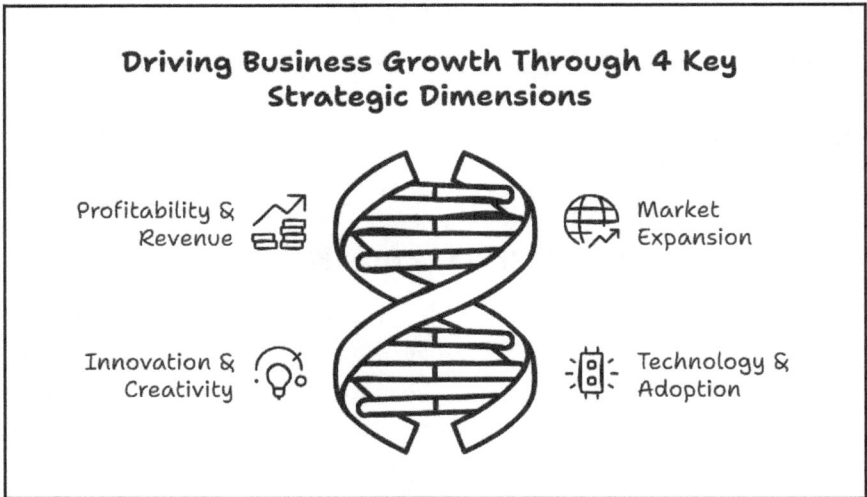

Driving Business Growth Through 4 Key Strategic Dimensions

Profitability & Revenue

Market Expansion

Innovation & Creativity

Technology & Adoption

1. Profitability and Revenue Growth

- **What It Is:** Sustainable business success demands more than just making money; it requires strategic growth in revenue and profitability. This means developing new revenue streams, optimizing costs, expanding market share, and maximizing customer value. Strong profitability creates the resources needed for future investment and expansion.

- **How L&D Supports:** Your role is to build critical capabilities that drive financial performance. Create programs that develop consultative selling skills and strategic account management expertise. Help teams sharpen their financial acumen through training in business case development, financial analysis, and resource allocation.

- **The Impact:** When organizations focus strategically on profitability, the benefits multiply. Revenue per customer increases while profit margins improve. Better cost management creates resources for new investments. Strong market position and operational efficiency drive sustainable growth.

- **Example:** Imagine a global technology company seeking to boost its revenue generation by refining its sales strategies. The organization introduced a robust development program that integrated consultative selling techniques with strategic account planning. Sales leaders participated in performance coaching certification to ensure these skills were applied effectively. The results were remarkable: Sales close rates increased by 15 percent, contributing $10 million in additional annual revenue. Deal sizes grew by 25 percent. The sales cycle was shortened by 30 percent, and customer retention improved by 40 percent, showcasing the program's long-term impact on sustainable growth.

2. Market Expansion

- **What It Is:** Market expansion drives growth by strategically pursuing new opportunities, whether entering new territories, reaching untapped customer segments, or moving into adjacent industries. Success requires powerful market insight, cultural understanding, and consistent execution capabilities.

- **How L&D Supports:** Your role is to prepare teams for successful market expansion. Develop programs that build expertise in market analysis, competitive intelligence, and customer needs assessment. Create learning experiences that strengthen cross-cultural communication skills and knowledge of local business practices. Ensure consistent execution through operational excellence training.

- **The Impact:** Successful market expansion creates multiple growth engines. Revenue streams diversify as the customer base expands. Teams develop valuable global capabilities and operational flexibility. The organization becomes more adaptable as it learns to operate effectively in diverse markets.

- **Example:** Consider a global pharmaceutical company aiming to enhance its market expansion efforts. The organization implemented a strategic initiative to achieve this, including cultural intelligence certification, tailored market entry play-books, and comprehensive regulatory compliance training. As a result, the company successfully entered five new markets, driving a 20 percent revenue increase. Local partnerships thrived, with success rates rising by 35 percent, while market entry timelines were reduced by 40 percent. Additionally, cross-border collaboration effectiveness improved by 50 percent, highlighting the initiative's transformative impact on global operations.

3. Innovation and Creativity

- **What It Is:** Innovation transforms ideas into market-winning solutions that set your organization apart. Success requires balancing creative thinking with disciplined execution— knowing how to generate breakthrough ideas and turn them into practical reality. This capability helps organizations solve customer problems in unique ways while staying ahead of competitors.

- **How L&D Supports:** Your role is to build innovation capabilities across the organization. Design programs that teach practical approaches like design thinking and rapid prototyping. Create learning experiences that develop both creative problem-solving and implementation skills. Help teams measure and track their innovation success to drive continuous improvement.

- **The Impact:** Strong innovation capabilities deliver powerful results. Organizations develop better solutions faster and respond more quickly to market changes. New revenue streams emerge as teams find novel ways to solve customer problems. Employee engagement rises as people see their ideas make a real difference.

- **Example:** Consider a healthcare organization establishing an innovation academy to inspire creative problem-solving and drive operational improvements. In this scenario, the program might include design thinking certification workshops and a dedicated innovation lab to foster collaboration and experimentation. Such an initiative could lead to outcomes like a 30 percent reduction in patient readmissions through innovative care protocols, a 40 percent increase in innovation initiatives, and a 25 percent improvement in solution time-to-market, generating $15 million in cost savings. Additionally, employee-driven improvements might rise by 45 percent, demonstrating how a focus on innovation can transform both culture and results.

4. Technology Adoption

- **What It Is:** Successful technology adoption transforms how organizations work and serve customers. It combines smart automation, data-driven insights, and enhanced customer experiences to create a competitive advantage. More than just implementing new tools, it's about changing how people work to capture technology's full value.

- **How L&D Supports:** Your role is to help people embrace and effectively use new technologies. Build programs that progress from digital literacy basics to advanced feature mastery. Support change management through hands-on training and performance support tools. Create networks of technology champions who can help others succeed.

- **The Impact:** Effective technology adoption drives improvements throughout the organization. Processes become more efficient while costs decrease. Teams make better decisions using data insights. Customer satisfaction improves through enhanced digital experiences. The organization becomes more agile and competitive in the digital marketplace.

- **Example:** A global logistics company could address operational inefficiencies by introducing a digital skills academy, platform certification programs, and a network of change champions to drive adoption. With this approach, delivery times might decrease by 10 percent, resulting in $5 million in annual savings. Additionally, user adoption could improve by 30 percent, support tickets might drop by 40 percent, and employee satisfaction could increase by 25 percent, illustrating the potential impact of combining upskilling with strategic change management.

⚡ REFLECTION QUESTIONS:

Effective growth initiatives require regular assessment of alignment and impact. Consider these questions when evaluating your growth initiatives:

- How well do your learning programs support profitability, innovation, and market expansion?
- Which organizational goals require stronger alignment with learning initiatives?
- What metrics best demonstrate learning's impact on business performance?
- How effectively does your learning strategy support innovation and digital transformation?

Resilience as the Foundation for Growth

Strategic business growth transforms organizational potential into market leadership through deliberate capability development. Success comes from the synergy between an empowered workforce, resilient operations, and an innovation-ready culture—all enabled by technology and guided by market-responsive strategies.

Growth initiatives create powerful internal momentum. Their ultimate success, however, hinges on an organization's ability to sustain and adapt that momentum over time. As we turn to the south direction of our Value Creation Compass, we explore how resilience becomes the foundation for sustaining growth, navigating disruption, and ensuring long-term success. This shift highlights how building organizational resilience transforms internal capabilities into enduring strength, empowering organizations to weather challenges and thrive in an ever-changing environment.

SOUTH: BUILDING ORGANIZATIONAL RESILIENCE

In today's unpredictable world, organizational resilience enables companies to navigate complexity and change while creating sustainable success. Resilient organizations harness change as a catalyst for growth and innovation, creating systems and cultures that thrive under pressure and evolve with changing demands.

Building resilience means developing a workforce prepared for today's challenges and tomorrow's unknowns. This requires cultivating operational efficiency, strengthening cultural foundations, supporting employee well-being, and instilling agility across teams.

FOUR PILLARS OF ORGANIZATIONAL RESILIENCE

4 Pillars of Organizational Resilience

| Operational Excellence | Cultural Alignment | Employee Well-Being | Agility & Flexibility |

1. Operational Excellence

- **What It Is:** Operational excellence is about making work flow better—finding smarter ways to get things done and keeping

91

those improvements going. It means carefully examining how work happens, removing obstacles that slow people down, and using real data to make better decisions. Think of it as fine-tuning an engine to run at its best, consistently and reliably.

- **How L&D Supports:** You create a pathway to operational excellence through methodology training and implementation support. This includes Lean and Six Sigma certification programs, continuous improvement workshops, and problem-solving training. Implementation support ensures learning translates into results through project-based opportunities and coaching programs.

- **The Impact:** When organizations focus on operational excellence, they see benefits across performance, capability, and culture. Organizations see increased productivity, reduced costs, enhanced process stability, and improved resource utilization. Work gets done more efficiently with less waste. Processes become more reliable and adaptable. Teams solve problems more effectively and work better together. Most importantly, the organization becomes more competitive and better equipped to meet customer needs.

- **Example:** A global manufacturing organization could enhance its operational efficiency through a targeted improvement program. In this scenario, the initiative might begin with tiered Lean or Six Sigma certifications, complemented by weekly improvement workshops and cross-functional project teams. Real-time digital monitoring systems could provide actionable feedback to drive ongoing progress. Over a year, such efforts might reduce process waste, boost production output, improve first-pass quality by 19 percent, and decrease customer complaints by 16 percent. These combined efficiency gains could result in $2 million in annual cost savings, showcasing the potential impact of a structured approach to operational transformation.

2. Cultural Alignment

- **What It Is:** Cultural alignment means creating an organization where values aren't just words on a wall but reflected in how people work daily. It ensures everyone understands what the organization stands for and how to implement those values. Strong cultural alignment helps people make better decisions and work together more effectively toward shared goals.

- **How L&D Supports:** Your role is to help bring organizational values to life through targeted development programs. Create learning experiences that help leaders model and reinforce cultural values. Design team activities that build collaboration skills and cultural understanding. Develop programs that help people work effectively across different backgrounds and perspectives.

- **The Impact:** When culture and actions align, organizations thrive. Teams work together more effectively and adapt more easily to change. People feel more engaged and safer to share ideas. Customer experience improves as employees consistently deliver on organizational values. Innovation increases as people feel empowered to contribute their best thinking.

- **Example:** Imagine a global consulting firm aiming to transform its culture through an integrated development initiative. In this scenario, the effort might begin with immersive cultural onboarding sessions, followed by regular workshops focused on core values and a cultural ambassador certification program to reinforce alignment. Hypothetically, these efforts could lead to significant outcomes: a 20 percent improvement in employee retention, a 35 percent increase in engagement scores, a 25 percent boost in client satisfaction, and a 40 percent enhancement in internal collaboration, demonstrating how intentional cultural development can drive measurable success.

3. Employee Well-Being

- **What It Is:** An organization's success depends on employees who bring their full energy and capability to work each day. Strong well-being initiatives integrate physical health, mental wellness, and emotional resilience to create sustainable high performance. This comprehensive approach ensures people flourish while building organizational resilience.

- **How L&D Supports:** Your role centers on building a workplace that sustains both performance and wellness. Design programs that develop practical stress management and work-life balance skills. Equip managers with capabilities to support team well-being while maintaining high standards. Create resources and networks that provide timely, accessible support.

- **The Impact:** Investment in well-being reduces absenteeism and healthcare costs while improving talent retention. Teams perform better through increased energy and focus. The workplace becomes more positive and resilient, strengthening relationships and collaboration. Change initiatives succeed more often because people are resilient enough to adapt effectively.

- **Example:** Suppose a multinational healthcare company wanted to address workforce well-being through a comprehensive, integrated program. This initiative might combine resilience training with a certification in providing well-being support, supported by a digital platform offering on-demand resources and peer networks fostering community-based assistance. Such an approach might result in reported burnout decreasing by 30 percent, stress-related absences reducing by 25 percent, team cohesion improving by 40 percent, and employee satisfaction increasing by 35 percent, demonstrating the potential impact of a holistic well-being strategy.

4. Agility and Flexibility

- **What It Is:** Organizational agility combines the speed to adapt with the foresight to anticipate change. In today's dynamic environment, successful organizations must pivot quickly in response to market shifts while simultaneously scanning for emerging opportunities. This dual capability requires flexible structures, rapid decision-making processes, and teams skilled in execution and innovation. More than just quick reactions, true agility builds systematic approaches for sensing market changes, evaluating options, and implementing solutions before competitors can respond.

- **How L&D Supports:** Your role focuses on building the mindsets and skills that enable organizational agility. Design learning experiences that strengthen adaptive thinking and drive innovation. Develop practical capabilities in change management and agile methodologies. Provide frameworks that help teams collaborate effectively and transform ideas into reality.

- **The Impact:** Agile organizations maintain competitive advantage through superior market responsiveness. They identify and capture opportunities ahead of competitors. Teams excel at solving complex problems and embracing change. The organization builds a reputation for innovation and adaptability, creating sustainable market leadership.

- **Example:** An international NGO could enhance its agility and effectiveness by implementing a comprehensive capability development initiative. This program might include adaptive leadership academies, collaborative innovation hubs, scenario planning workshops tailored to humanitarian challenges, and digital transformation training for remote teams. Such an approach might result in a 25% reduction in operational disruptions during crisis response, a 40% improvement in the success of change initiatives, a 30% increase in innovative solutions for community impact, and a 50% acceleration in the delivery of critical services, demonstrating how focused development can strengthen an NGO's ability to adapt and deliver.

⚡ REFLECTION QUESTIONS:

Strategic readiness requires careful consideration of how effectively your organization anticipates and prepares for future challenges. Consider these questions when assessing your organization's resilience:

- How are you preparing teams to anticipate and adapt to future challenges?
- What mechanisms identify emerging opportunities and threats?
- What barriers hinder your organization's ability to thrive under pressure?
- Where can you enhance operational efficiency?
- How are you building psychological safety and well-being?
- How effectively do teams collaborate across functions?

Transforming Resilience into Value

Organizations today face unprecedented change, from technological disruptions to shifting economic landscapes. Building resilience enables navigation through this complexity by creating adaptable systems and mindsets. Organizations that master resilience transform challenges into opportunities for innovation and growth.

As we turn to the West direction of our Value Creation Compass, we explore how organizations must channel their growth and capabilities toward delivering exceptional customer experiences. This progression from internal capability to external impact demonstrates how sustainable success flows from organizational strength to market leadership through meaningful customer value creation.

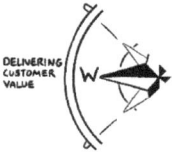

WEST: DELIVERING CUSTOMER VALUE

Creating exceptional customer value stands as the ultimate measure of organizational effectiveness.

This direction combines organizational capabilities with customer needs to build lasting trust and loyalty. Success comes from delivering meaningful solutions and fostering connections that strengthen relationships between organizations and customers.

You empower employees to deeply understand customer needs, resolve challenges proactively, and continuously improve the customer experience. Organizations establish themselves as trusted partners by equipping teams to deliver resonant value, creating competitive advantages that drive immediate and long-term success.

THREE ELEMENTS OF DELIVERING CUSTOMER VALUE

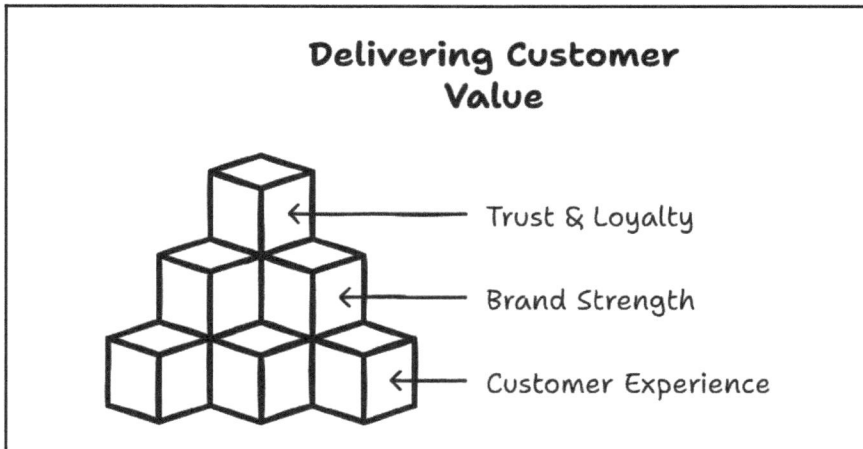

Delivering Customer Value

- Trust & Loyalty
- Brand Strength
- Customer Experience

1. Customer Experience

- **What It Is:** Exceptional customer experience connects every interaction into a seamless journey that builds lasting relationships. It transforms routine touchpoints—from first contact to ongoing support—into meaningful moments that delight customers and strengthen their connection to your organization.

- **How L&D Supports:** Your role is to build the skills that create outstanding customer experiences. Design programs that develop empathetic communication and active listening abilities. Create learning scenarios that help people master personalized interactions while staying true to your brand. Teach teams how to turn service challenges into opportunities to strengthen relationships.

- **The Impact:** Great customer experiences create ripple effects throughout the organization. Customers stay longer and spend more. They become advocates who bring in new business through referrals. The organization builds the kind of trust and loyalty that competitors find hard to match.

- **Example:** A global retail chain might enhance its customer experience through an integrated capability development initiative. In this example, the program could begin with immersive scenario-based training designed to build advanced empathy and problem-solving skills among employees. Over six months, such efforts might result in a 20 percent increase in positive customer feedback, a 12 percent rise in sales conversions, and a 25 percent improvement in customer retention. Additionally, employee engagement scores could improve as teams gain confidence in their ability to deliver exceptional customer experiences.

2. Brand Strengthening

- **What It Is:** Strong brands create emotional connections that transform your organization from just another provider into a trusted partner. This happens when every employee understands and delivers on your brand promise, creating authentic experiences that stand out in crowded markets.

- **How L&D Supports:** Your role is to help employees bring the brand to life. Create immersive experiences and storytelling workshops that make brand values real and personal. Develop communication skills that help teams connect brand value to customer needs. Build programs that align internal actions with external promises.

- **The Impact:** When organizations deliver consistently on their brand promise, they create lasting competitive advantage. Authentic brand experiences build customer loyalty and advocacy. Trust deepens into long-term relationships that support sustainable growth and market leadership.

- **Example:** A luxury automotive retailer could elevate its brand experience through a focused employee development initiative. Such a program might include brand storytelling workshops, personalized coaching sessions, and regular brand immersion experiences to deepen employees' connection to the brand. The potential outcomes of these efforts could include an 18 percent increase in customer satisfaction scores, a 10 percent growth in flagship model sales, and significant improvements in employee engagement. Customer feedback might consistently highlight the authenticity and expertise of the brand experience, demonstrating the program's impact.

3. Trust and Loyalty

- **What It Is:** Trust and loyalty form the bedrock of strong customer relationships. Trust grows when organizations consistently demonstrate reliability, transparency, and genuine care for customer success. Loyalty deepens when experiences consistently exceed expectations and create meaningful connections.

- **How L&D Supports:** Your role is to develop the capabilities that build and maintain trust. Create programs that strengthen ethical decision-making and authentic communication. Help teams balance technical expertise with emotional intelligence. Prepare people to maintain trust even during challenging situations.

- **The Impact:** Organizations that earn deep trust and loyalty gain significant advantages. They enjoy more stable revenue and less price sensitivity. Their customers provide valuable feedback and strong referrals. This creates a foundation for sustainable growth that's difficult for competitors to replicate.

- **Example:** A financial services firm could enhance its client relationships by introducing ethics-centered leadership training alongside transparent communication workshops. Such an initiative might lead to a 30 percent reduction in customer complaints, a 20 percent improvement in client retention, and a 40 percent increase in referral business. Additionally, prioritizing ethical practices and open communication could help the firm maintain strong client partnerships during periods of market volatility, showcasing the potential resilience of trust-based approaches.

⚡ REFLECTION QUESTION:

Delivering exceptional customer value requires careful consideration of your organization's current capabilities and opportunities for enhancement. Consider these questions when evaluating your customer value creation:

- What capabilities need strengthening to enhance customer experience delivery?

- How effectively do teams collaborate to deliver superior customer value?

- How do you measure the impact of customer experience initiatives?

- Where are the greatest opportunities to strengthen customer trust and loyalty?

THE DYNAMIC INTEGRATION OF THE COMPASS

The true power of the Value Creation Compass lies not in each direction individually but in how they work together as an integrated system. Each direction reinforces and amplifies the others, creating a multiplier effect that drives organizational success. Understanding these relationships helps leaders design initiatives that create cascading benefits across the organization.

North → East: Building Capabilities that Drive Growth

When organizations invest in people development (north), they build the capabilities that fuel business growth (east). This relationship creates a powerful engine for sustainable success:

- Leadership development programs create managers who can identify market opportunities and execute growth strategies.

- Technical skill development enables teams to innovate and implement new technologies more effectively.

- Enhanced employee engagement leads to improved productivity and customer service, driving revenue growth.

- Example: A software company's investment in advanced AI training enables their teams to develop new product features that open entirely new market segments, driving 30 percent revenue growth.

South → West: Converting Resilience into Customer Value

Organizational resilience (south) directly strengthens the ability to deliver consistent customer value (west). This connection builds trust and competitive advantage:

- Stable operations ensure reliable product and service delivery.

- Adaptable teams respond more effectively to changing customer needs.

- Strong culture translates into authentic customer experiences.

- Example: A manufacturing company's investment in operational excellence leads to 99.9 percent on-time delivery, dramatically increasing customer satisfaction and retention.

East → North: Reinvesting Success into People

Business growth (east) generates resources that can be reinvested in people development (north), creating a virtuous cycle of improvement:

- Increased profits fund expanded training programs.
- Market success creates new career opportunities.
- Innovation initiatives spark learning and development.
- Example: A retail chain's expansion into new markets funds an advanced management program that develops the next generation of leaders.

West → South: Using Customer Insights to Build Resilience

Customer value creation (west) provides insights and motivation that strengthen organizational resilience (south):

- Customer feedback guides operational improvements.
- Market demands drive cultural evolution.
- Success with customers validates adaptation strategies.
- Example: A healthcare provider's patient experience program reveals process improvements that increase both efficiency and staff satisfaction.

Understanding these dynamic relationships transforms the Compass from a simple framework into a powerful tool for creating compound organizational value. As we'll see in the following case studies, organizations that master these relationships can create extraordinary impact from seemingly ordinary initiatives.

ILLUSTRATIVE EXAMPLE 1: TRANSFORMING HEALTHCARE RETENTION

Consider the following hypothetical example that demonstrates how the Value Creation Compass framework can address critical organizational challenges. Imagine a large regional hospital grappling with a nurse turnover rate of 27 percent, which significantly strained both patient care quality and team morale. Increased reliance on agency staffing created unsustainable costs, and team cohesion began to erode. Leadership recognized that solving this complex issue required more than short-term fixes; it demanded a comprehensive, systemic approach.

Using the Value Creation Compass as a framework, the hospital designed a comprehensive retention strategy that touched all four directions:

North - People Development

- Launched a Nurse Leadership Academy providing 120 hours of advanced clinical and leadership training
- Created individualized career development plans
- Established a mentorship program pairing experienced nurses with new hires
- Implemented quarterly skill-building workshops based on staff feedback

East - Operational Impact

- Decreased agency staffing costs by $1.8 million annually
- Reduced recruitment and onboarding costs by $300,000
- Improved unit efficiency scores by 22 percent
- Reinvested savings into staff development

South - Cultural Transformation

- Introduced daily huddles focusing on patient outcomes and team recognition
- Created unit-based councils giving nurses direct input into protocols
- Established wellness programs addressing burnout
- Developed cross-unit collaboration protocols

West - Patient Outcomes

- Increased HCAHPS patient satisfaction scores from seventy-two to eighty-eight
- Reduced average length of stay by 0.8 days
- Decreased medication errors by 45 percent
- Improved care coordination scores by 35 percent

After twelve months, nurse turnover decreased to 16 percent, employee engagement rose to 82 percent, and the program generated $2.1 million in savings while pushing patient satisfaction into the top quartile nationally.

The initiative demonstrated how simultaneously addressing multiple dimensions of organizational value creation could transform a critical challenge into an opportunity for sustainable improvement. By focusing on individual growth and systematic change, the organization created an environment that supported excellence in patient care and professional fulfillment.

⚡ **Reflection Question:** Instead of just cutting costs, the hospital invested in its people first—and the financial savings followed. What current challenge in your organization could benefit from this people-first approach? What might that look like?

ILLUSTRATIVE EXAMPLE 2: SARAH'S SAFETY TRANSFORMATION

In Chapter 3, we met Sarah, an L&D leader who turned a routine safety training request into a cultural transformation. By applying the Value Creation Compass, Sarah expanded her initiative, ensuring it created measurable value across her organization. The Compass provided both clarity and direction, helping Sarah design a balanced, high-impact solution.

True North – Empowering People

Sarah began her initiative by focusing on people development. She recognized that safety improvements couldn't happen without leadership at the frontline. To empower her teams, Sarah launched targeted leadership training for supervisors. These programs focused on enhancing communication, coaching skills, and accountability—skills critical for promoting a culture of safety. Supervisors gained confidence and the ability to engage employees in adopting new protocols.

East – Driving Business Growth

Enhanced leadership skills led to improved safety protocols, more efficient workflows, and engaged employees. Reduced incidents lowered insurance claims and compliance costs, freeing resources for development while improving productivity.

South - Building Organizational Resilience

Recognizing that safety reflected deeper cultural and operational habits, Sarah introduced cross-functional knowledge-sharing sessions. Teams collaborated to identify risks proactively, share best practices, and brainstorm solutions. This transformed safety from a checklist into an organizational mindset.

West – Delivering Customer Value

As Sarah's teams became more effective, the improvements didn't go unnoticed by customers. Enhanced safety protocols led to fewer production delays and greater reliability in delivering products on time. This strengthened customer trust and became a market differentiator, transforming internal improvements into customer value.

When Sarah encountered initial resistance, she used the Compass diagnostically to identify the root cause: confusion about the new protocols' value. This led her to implement targeted communication sessions that shared success stories and demonstrated business impact, restoring momentum to the initiative.

> ⚡ **Reflection Question:** Sarah showed how improving safety could help the business grow and make customers happier. What's one challenge in your workplace that might have similar hidden benefits if you looked at it from different angles?

ALIGNING THE COMPASS WITH STAKEHOLDER VALUE

The Value Creation Compass ensures learning initiatives resonate with the unique goals of executives, managers, employees, and customers. Aligning L&D efforts with stakeholder priorities—advancing executive strategies, improving team performance, enhancing employee growth, and elevating customer experiences—positions learning professionals as true strategic partners. The Compass bridges the gap between intent and impact

The Value Creation Compass also helps us communicate with stakeholders more effectively. When presenting to executives, we can speak in all four directions, addressing both their immediate concerns and longer-term strategic objectives. We can show how a single initiative creates multiple layers of value, making our proposals more compelling and our impact more visible.

STAKEHOLDER ALIGNMENT

Stakeholder	Focus	Application	Example
Executives	Profitability, innovation, and business resilience	Connect learning initiatives to revenue growth, market differentiation, and sustainable performance	Frame innovation training in terms of market share growth and competitive advantage
Managers	Team performance, efficiency, and retention	Demonstrate how initiatives close skill gaps and enhance operational results	Show how leadership development directly improves team engagement and productivity
Employees	Personal growth, career advancement, and work-life balance	Link development opportunities to career progression and job satisfaction	Highlight how skill development creates new career opportunities while building resilience
Customers	Service quality, reliability, and trust	Connect employee development to enhanced customer experience	Demonstrate how service excellence training improves satisfaction scores and retention
Partners & Suppliers	Collaboration, reliability, and mutual growth	Align L&D with shared goals like efficiency, compliance, and innovation	Show how co-training initiatives improve supplier relationships, reduce errors, and drive innovation

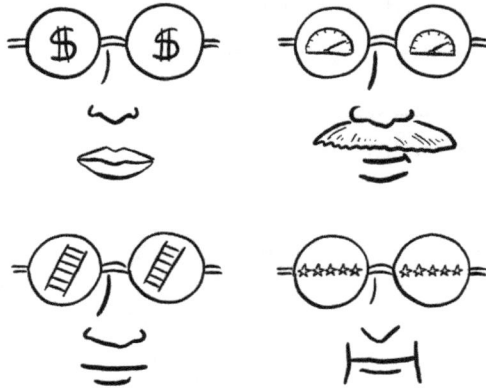

TURNING UNDERSTANDING INTO ACTION

The Value Creation Compass is a transformative tool for redefining how we deliver impact. Understanding its potential is only the first step; the true value lies in using it. This is your opportunity to step into the role of a strategic leader, using the Compass to align your work with the priorities that matter most to your organization and its stakeholders.

👣 NEXT STEPS: TAKING ACTION WITH THE COMPASS

1. Assess Current State

- Map existing initiatives to compass directions.
- Identify areas of strengths and opportunities.
- Evaluate alignment with stakeholder priorities.
- Look for existing connections between directions.

2. Start Small but Strategic

- Select one direction to prioritize as your starting point.

- Design initiative to intentionally activate multiple compass connections.
- Define clear success metrics for each direction involved.
- Start with a scope that's manageable but allows for relationship-building between directions.

3. Engage Stakeholders

- Use the compass as a collaborative tool.
- Present both individual directions and their relationships.
- Seek input on how stakeholders see L&D contributing to success.
- Communicate potential compound benefits to build support.
- Create space for stakeholder suggestions on metrics and value creation.

4. Measure, Reflect, and Iterate

- Implement clear metrics for each direction involved.
- Track how improvements in one direction create opportunities in others.
- Monitor outcomes and gather feedback.
- Look for opportunities to create virtuous cycles of improvement.
- Celebrate wins to build momentum for broader adoption.
- Adjust approach based on learning.

By acting intentionally and collaboratively, the Compass becomes a guide and catalyst for transformational impact, aligning your work with what matters most to your organization.

CHARTING YOUR COURSE FORWARD

The Darien Library story demonstrates a powerful lesson:

Value creation begins with intentionality.

By aligning vision, strategy, and action, Gray turned a declining library into a thriving hub that empowered people, strengthened resilience, and delivered measurable growth. His story challenges us to see the untapped opportunities within our organizations and take deliberate steps to activate them.

We can use the Value Creation Compass to:

- Identify untapped opportunities
- Align initiatives with strategic priorities
- Create measurable impact across all dimensions
- Build sustainable organizational success

Like Alan Gray, you stand at the helm of possibility, equipped with the Value Creation Compass to guide your journey from support function to strategic catalyst. You create cascading benefits that touch every corner of your organization by systematically aligning initiatives across all four directions—empowering people, driving growth, building resilience, and delivering customer value.

> VALUE CREATION BEGINS WITH INTENTIONALITY.

As we move into Chapter 5, we'll tackle our next challenge: measuring and demonstrating impact. We'll explore measurement frameworks and practical tools that help transform tangible and intangible value into compelling evidence that resonates with stakeholders and drives strategic decisions. Through these approaches, we'll ensure your compass guides your journey and validates the wisdom of your chosen course.

🔑 KEY LEARNINGS

- **The Navigator's Tool:** Like Alan Gray transforming a fading library into a vital community hub, the Value Creation Compass guides L&D's evolution from support function to strategic catalyst by aligning initiatives across four essential directions: empowering people, building resilience, driving growth, and delivering customer value.

- **The Multiplier Effect:** As a single stone creates expanding ripples across still water, powerful L&D initiatives generate multiple layers of value—simultaneously developing people (north), accelerating business growth (east), strengthening organizational fabric (south), and enriching customer experiences (west).

- **The People Foundation:** When organizations deeply invest in developing their people, they create a cascade of positive change where individual growth catalyzes team excellence and operational mastery, building the bedrock of sustainable success.

- **The Resilient Core:** Much as a strong foundation enables a building to weather any storm, organizational resilience emerges from the careful cultivation of robust operations, vibrant culture, employee well-being, and adaptive agility—transforming challenges into springboards for growth.

- **The Growth Engine:** A coordinated symphony of enhanced profitability, market expansion, continuous innovation, and technology adoption drives sustainable business growth—working in harmony to create lasting market leadership.

- **The Trust Anchor:** Customer value stands as the true measure of organizational success, where aligned capabilities and authentic culture forge business relationships into enduring partnerships anchored in trust and mutual growth.

5

ANCIENT TRACKS:
MEASURING WHAT MATTERS

"Not everything that can be counted counts,
and not everything that counts can be counted."

—Unknown

THE UNSEEN TRACKS

I n the limestone quarries of Oxfordshire in June 2024, a worker paused during routine excavation, something catching their experienced eye. Where others might have seen random bumps in the rock, they recognized an emerging pattern that would soon reveal an ancient thoroughfare frozen in time.

What unfolded next demonstrated a masterclass in unveiling the hidden. Scientists meticulously documented what would come to be known as a "dinosaur highway"—nearly two hundred perfectly preserved footprints stretching across the quarry like an ancient roadmap, each impression a 166-million-year-old testament to the giants that once ruled these lands. Advanced technology, including drone photography and 3D modeling, brought this prehistoric pathway back to life. However, the true breakthrough wasn't just finding the footprints but what this ancient highway revealed about the past. Each track told a story: here, the ponderous steps of massive herbivorous sauropods like Cetiosaurus; there, the purposeful stride of the predatory Megalosaurus. A seemingly unremarkable quarry transformed into a busy intersection of prehistoric life, complete with its dramas and daily rhythms.

This discovery carries a powerful lesson. Like those ancient tracks, the value of our work exists in measurable evidence, waiting for the right tools and methods to bring it to light. When a leadership program transforms a struggling manager into an inspiring team leader or when a skills initiative enables an entire department to embrace new technology—these changes leave measurable footprints. They're evidence of real impact and quantifiable transformation. Yet, we often lack the right measurement tools to capture and communicate this value. In today's business environment, where every investment competes for limited resources, this measurement gap puts learning initiatives at risk. Without clear evidence of an impact that resonates with financial decision-makers, potentially transformative programs get cut in favor of investments with more easily measured returns.

While previous chapters explored how to recognize hidden value, this chapter focuses on how to measure value systematically and rigorously. Like those scientists in Oxfordshire, we need precise tools and proven methodologies to quantify what others might miss. This chapter will show you how to become a skilled measurer of impact and, more importantly, how to translate that measurement into compelling evidence of strategic value.

Throughout this chapter, we'll explore four essential dimensions of measurement:

1. **The Foundation of Measurement:** Establishing why evidence matters and crafting core principles for measurement

2. **The Evolution of Measurement:** Analyzing proven frameworks that reveal learning's full value

3. **Broadening the Lens:** Uncovering both immediate results and deeper transformations

4. **Turning Insights into Action:** Deploying practical strategies that demonstrate strategic value

By mastering these dimensions, you'll develop the mindset and toolkit needed to transform L&D from a support function into what it truly represents: a strategic driver of organizational success. Let's begin with understanding why measurement matters and how to build a solid foundation for capturing learning's value.

PART 1: THE FOUNDATION OF MEASUREMENT

THE POWER OF PROOF: WHY EVIDENCE MATTERS

Every day, transformative initiatives are abandoned in proverbial boardrooms—not because they lack value but because they lack evidence. A breakthrough sales training program loses funding to an automation project. A culture change initiative gets shelved in favor of new accounting software. Time and again, measurable efficiency prevails over *potential* impact.

Consider two identical learning programs in different organizations. One thrives and expands, becoming central to company strategy. The other gets cut in the next budget cycle. The difference? Evidence.

When a CFO reviews competing investment proposals—for example, a new technology platform versus a leadership development program—the technology proposal typically wins. It comes armed with clear ROI projections and immediate efficiency gains. Despite its transformative potential, the leadership program faces an uphill battle—not because it delivers less value but because that value remains obscured without compelling evidence.

This scenario unfolds daily in organizations worldwide and illuminates three fundamental truths about evidence in L&D:

1. EVIDENCE TRANSFORMS PERCEPTION

When C-suite leaders recognize clear, data-backed connections between learning initiatives and business goals, their perception of L&D shifts dramatically. Deloitte's research reveals that 95 percent of L&D organizations struggle to use data effectively to align learning with business goals or measure its impact, leaving significant potential untapped. This disconnect underscores the urgent need to use evidence to demonstrate strategic value.

Research further supports the transformative power of alignment. Top-performing L&D teams, according to Mind Tools for Business, are twice as likely to collaborate closely with business leaders to integrate learning initiatives into the broader strategy. Similarly,

Training Industry, Inc. found that executives are far more likely to champion L&D when its outcomes directly support strategic goals and address pressing organizational needs.

By anchoring learning initiatives in measurable outcomes, you can elevate your function from perceived cost centers to indispensable drivers of organizational success.

2. EVIDENCE ENABLES EVOLUTION

Adapting and thriving in a dynamic business landscape demands evidence. McKinsey research demonstrates that data-driven organizations are twenty-three times more likely to acquire customers, six times more likely to retain them, and nineteen times more likely to achieve profitability. This correlation highlights a simple but critical truth: Evidence enables precise, informed decision-making, allowing organizations to confidently adapt their strategies.

With data as their compass, these organizations identify customer needs, predict trends, and align efforts with measurable outcomes. Without this clarity, decisions rely on assumptions, and opportunities for growth risk being missed.

In a rapidly evolving business environment, evidence isn't just a guide; it's an accelerant for innovation and sustained growth. When organizations embed data into decision-making processes, they create a culture of continuous improvement and position themselves to thrive amid uncertainty.

3. EVIDENCE BRIDGES THE KNOWING-DOING GAP

The gap between intuition and measurable impact has long challenged L&D teams. According to Brandon Hall Group's *Learning Measurement Study*, fewer than 16 percent of organizations are highly effective at tracking critical metrics like participation, knowledge transfer, behavior change, and business outcomes. As a result, many of the transformative stories behind learning initiatives remain untold.

The stakes have never been higher. Research from Watershed reveals that 60 percent of L&D managers face increasing executive pressure to measure learning's impact—up sharply from just 35 percent in previous years. Despite this, fragmented data systems and lacking alignment with stakeholders undermine efforts to demonstrate value.

Without robust measurement frameworks, we risk losing the ability to tell the most compelling narratives of learning's impact—stories that show how L&D drives transformation, growth, and measurable success. To bridge the knowing-doing gap, L&D must adopt data-driven approaches that bring these stories to the forefront. Evidence doesn't merely justify investment; it secures strategic influence and ensures continuous improvement.

Together, these three truths challenge you to take action and seize an extraordinary opportunity. As an L&D practitioner, you hold the power to transform how others perceive the value of learning, drive meaningful evolution within your organization, and bridge the critical gap between knowing and doing. However, without measurable evidence, your initiatives are at risk.

In times of economic pressure, learning programs without documented results often become the first casualties of budget cuts. Beyond the financial risks, failing to measure and communicate impact weakens your influence and limits your ability to optimize programs for lasting results. By closing this gap, you can secure L&D's place as an essential driver of growth, resilience, and organizational success.

The question isn't whether measurement matters; it's how to measure results effectively. This challenge has captivated learning practitioners for decades, leading to powerful frameworks and approaches that shape our work today.

Reminder: These three fundamental truths about evidence remain constant:

1. Evidence transforms perception.
2. Evidence enables evolution.
3. Evidence bridges the knowing-doing gap.

STANDING ON THE SHOULDERS OF GIANTS

The challenge of measuring learning's impact has deep historical roots. For decades, learning practitioners have worked to capture and communicate the value created through their efforts. These contributions have led to the development of widely recognized frameworks and approaches:

- Kirkpatrick's Four Levels shows how to track learning from reaction to results.

- Phillips' ROI methodology helps translate learning outcomes into financial terms.

- Brinkerhoff's Success Case Method demonstrates the value of strategic sampling and storytelling.

- Thalheimer's Learning Transfer Evaluation Model (LTEM) clarifies the complex path from knowledge to performance.

Each framework sheds light on different aspects of learning's impact, providing essential tools for our measurement toolkit. Yet despite these valuable approaches, many organizations still struggle to demonstrate learning's full value. The problem lies not in a lack of measurement approaches but in how we use them.

Organizations typically stumble in one of two ways: turning these frameworks into mechanical checklists that reveal no insights or getting lost in their complexity and measuring everything while understanding nothing. Our opportunity isn't to create new frameworks but to develop the expertise to use our existing tools effectively.

Consider how those paleontologists in Wyoming approached their discovery. They didn't need to invent new scientific methods; they needed to apply existing tools with precision and insight. Similarly, your mission isn't to reinvent measurement but to develop the expertise to spot the tracks you're already leaving: the subtle shifts in behavior, the gradual improvements in performance, and the moments when learning translates into breakthrough results.

To use these frameworks effectively, you must focus on:

- Understanding each framework's strengths and limitations
- Combining approaches strategically
- Focusing on what matters most to stakeholders
- Building measurement into program design
- Creating compelling narratives from measurement data

These principles guide our use of any measurement framework. However, perhaps no approach better illustrates the power and limitations of traditional measurement than ROI. While it provides valuable insights, overreliance on this single metric can blind you to learning's deeper impact.

THE ROI ILLUSION

In the 1970s, a major airline made a bold bet: invest millions in revolutionizing their onboard meal service. The logic was simple: exceptional meals would delight passengers and build loyalty. The verdict seemed clear when the finance team tallied up the costs against measurable returns months later. Traditional ROI calculations deemed it a failure. Yet looking beyond the numbers revealed a transformative success story.

The rigid financial metrics failed to capture the remarkable transformation: Passenger loyalty soared, the airline's reputation for service excellence took flight, and enthusiastic customers became brand ambassadors. The program's true value lay precisely where ROI couldn't measure—in the intangible elements that build sustainable competitive advantage.

This decades-old lesson resonates even more powerfully in our current context. According to Bersin, only 8 percent of organizations believe their ROI measurements capture the full impact of their learning programs. The problem isn't ROI itself but the overreliance on it as the single measure of success.

ROI: WHEN SIMPLICITY BECOMES A LIABILITY

The allure of ROI lies in its straightforward calculation:

$$\text{ROI (\%)} = [(\text{Net Benefits} - \text{Costs}) \div \text{Costs}] \times 100$$

This basic formula appears deceptively complete. A leadership development program illustrates the limitations: With a $100,000 investment generating $150,000 in measurable benefits, the 50 percent ROI looks solid on paper but misses vital value creators:

- Costly mistakes avoided through improved decision-making

- Projects accelerated by stronger team dynamics

- Innovations sparked by increased confidence

- Cultural shifts that enable long-term performance

This simplified calculation masks three fundamental limitations that can significantly impact organizational decision-making:

1. **Time Horizon Blindness:** Leadership development programs plant seeds that may take years to fully bloom, yet ROI demands immediate returns.

   This limitation is particularly evident in leadership development initiatives. While training costs hit the books immediately, the true value often emerges gradually over the years. A leader's growth ripples through the organization as they advance, mentor others, and shape strategic decisions. These compound benefits, though profound, remain hidden under traditional ROI calculations focused on immediate returns.

2. **Cultural Impact Oversight:** Programs that transform workplace culture create value in ways that resist simple financial calculations.

A diversity and inclusion program illustrates this challenge perfectly. As psychological safety grows, employees who previously stayed silent share innovative ideas. Silos begin to fall as teams collaborate in new ways. Top talent stays longer as people find a sense of belonging and connection. While these cultural shifts ultimately drive financial success, their value unfolds through intricate human connections and behavioral changes that defy simple ROI calculations.

3. **Network Effect Neglect:** Team development strengthens the entire organizational fabric, creating compound value far beyond the original investment.

    Consider a customer service training program boasting a 200 percent ROI. While the number appears impressive, it fails to capture how improved service capabilities spread throughout the organization. As team members collaborate more effectively, share best practices, and build on each other's successes, the program's impact multiplies in ways that transcend individual performance metrics.

THE ILLUSION OF PRECISION

The mathematical precision of ROI calculations creates a deceptive sense of objectivity, masking significant vulnerabilities. Every calculation rests on assumptions:

- Which costs truly belong to this initiative?
- How much of an improvement can we attribute to learning versus other factors?
- What timeline should we consider for benefits?

Each assumption shapes the final number, creating a misleading appearance of precision that can compromise decision-making and program credibility.

This false precision often leads you to miss crucial strategic questions:

- Which program elements drive the greatest impact?
- How do different teams respond to the initiatives?
- What aspects need refinement to create even better results?

Without these insights, you risk misallocating resources and losing the ability to continuously improve and optimize learning initiatives. The challenge, therefore, lies not in abandoning ROI entirely but in developing a more nuanced approach that acknowledges quantifiable returns and the deeper, more complex value that emerges over time.

THE PATH FORWARD

While ROI remains a valuable instrument in the measurement tool-kit, it cannot serve as the sole arbiter of success—though a CFO might argue otherwise. ROI's ability to translate outcomes into monetary terms makes it a powerful metric, particularly for financial decision-makers. Yet, as discussed earlier in this book, CFOs often overlook the intangible but critical benefits of learning initiatives—like improved employee engagement, cultural transformation, or long-term organizational resilience.

Just as a physician employs multiple diagnostic tools rather than relying solely on a thermometer, you need a comprehensive measurement approach. ROI serves as one instrument in a broader orchestra of metrics, each contributing to a nuanced understanding of value. By combining financial, strategic, and operational measures, you can present a more complete picture that resonates with CFOs and all the stakeholders seeking to understand the true impact of learning.

This expanded perspective rests on three core principles:

1. **Strategic Alignment:** Every metric must connect directly to organizational priorities and demonstrate clear lines of sight between learning initiatives and business outcomes. This means revealing how learning drives organizational

success in the short term and through sustained performance improvement.

2. **Balanced Measurement:** You need to capture both immediate indicators and long-term results, understanding that true transformation often emerges through the interplay of multiple factors over time. This requires balancing tangible and intangible value, measuring both what's easily counted and what truly counts.

3. **Actionable Insights:** Generate data that drives decision-making and continuous improvement, moving beyond measurement for measurement's sake. These insights should enable better program design, more strategic resource allocation, and clearer paths to organizational impact.

Embracing these principles transforms measurement from a mechanical exercise into a strategic insight engine. Like those paleontologists who combined basic tools with advanced technology, you must learn to use different frameworks in concert, revealing what single metrics alone might miss. This sets the stage for exploring how measurement approaches have evolved and how you can combine them effectively to demonstrate learning's full impact.

⚡ YOUR TURN: IDENTIFY HIDDEN VALUE

Think about a recent or ongoing learning initiative in your organization. Take ten minutes to:

1. List three valuable outcomes that wouldn't show up in a traditional ROI calculation

2. For each outcome, describe:
   o How it creates value for your organization
   o Why it's difficult to measure in purely financial terms
   o One alternative way to track its impact

PART 2: THE EVOLUTION OF MEASUREMENT

THE CARTOGRAPHER'S TOOLS

When sixteenth-century explorers ventured into unknown waters, they faced a terrifying challenge: how to measure their position in a seemingly endless ocean. Their tools were basic—crude compasses and hand-drawn maps marked with "here be dragons." Yet these simple instruments launched an age of discovery that would transform our understanding of the world.

Like those early explorers, we face a similar challenge. How do we measure the impact in the vast sea of organizational performance? Like those early navigators, we've evolved from basic tools to sophisticated systems. Just as modern ships use multiple technologies—GPS, radar, and weather monitoring—to navigate safely, effective L&D measurement requires a constellation of frameworks working in concert.

MAPPING THE MEASUREMENT LANDSCAPE

As navigation evolved from basic compasses to integrated systems, learning measurement has developed through distinct approaches over time. Throughout L&D's history, four key measurement frameworks have emerged as foundational approaches to evaluating training impact. Each framework emerged to address specific challenges of its era, building upon and sometimes challenging the assumptions of earlier models. From measuring basic learner reactions to calculating financial returns, these four approaches—Kirkpatrick, Phillips, Thalheimer, and Brinkerhoff—represent tools available to measure value and impact.

THE FOUR FRAMEWORKS: A NAVIGATOR'S TOOLKIT

1. **Kirkpatrick's Four Levels: The Foundation**

   Developed in the 1950s, Kirkpatrick's model provides a hierarchical structure for evaluating training programs through four progressive levels:

- Level 1: Reaction - Measures participant satisfaction and engagement with the training
- Level 2: Learning - Assesses knowledge acquisition and skill development
- Level 3: Behavior - Evaluates changes in on-the-job performance
- Level 4: Results - Examines business outcomes and organizational impact

While this model offers a structured approach to measurement, research shows most organizations struggle to move beyond Level 1 and 2 evaluations. The challenges of isolating training's impact on behavior change and business results, combined with resource constraints, often limit the implementation of the full framework.

2. **Phillips' ROI Model: The Accountant's Lens**

Jack Phillips added what many stakeholders craved: financial accountability. While Kirkpatrick's Level 4 examines broad business outcomes, Phillips' framework specifically translates learning outcomes into monetary terms—the language of business. It's like adding a fuel gauge to your toolkit; it's essential but insufficient alone. While ROI calculations add important perspectives, they work best as part of a more comprehensive approach, especially when measuring complex initiatives like leadership development or cultural transformation.

3. **Thalheimer's LTEM: The Microscope**

Dr. Will Thalheimer's Learning-Transfer Evaluation Model (LTEM) revolutionized how we view learning transfer. Where previous models saw a simple handoff from classroom to workplace, LTEM revealed an intricate transformation journey. It's like switching from a telescope to a microscope; suddenly, we can see the crucial details of how knowledge becomes performance. The challenge is that its precision can make it resource-intensive to implement.

4. **Brinkerhoff's Success Case Method: The Storyteller**

Robert Brinkerhoff offered a radical suggestion: Instead of measuring everything, study what works exceptionally well. His Success Case Method is like a detective's magnifying glass, examining instances of outstanding success to understand what made them possible. While this approach excels at capturing learning's human impact, its qualitative nature requires careful handling when extrapolating to larger populations.

CREATING SYMPHONY FROM INSTRUMENTS: INTEGRATED MEASUREMENT

Each framework, while valuable, illuminates only part of learning's impact—like trying to create a gourmet dish with a single ingredient. Salt might be essential, but it can't create flavor complexity alone. The art lies in combining these tools strategically, letting each ingredient enhance the others. Consider a leadership development program: Kirkpatrick's levels provide the foundation like a primary protein, while Success Case stories add the spice of human narrative. Phillips ROI adds the umami of financial validation, and LTEM's precision helps perfect the seasoning. Together, they create a rich, nuanced understanding that satisfies multiple stakeholders' appetites for insight.

Different initiatives call for different combinations. Technical training might leverage Phillips' ROI methodology alongside LTEM's granular analysis, revealing business impact and skill transfer mechanics. Cultural initiatives often shine brightest through Success Case studies paired with organizational metrics, capturing individual stories and systemic shifts.

🔖 **Remember:** Match your measurement recipe to your specific context—what works for technical training may not serve leadership development.

FRAMEWORK SELECTION GUIDE

Framework	Best For	Time Frame	Complexity	Key Strengths
Kirkpatrick	Training Programs	Short–Medium	☆ ☆	Systematic Evaluation Process
Philips ROI	Financial Impact	Medium–Long	☆ ☆ ☆	Money Talk
LTEM	Learning Transfer	Medium	☆ ☆ ☆ ☆	Detailed Focus
Success Case	Impact Stories	Short–Long	☆ ☆	Human Impact

IMPLEMENTATION: FROM THEORY TO PRACTICE

The Smart Start Approach

Implementing a comprehensive measurement strategy requires patience and strategic progression. Begin with foundational elements—Kirkpatrick Levels 1–2 across all programs—to establish basic measurement discipline. Selectively add Success Case studies for high-priority initiatives as your team builds confidence. This combination provides both breadth of basic metrics and depth where it matters most. Over time, incorporate ROI analysis for major investments and LTEM for detailed learning transfer insights.

Building Momentum for the Future

Success in measurement follows a clear pattern but demands a balance between aspiration and practicality. Start strategic—select high-visibility pilot programs where clear metrics can generate compelling early wins. Let these initial successes build credibility as results tell their story. This foundation makes thoughtful expansion possible, introducing new perspectives while maintaining clear links to business priorities. The most effective approaches capture immediate and long-term impact, adapting and scaling across diverse initiatives without losing sight of strategic outcomes.

> ✎ **Remember:** Your measurement journey resembles those of early explorers. Start with proven tools, add sophistication gradually, and keep your destination in sight, demonstrating learning's full impact on organizational success.

Our journey through measurement frameworks reveals a crucial truth: Tools alone aren't enough. Like craftspeople selecting instruments with purpose, we must understand how to measure and what deserves measurement. This insight reveals learning's dual nature—its power to create immediate results and deeper transformations.

PART 3: BROADENING THE LENS: THE DUAL NATURE OF LEARNING IMPACT

In my years of studying organizational learning, I've found an analogy that resonates with the complexity of measuring impact. When scientists first mapped icebergs, they were surprised to discover that only about 10 percent of the iceberg's mass is visible above the water. The vast majority, its true power and structure, lies hidden beneath the surface. In the same way, learning initiatives create both visible and hidden transformations in an organization.

The metrics we often track—improved performance, increased revenue, and faster processes—represent just the "visible peak" of learning's impact. However, beneath these surface-level results lies a deeper, more profound transformation: shifts in mindset, the evolution of culture, and the strengthening of capabilities. These unseen elements support, amplify, and sustain the visible outcomes.

Many organizations face this challenge: They either focus solely on tangible, surface-level metrics or get lost in intangible changes without understanding their broader context. This creates a false dichotomy that can derail even the most promising learning initiatives. The truth is that both dimensions—surface and deep—work in powerful synergy, reinforcing and amplifying each other.

Here are three examples that demonstrate how surface and deep impacts work together:

1. TIME MANAGEMENT MASTERY

- Surface Impact: 15 percent faster project completion
- Deep Change: Enhanced sense of control and well-being
- Result: A self-reinforcing cycle where improved capabilities drive better results, building further confidence and effectiveness

2. SALES EXCELLENCE PROGRAM

- Surface Impact: $1 million quarterly revenue increase
- Deep Change: Transformed team collaboration, innovation, and sales expertise
- Result: A virtuous cycle where strengthened team dynamics continuously improve sales performance

3. ETHICS AND COMPLIANCE INITIATIVE

- Surface Impact: 30 percent reduction in regulatory fines
- Deep Change: Shift from rule-following to value-driven behavior
- Result: Sustainable compliance through cultural transformation

These examples reveal a crucial insight: While surface impacts provide immediate evidence of success, the deeper transformations sustain and amplify these results over time. Like an iceberg, the visible metrics above the water line are supported by massive, unseen changes below—shifts in mindset, behavior, and capability that create lasting organizational value.

By recognizing and measuring this interplay, we can demonstrate how L&D initiatives achieve immediate, visible results and create the conditions for sustainable growth and transformation.

MOVING FROM METRICS TO MEANING

Measuring the impact of learning once seemed straightforward to me until I noticed a pattern that kept showing up in my research. I realized the metrics we often rely on weren't telling the full story. Here's what I discovered:

- Programs with 100 percent completion rates that changed nothing about how people worked
  - **High completion rates ≠ behavior change**
- Packed training rooms often masked the empty impact
  - **Strong attendance ≠ transformation**
- Teams hitting all their learning targets while missing the real point of transformation
  - **Activity metrics ≠ achievement**

After studying measurement approaches across industries for years, I've found that real transformation goes beyond surface-level metrics. Here's what the most successful organizations do differently:

1. **Define Holistic Success Criteria**

   I once sat with a chief learning officer who had spent millions on a leadership program. "Our completion rates are perfect," she told me, "but nothing's really changed." That's when she realized they'd been starting in the wrong place. The successful organizations didn't focus on metrics first. Instead, they first brought everyone to the table—business leaders, participants, and even customers—to define success. They didn't look at only numbers; they looked at the stories, the shifts, and the moments that matter.

2. **Blend Methods Strategically**

"We need hard data," a CFO once told me. "Stories don't count." Six months later, he called back: "I was wrong." The breakthrough came when his team started combining multiple threads of evidence—quantitative data for precision, qualitative insights for depth, and real-time feedback for agility. It was like combining the right ingredients in a recipe—each method added something valuable to the overall picture.

3. **Leverage Advanced Analytics**

The most innovative organizations didn't just collect more data; they used it more effectively. One team used AI to uncover hidden patterns in their learning data that completely transformed their approach. They found that:

- Small behavior changes were predicting major performance shifts.
- Seemingly unrelated improvements were deeply connected.
- Team dynamics were evolving in ways traditional metrics missed completely.

4. **Create Clear Connections**

The real breakthrough came when I saw how the pieces fit together. Tracking individual metrics wasn't enough; the real value came when organizations connected the dots. For example:

- A tech company traced how personal growth sparked team innovation
- A healthcare provider linked skill development directly to patient outcomes
- A manufacturer showed how culture shifts drove operational excellence

This journey led to a surprising revelation about how transformation happens in organizations. Imagine learning's impact as two intertwining streams flowing through an organization. The first stream is easy to spot; it's the improved metrics, bigger sales numbers, and faster processes that executives love to see in their dashboards. However, there's a second stream that most organizations miss entirely. It flows deeper, quieter, but with remarkable power. It's the shifts in how people think differently about challenges, how teams find new ways to collaborate, and how organizational cultures evolve. Traditional measurement approaches catch the first stream easily enough but often miss the second, and that's where the real magic of sustainable transformation lives.

This dual-stream perspective isn't just theoretical; it shapes real organizational transformation. Consider a global pharmaceutical company's leadership development initiative. On the surface, the numbers told an impressive story: 20 percent faster project completion, 15 percent improved team engagement scores, and $3 million in cost savings. However, the program's true power emerged in how it transformed the organization itself. Leaders approached challenges differently, teams found new ways to collaborate, and the entire organization became more adaptable to change. Though harder to measure, these deeper transformations ultimately drove and sustained the surface improvements.

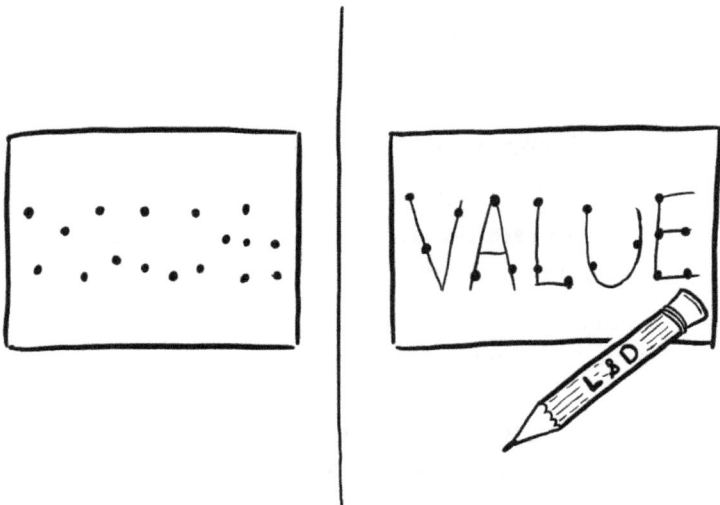

USING THE VALUE CREATION COMPASS AS YOUR MEASUREMENT GUIDE

The Value Creation Compass, which we introduced in Chapter 4, offers a powerful framework for capturing both streams of learning impact. By examining value creation through four essential dimensions—human potential, organizational resilience, business growth, and customer impact—we can reveal learning's full contribution to organizational success.

Earlier, we reviewed four distinct measurement methodologies. Now, we'll see how the Compass helps us deploy these tools more strategically. Think of the Compass as your navigation system, helping you determine where and how to apply different measurement approaches to capture the complete picture of value creation. This ensures we measure not just what's easily counted but what truly counts in building sustainable competitive advantage.

Let's explore how each direction of the Compass illuminates different aspects of learning's impact, creating a comprehensive view of how learning initiatives strengthen organizational capability and drive lasting success.

Note: Detailed measurement frameworks for each compass direction can be found in Appendix.

TRUE NORTH: EMPOWERING PEOPLE

The foundation of organizational value lies in human potential. When you look north, you measure how learning empowers people and transforms individual capability into organizational strength. This dimension focuses on three core areas: strategic skill development, leadership capability, and employee engagement.

1. Strategic Skill Development

To measure skill development comprehensively, start with establishing clear baselines using validated assessment tools. Pre-training assessments should capture technical knowledge and practical application ability. During the learning journey, implement periodic checkpoint assessments that examine knowledge retention and actual skill application in real work situations.

For deeper measurement, combine quantitative and qualitative approaches. Use structured observation protocols where managers document specific examples of skill application in complex situations. Implement regular reflection sessions where employees document how they're applying new capabilities and where they see growth opportunities. Gather team feedback through focused surveys examining how skill development influences collaboration and project outcomes.

The key lies in measuring sustainability. Track not just immediate skill gains but how capabilities evolve:

- Conduct follow-up assessments three, six, and twelve months post-training.
- Monitor knowledge-sharing and mentoring activities.
- Track career progression and role complexity.

2. Leadership Development

Leadership development represents one of our most powerful levers for organizational transformation. While traditional metrics might track promotion rates or program completion, the true impact of leadership development ripples throughout the organization in visible and subtle ways. Leaders who grow catalyze change far beyond their immediate sphere of influence—inspiring innovation, accelerating strategic execution, and strengthening organizational culture.

To measure surface impact, track the immediate indicators of leadership growth. Use validated 360-degree feedback tools to assess behavioral change. Monitor team performance metrics for underdeveloped leaders. Track strategic initiative success rates and measure improvements in decision-making effectiveness.

For deeper measurement, examine how enhanced leadership capability transforms organizational dynamics. Assess cultural impact through regular climate surveys. Study how leadership behaviors cascade through teams. Document instances of innovation and strategic thinking that emerge from stronger leadership. Analyze how improved leadership shapes team dynamics and enables better execution of strategic initiatives.

The key to sustainable measurement lies in tracking leadership development's ripple effects:

- Monitor succession pipeline strength through regular talent reviews.

- Track the success rates of leaders' direct reports and team members.

- Assess knowledge transfer through mentoring program effectiveness.

- Measure the spread of leadership practices across departments.

3. Employee Engagement and Growth

Employee engagement acts as a critical driver of organizational performance and innovation. It goes beyond satisfaction or happiness at work, reflecting the depth of commitment, sense of purpose, and discretionary effort employees bring to their roles. While traditional metrics track basic satisfaction, measuring true engagement provides insight into how deeply employees connect with their work and organization—connections that fuel productivity, collaboration, and innovation.

For surface measurement, begin with the fundamentals of engagement tracking. Conduct regular pulse surveys to gauge satisfaction levels. Monitor participation rates in development programs and voluntary initiatives. Track basic retention metrics and time-to-proficiency in new roles. These indicators provide important baseline data about engagement levels.

Deeper measurement reveals how engagement transforms organizational culture and capability. Implement psychological contract assessments to understand the evolving relationship between employees and the organization. Study how engagement enables innovation and collaboration. Document instances where enhanced engagement leads to breakthrough thinking or problem-solving. Analyze how stronger engagement influences team dynamics and organizational resilience.

Build sustainable engagement measurement through systematic tracking:

- Design longitudinal studies to track career progression patterns.

- Monitor the development of informal leadership and mentoring relationships.

- Assess the growth of cross-functional collaboration and knowledge sharing.

- Evaluate the emergence of employee-driven improvements and innovations.

When we empower people through learning, we create the foundation for organizational excellence. Strategic skill development closes immediate performance gaps while building future capability. Leadership development catalyzes innovation and strengthens team effectiveness. Engagement and retention programs ensure these capabilities translate into sustained high performance. Together, these elements create a virtuous cycle of individual and organizational growth.

While individual capability forms the foundation, success requires weaving these capabilities into the organizational fabric. As we turn east, we'll explore how personal growth transforms into collective strength, enabling organizations to adapt and thrive amid constant change.

EAST: DRIVING BUSINESS GROWTH

Looking east on our compass, you measure how learning drives market success and financial performance. While traditional metrics focus on immediate returns, sustainable business growth emerges from developing lasting capabilities in revenue generation, market expansion, innovation, and technology adoption. Each area requires measurement that captures immediate gains and growing organizational capacity.

1. Revenue and Profitability Growth

Revenue and profitability growth represent the most visible evidence of learning's impact on business success. Yet sustainable financial performance requires more than just improved sales techniques; it demands building lasting capabilities that consistently create value for customers and the organization.

For surface measurement, track immediate financial indicators. Monitor revenue per trained employee and sales growth rates. Analyze deal win rates and average deal sizes. Calculate customer acquisition costs and conversion rates. These metrics demonstrate direct financial impact and validate learning investments.

Deeper measurement reveals how learning transforms revenue-generating capabilities. Study how sales teams approach complex opportunities differently. Examine the evolution of customer relationships and strategic account development. Analyze how enhanced capabilities influence pricing power and margin management. These insights show how learning creates a sustainable competitive advantage.

Build sustainable measurement through systematic tracking:

- Monitor the development of consultative selling capabilities.
- Track how teams identify and capture new revenue opportunities.
- Assess the growth of strategic account relationships.
- Measure the evolution of team selling effectiveness.

2. Market Expansion

Market expansion success requires more than just entering new territories; it demands building a deep understanding of diverse markets and creating lasting customer relationships. Effective measurement captures both immediate market penetration and the development of sustainable market presence.

For surface measurement, focus on market entry metrics. Track new market revenue growth and market share gains. Monitor customer acquisition rates in new segments. Measure local partnership success rates. These indicators show immediate market traction.

Deeper measurement examines how organizations build lasting market presence. Assess the development of cross-cultural competencies. Study how teams adapt offerings for local markets. Analyze the evolution of market understanding and customer insight. These measurements reveal a growing capacity for sustainable market success.

Create sustainable market expansion measurement by tracking:

- Development of market-specific capabilities
- Growth of local relationship networks
- Evolution of cultural adaptation skills
- Strengthening of market intelligence capabilities

3. Innovation Capability

Innovation capability transforms organizations from market followers into market leaders. While patents and product launches provide visible metrics, true innovation measurement reveals an organization's growing capacity to consistently identify opportunities and create novel solutions.

Surface measurement tracks immediate innovation output. Monitor new product launch rates and success metrics. Measure revenue from new solutions. Track time-to-market improvements. These metrics demonstrate tangible innovation results.

Deeper measurement reveals how innovation capability becomes embedded in organizational DNA. Study how teams approach problems differently. Examine the evolution of creative confidence across departments. Analyze how innovation spreads between teams and divisions. These insights show innovation's transformative impact.

Establish sustainable innovation measurement through:

- Tracking the development of innovation mindsets
- Monitoring the growth of collaborative problem-solving
- Assessing the evolution of experimentation approaches
- Measuring the strengthening of innovation networks

4. Technology Adoption

Technology adoption transcends simple tool usage; it transforms how organizations operate and create value. Effective measurement captures immediate utilization and growing digital transformation capabilities.

For surface measurement, track adoption metrics. Monitor system utilization rates and feature adoption. Measure efficiency gains from new tools. Track user proficiency levels. These indicators show basic technology uptake.

Deeper measurement reveals how technology transforms work approaches. Study how teams leverage digital tools for innovation. Examine the evolution of digital collaboration patterns. Analyze how enhanced capabilities create new possibilities. These insights demonstrate technology's transformative power.

Build sustainable technology measurement by tracking:

- Development of digital fluency across teams
- Growth of technology-enabled innovation
- Evolution of digital collaboration capabilities
- Strengthening of change readiness

This comprehensive approach to measuring business growth reveals how learning initiatives drive sustainable market success. You demonstrate learning's crucial role in building lasting competitive advantage by capturing immediate gains and deeper capability development.

A resilient organization creates the perfect platform for sustainable growth. As we turn south, we'll explore how organizational resilience enables bolder market moves, faster innovation, and stronger financial performance.

SOUTH: BUILDING ORGANIZATIONAL RESILIENCE

BUILDING
ORGANIZATIONAL
RESILIENCE

Looking south on our compass, you measure how learning builds organizational strength and adaptability. In today's unpredictable environment, resilience isn't just about surviving challenges but emerging stronger from them. This dimension examines four critical areas that create sustainable organizational resilience: operational excellence, cultural alignment, workforce well-being, and organizational agility.

1. Operational Excellence

Operational excellence goes beyond efficient processes; it's about building an organization's capacity for continuous improvement and sustained high performance. While traditional metrics focus on immediate efficiency gains, true operational excellence transforms how organizations approach quality, innovation, and problem-solving.

For surface measurement, focus on immediate operational indicators. Track process efficiency through cycle time improvements and resource utilization rates. Monitor quality metrics like error rates and first-time-right percentages. Calculate cost savings and productivity gains from process improvements. These metrics provide clear evidence of operational enhancement.

Deeper measurement reveals how operational excellence transforms organizational capability. Assess problem-solving competency through structured observations. Document the evolution of continuous improvement mindsets. Study how teams approach complex challenges differently. Evaluate the spread of best practices across departments and divisions.

Build sustainable measurement by tracking operational evolution:

- Monitor the emergence and success of improvement initiatives.
- Assess the depth and breadth of problem-solving capabilities.
- Track how innovations spread between teams and departments.
- Measure the organization's growing capacity for systematic improvement.

2. Cultural Alignment

Cultural alignment represents the invisible force that turns strategic intent into consistent action. While surface metrics might show behavioral compliance, true cultural alignment creates an environment where organizational values naturally guide decisions and actions at every level.

For surface measurement, begin with observable behaviors. Use structured assessments to evaluate values-based actions. Monitor cross-functional collaboration frequency. Track participation in cultural initiatives. These metrics provide important indicators of cultural adoption.

Deeper measurement examines how values become embedded in organizational DNA. Study how decisions reflect cultural principles. Analyze how teams navigate conflicts and challenges through the lens of organizational values. Document instances where culture drives innovation or resilience. These insights reveal culture's transformative power.

Create sustainable cultural measurement through systematic tracking:

- Conduct regular cultural impact assessments.
- Monitor the evolution of informal leadership behaviors.
- Track how values influence strategic decisions.
- Assess cultural resilience during challenging periods.

3. Workforce Well-being

Workforce well-being forms the foundation of sustainable organizational performance. Beyond basic health metrics, true well-being measurement reveals how organizations create environments where people can thrive personally and professionally.

Surface measurement focuses on immediate health indicators. Track stress and burnout levels through regular assessments. Monitor work-life balance through time utilization studies. Analyze healthcare utilization patterns and wellness program participation. These metrics provide crucial baseline data about workforce health.

Deeper measurement reveals how well-being transforms organizational capacity. Study the relationship between well-being and innovation. Examine how team resilience develops through strong well-being practices. Analyze how enhanced well-being influences collaboration and problem-solving capability.

Establish sustainable well-being measurement through ongoing monitoring:

- Design longitudinal studies of performance sustainability.
- Track the development of team resilience patterns.
- Assess the impact of well-being on organizational adaptability.
- Measure how well-being influences talent retention and growth.

4. Organizational Agility

Organizational agility determines how effectively companies navigate change and seize opportunities. While traditional metrics might focus on change implementation speed, true agility measurement reveals an organization's capacity for continuous adaptation and innovation.

Surface measurement tracks immediate adaptation capabilities. Monitor change implementation speed and success rates. Measure innovation adoption across departments. Track how quickly teams respond to market shifts. These metrics show basic agility in action.

Deeper measurement reveals how agility becomes embedded in organizational capability. Study how teams anticipate and prepare for change. Analyze decision-making patterns during uncertainty. Document how organizations learn from both successes and failures. These insights show agility's transformative impact.

Build sustainable agility measurement through systematic tracking:

- Assess the evolution of change readiness across teams.

- Monitor the development of adaptive leadership capabilities.

- Track how innovation spreads throughout the organization.

- Measure growing capacity for market responsiveness.

Together, these four elements of organizational resilience create a comprehensive picture of how learning strengthens an organization's ability to thrive amid constant change. By measuring both immediate improvements and deeper transformations, you reveal learning's full contribution to organizational resilience.

While business growth provides clear evidence of learning's impact, sustainable growth ultimately depends on our ability to create exceptional customer value. As we turn west to examine customer value metrics, we'll explore how learning initiatives strengthen our ability to understand, serve, and delight customers. This closing dimension reveals how all our previous measures—people capability, organizational resilience, and business growth—ultimately converge in the customer experience.

WEST: DELIVERING CUSTOMER VALUE

Looking west on your compass, you measure how learning strengthens customer relationships and creates lasting value. Customer experience has emerged as the ultimate differentiator in today's competitive landscape. This dimension reveals how learning transforms customer relationships through three essential areas: experience excellence, brand strength, and customer trust.

1. Customer Experience Excellence

Creating exceptional customer experiences has become the ultimate competitive differentiator in today's market. While traditional metrics track transaction efficiency, true customer experience excellence emerges from how deeply employees understand and connect with customer needs, turning routine interactions into meaningful moments.

For surface measurement, track immediate service indicators. Monitor customer satisfaction scores (CSAT) and net promoter score (NPS) trends. Measure resolution times and first-contact resolution rates. Track service quality metrics and completion rates. These indicators show basic service effectiveness.

Deeper measurement reveals how learning transforms service delivery at a fundamental level. Study how employees develop stronger customer understanding. Analyze the evolution of problem-solving approaches in complex situations. Examine how teams create memorable experiences that strengthen relationships. These insights show the shift from transactional service to transformational partnerships.

Build sustainable experience measurement through systematic tracking:

- Monitor the development of service intuition and empathy.
- Assess the growth of proactive problem-solving capabilities.
- Track how customer insights spread across teams.
- Measure the evolution of customer journey understanding.

2. Brand Strength

A brand lives or dies through numerous daily interactions between employees and customers. While marketing shapes brand perception, learning ensures consistent brand delivery through every customer touchpoint. True brand measurement reveals how effectively employees embody and deliver on brand promises.

For surface measurement, track fundamental brand metrics. Monitor brand awareness and preference scores. Measure customer advocacy rates. Track basic brand delivery consistency. These indicators show immediate brand impact.

Deeper measurement examines how thoroughly employees internalize and authentically deliver brand values. Study how teams translate brand promises into meaningful actions. Analyze how brand values influence decision-making. Document instances where employees go beyond scripts to create brand-aligned solutions. These insights reveal genuine brand embodiment.

Create sustainable brand measurement by tracking:

- Development of brand understanding and alignment
- Growth of authentic brand advocacy
- Evolution of value-driven decision-making
- Strengthening of brand-aligned innovation

3. Customer Trust and Loyalty

In an age of endless choices, customer trust and loyalty represent the ultimate measure of organizational effectiveness. While standard metrics track retention, true loyalty measurement reveals how learning enables employees to build lasting partnerships based on genuine value creation.

Surface measurement focuses on basic loyalty indicators. Track customer retention rates and repeat purchase patterns. Monitor customer lifetime value trends. Measure share of wallet and account growth. These metrics demonstrate basic relationship strength.

Deeper measurement reveals how learning transforms transactional relationships into strategic partnerships. Study how teams build and maintain trust through challenging situations. Examine the evolution of strategic account relationships. Analyze how enhanced capabilities enable deeper customer understanding. These insights show the development of lasting loyalty.

Establish sustainable loyalty measurement through:

- Tracking the development of strategic relationship capabilities
- Monitoring the growth of trust-building behaviors

- Assessing the evolution of partnership depth
- Measuring the strengthening of customer advocacy

This comprehensive approach to measuring customer impact reveals how learning initiatives transform customer relationships from transactional interactions into lasting partnerships. By capturing immediate service improvements and deeper relationship development, you demonstrate learning's essential role in creating sustainable competitive advantage through superior customer experience.

SYNTHESIZING THE COMPLETE PICTURE

The Value Creation Compass transforms how we understand and measure learning's impact. By examining surface metrics and deeper transformations across all four directions, patterns emerge that tell a powerful story about organizational transformation. Like a master weaver working with multiple threads, each measurement direction adds essential color and texture to the final tapestry.

Consider how improvements in one direction naturally strengthen others. Employees who develop stronger capabilities (north) deliver better customer experiences (west). As operational excellence grows (east), it enables innovation and market expansion (south). These interconnections create a virtuous cycle of value creation that builds sustainable competitive advantage.

The Value Creation Compass helps us avoid the "either/or" trap by:

1. Identifying both surface and deep metrics in each direction
2. Revealing connections between immediate and long-term impact
3. Showing how different types of value reinforce each other
4. Creating a complete picture of learning's contribution

Remember that measurement itself should evolve as your organization grows. The Value Creation Compass provides a flexible framework that can adapt to changing strategic priorities while maintaining focus on both immediate results and lasting capability building.

After exploring the *what*, *why*, and *how* of measurement, we now turn our focus to practical implementation, offering concrete strategies for turning these insights into action.

PART 4: TURNING INSIGHTS INTO ACTION: MAKING LEARNING IMPACT VISIBLE

THE GARDENER'S GUIDE TO GROWTH

Like master gardeners who understand that different plants need different care, successful measurement requires both vision and precision. You wouldn't use the same approach to nurture a delicate orchid and a hardy oak. Similarly, each learning initiative demands its own measurement strategy, carefully calibrated to reveal its unique value.

The following strategies and approaches will help you develop measurement practices that capture learning's full impact. Whether building a new measurement system or enhancing existing practices, these insights will help you demonstrate learning's strategic value.

1. **Map Stakeholder Priorities:** Effective measurement begins with clearly understanding what matters most to your organization. Start by engaging deeply with stakeholders to understand their strategic priorities and concerns. Through focused conversations and careful listening, identify the outcomes and evidence that will resonate most strongly with decision-makers. This foundation of understanding guides all subsequent measurement choices.

   o **Essential Questions:**
      1. What does success look like for your department?
      2. What outcomes would demonstrate value to you?
      3. How do you define and measure success?

147

- o **Action Steps:**

  1. Create stakeholder priority maps.
  2. Document and validate key concerns with stakeholders.
  3. Build alignment on success metrics.

2. **Plant SMART Goals:** Once you understand stakeholder priorities, translate them into specific, measurable targets that connect learning initiatives to organizational success.

- **SMART Goals:** Set goals using the SMART methodology.

  - o **Specific, Measurable, Achievable, Relevant, Timebound**

- **Instead of:** "Improve leadership capabilities."

- **Try:** "Increase leadership effectiveness scores by 20 percent within six months, measured through 360-degree feedback."

3. **Choose Your Measurement Tools:** Strategic metric selection requires balancing different types of evidence. Combine performance metrics with rich qualitative feedback about how learning changes behavior.

- o **Strategic Pairs:**

  1. Performance metrics + Employee feedback
  2. Business outcomes + Learning impact stories
  3. Promotion rates + Employee testimonials about career growth

4. **Start Small and Scale:** Begin your measurement journey with focused pilot efforts that allow you to test and refine your approach.

  - o **Pilot First:** Test your approach with one team or one program.

  - o **Learn and Adjust:** Gather feedback and refine methods.

  - o **Action Step:** Design a thirty-day pilot program.

5. **Craft your Impact Story:** Evidence becomes powerful when woven into compelling narratives demonstrating impact.

   o **Data + Narrative:** Combine data with compelling narratives to show not just *what* happened but *why* it matters.

   o **Structure:**

      1. **Challenge:** What problem needed solving?
      2. **Solution:** How did learning address it?
      3. **Impact:** What changed, and why does it matter?
      4. **Future:** What possibilities have opened up?

6. **Create Feedback Loops:** Sustainable measurement requires regular rhythms for reflection and adjustment.

   o Weekly team check-ins
   o Monthly stakeholder updates
   o Quarterly impact reviews

7. **Share Success Strategically:** Multiple channels, consistent message:

   o Executive briefings
   o Team newsletters
   o Success story database
   o Visual impact dashboards

📌 **Remember:** Strategic measurement isn't about measuring everything; it's about measuring what matters most to your stakeholders and organization. Start with their priorities and work backward to identify your most critical metrics.

EVIDENCE: YOUR TRANSFORMATION ENGINE

Throughout this chapter, we've explored how evidence powers organizational transformation by revealing the full impact of learning initiatives. Through frameworks like the Value Creation Compass, we've discovered ways to measure tangible and intangible outcomes, directly connecting learning to business success. However, here's the fascinating paradox I've observed in my research: The organizations that prove their value most effectively aren't necessarily the ones with the most sophisticated measurement systems; they're the ones that transform their evidence into unforgettable stories.

LOOKING AHEAD

As we turn toward Chapter 6, we move from the science of measurement to the art of narrative. Like a master photographer who knows that the perfect image requires both technical precision and artistic vision, we'll explore how to transform our carefully gathered metrics into stories that resonate, inspire, and drive action. The numbers tell us what happened; the stories show us why it matters.

🔑 KEY LEARNINGS

- **The Art of Deep Observation:** Like ancient dinosaur tracks that reveal complex stories to trained eyes, learning's true impact often lies beneath the surface. Strategic measurement requires the skill to uncover both immediate results and deeper organizational transformations.

- **Orchestrating Multiple Lenses:** Just as skilled trackers use various tools to read their environment, powerful measurement approaches weave together complementary frameworks like the Value Creation Compass, Kirkpatrick, Phillips ROI, and Success Cases to paint a complete picture.

- **The Four Dimensions of Impact:** The Value Creation Compass illuminates learning's transformative power across human potential, organizational resilience, business growth, and customer impact—essential markers of sustainable success in our rapidly changing world.

- **Beyond Surface Metrics:** Moving past ROI's deceptive simplicity, strategic measurement captures both tangible business outcomes and the deeper currents of change that drive lasting transformation. Each piece of evidence adds to the story.

- **Measurement as Evolution:** When you truly understand how learning creates value, each insight becomes a stepping stone to greater effectiveness. Through strategic measurement, you demonstrate impact, illuminate the path forward, and accelerate organizational transformation.

6

THE UNTOLD WELL:
BRINGING NUMBERS TO LIFE

"Those who tell the stories rule society."

—Plato (allegedly)

THE POWER OF STORY

In 2006, *Charity: Water* was just an idea—a bold vision to bring clean drinking water to millions of people suffering without it. Founder Scott Harrison had the statistics: 663 million people globally lacked access to clean water, and contaminated water caused more deaths than all forms of violence combined, including war. However, there was a problem. When Harrison shared these numbers with potential donors, the response was tepid. No matter how staggering, the data wasn't enough to move people to act.

Then, Harrison tried a different approach. Instead of leading with the statistics, he told the story of Lethebo, a thirteen-year-old girl from Rwanda. Every day, Lethebo walked miles to fetch water from a dirty pond. Harrison described the scene: the murky water crawling with bacteria, the heavy jugs cutting into Lethebo's hands, and the hours lost that she could have spent learning in school. Then, Harrison shared the transformation: Everything changed after a well was built in Lethebo's village. Lethebo had clean water; her family's health improved, and for the first time, she could attend school.

That story transformed the organization's outreach. Putting a human face to the crisis turned abstract numbers into a vivid, emotional narrative that resonated with donors. Donations poured in, enabling *Charity: Water* to fund hundreds of wells in its first year. Today, the organization has raised over $700 million, thanks largely to its mastery of storytelling—continuously sharing the personal, transformative stories of those whose lives have been changed by clean water.

Stories like Lethebo's don't just inspire action; they illustrate impact. They remind us that behind every number is a human experience. In L&D, storytelling has the same power to transform perceptions, connect with stakeholders, and demonstrate value. A single compelling narrative can elevate a program's significance, making the hidden visible and ensuring that the impact of learning is understood *and* felt.

In Chapter 5, we explored the science of measurement—the metrics, frameworks, and tools that capture our impact. Now, we turn to the art that brings these measurements to life. Stories transform raw data into compelling evidence of L&D's value, making our impact measurable, memorable, and meaningful.

WHY STORYTELLING MATTERS

Imagine Scott Harrison standing before a room of potential donors, sharing data about the global water crisis. The numbers were impressive, yet the audience remained unmoved. It wasn't until he shared Lethebo's story that he unlocked their attention and support. In that moment, storytelling didn't just complement the data; it elevated it, creating an emotional connection that made action inevitable.

We face a similar challenge: transforming data into compelling narratives that drive action. While metrics provide essential evidence of impact, their true power emerges when connected to stories that bring these numbers to life. Our work involves both tangible metrics and intangible outcomes—from completion rates and assessment scores to improved morale and greater collaboration. The key isn't just collecting data or telling stories but weaving them together to create a holistic picture of value. Storytelling bridges this gap, transforming abstract results and raw data into vivid, human-centered narratives that inspire action and drive change. Whether it's an individual finding their voice through leadership training or a team improving efficiency after a skills workshop, storytelling shows stakeholders the real-world impact of learning.

Let's explore five value propositions for storytelling.

1. Stories Build Trust and Advocacy

Storytelling is more than a communication tool; it's a bridge to connection. Storytelling builds credibility by demonstrating real-world impact through authentic experiences. When L&D professionals share specific examples of learning initiatives that solved business problems or transformed team performance, they establish themselves as trusted advisors rather than just training providers. For example, a story showing how a leadership development program helped a struggling team improve its performance metrics proves L&D's strategic value. These narratives also create advocates among successful participants, who share their experiences with colleagues and leadership, amplifying L&D's influence across the organization. The trust built through consistent, results-focused storytelling helps secure resources, gain executive support, and position L&D as an essential business partner.

2. Stories Create Emotional Connections

A statistic might inform, but a story moves. Stories humanize outcomes. Humans are wired to respond to stories because they resonate emotionally, engaging the part of our brain responsible for memory and decision-making.

Beyond the neuroscience of dopamine release, stories forge lasting emotional bonds by tapping into universal human experiences. Sharing a story about an employee overcoming imposter syndrome through targeted learning interventions resonates with others facing similar challenges. This emotional resonance creates a ripple effect, where one person's journey becomes the inspiration for others. L&D professionals can leverage this emotional connection to break down resistance to learning initiatives and create psychological safety for skill development. The empathy generated through storytelling also helps bridge gaps between different departments and hierarchical levels, fostering a more collaborative learning culture.

3. Stories Make the Abstract Concrete

While data tells us what happened, stories show us why it matters. Effective stories transform complex metrics and learning objectives into tangible outcomes by providing real-world context and applications. Instead of simply reporting completion rates or satisfaction scores, stories illuminate the journey from learning to application to results. For instance, rather than stating, "Leadership training improved decision-making by 45 percent," a story might show how a manager used specific frameworks from the training to navigate a critical business challenge, leading to measurable improvements in team performance. This concrete illustration helps stakeholders understand what was learned and how it created value in practice.

4. Stories Stick

The "stickiness" of stories extends beyond initial memory retention to influence long-term behavior change and decision-making. Learners who can recall and relate to specific success stories are more likely to apply new skills and approaches. The Princeton research on neural coupling shows that well-crafted stories create shared understanding between storyteller and audience, making complex concepts and behavioral changes more accessible and actionable. This lasting impact is particularly crucial in L&D, where the goal is not just knowledge transfer but sustained behavior change and performance improvement.

5. Stories Drive Change and Transform Organizations

Stories are catalysts for both individual motivation and systemic change. They inspire immediate action while laying the groundwork for lasting transformation. A compelling story about one team's successful adoption of new technologies can motivate other teams to embrace digital transformation. Similarly, narratives about cross-functional collaboration can break down organizational silos and foster innovation. By connecting individual success stories to broader organizational impact, such as improved customer satisfaction, reduced costs, or accelerated product development, these narratives demonstrate how learning initiatives contribute to strategic goals. The result is a powerful case for L&D as an essential driver of organizational evolution and competitive advantage.

By combining personal and collective success, storytelling elevates L&D from an operational function to a catalyst for cultural and business growth.

THE STORYTELLING ADVANTAGE

Just as Scott Harrison discovered with Charity: Water, the most powerful stories in L&D are those grounded in data but brought to life through narrative. When we weave metrics into our stories, we create compelling evidence of learning's impact that resonates with stakeholders at every level.

Consider a global technology company that transformed ordinary program metrics into an extraordinary story of organizational change. On the surface, their leadership development program showed strong completion rates—85 percent compared to the typical 60 percent. However, the real story emerged when they dug deeper. Those completions translated into a 40 percent surge in internal promotions within six months. As they followed the thread further, they discovered a 50 percent increase in cross-departmental collaboration, leading to three major product launches that traced directly back to relationships formed during the program.

This example illustrates three essential elements that make metrics story-worthy:

1. **Significant Changes:** Look for metrics that show notable improvements or unexpected results. These dramatic shifts—like the jump from 60 percent to 85 percent completion rates—signal the beginning of a compelling narrative.

2. **Human Connections:** Map how performance improvements link directly to learning interventions. The technology company's story resonated because it clearly connects leadership development and career advancement.

3. **Impact Chains:** Track how individual growth catalyzes team and organizational success. The progression from program completion to promotions to product launches demonstrates L&D's far-reaching impact.

When combined with data, storytelling creates a powerful one-two punch. Data provides the evidence that validates our impact; stories provide the emotional resonance that makes that impact memorable. Together, they humanize the value of L&D, ensuring our significance isn't just understood intellectually but felt viscerally.

As we move into the next section, we'll explore how to craft these evidence-based narratives using proven frameworks that ensure they stick, resonate, and inspire action.

CRAFTING COMPELLING NARRATIVES

Telling a story is one thing. Crafting a narrative that resonates with different audiences, inspires action, and highlights impact is another. To do this effectively, you need a structure that keeps your audience engaged and a strategy that ensures your story connects with their needs and priorities.

The Hero's Journey

Great stories follow a pattern—one that has been told for centuries. The Hero's Journey, first popularized by Joseph Campbell in *The Hero with a Thousand Faces*, is a timeless narrative structure found in myths, books, movies, and personal transformation stories. It's the framework behind many of the most compelling stories we know, from ancient legends to modern blockbusters like *Star Wars*.

At its core, the Hero's Journey follows a three-part arc:

- The struggle introduces a challenge or limitation that must be overcome.

- The journey explores how the hero steps into the unknown, learns, adapts, and grows, often with the help of mentors or new experiences.

- The transformation reveals the outcome, showing how the hero emerges stronger, wiser, and more capable, applying what they've learned to change themselves and their world.

This structure isn't just for Hollywood—it's how we make sense of real-life growth and transformation, including learning and development.

THE THREE-PART FRAMEWORK: STRUGGLE, JOURNEY, TRANSFORMATION

A compelling story often follows a similar structure: The beginning introduces a problem, the middle explores the actions taken to address it, and the end reveals the result. This format mirrors the Hero's Journey and is a powerful way to communicate the impact of learning initiatives in a way that engages stakeholders and demonstrates real change.

1. The Struggle

The struggle sets the stage by presenting a challenge that needs to be overcome. In L&D, this could be an employee grappling with a skills gap, a team struggling with collaboration, or an organization facing an external disruption.

- Example: Julia, a project manager, doubted her ability to lead. She hesitated to speak up in meetings and avoided leadership roles, feeling she wasn't a "natural leader."

This act creates empathy and establishes the stakes, encouraging your audience to root for the protagonist.

2. The Journey

The journey is where growth happens. It highlights how the protagonist confronts the struggle, using tools, resources, or experiences to move forward. For L&D stories, this is where learning programs and interventions shine.

- Example: Julia's manager encouraged her to enroll in the Leadership Development Program. Despite initial doubts, she joined, learned practical leadership skills, and began applying them in her team meetings. A classmate's success story inspired her, showing her that growth was possible.

This act demonstrates the value of the L&D initiative, showing how it provided the tools for transformation.

3. The Transformation

The transformation is the payoff. It reveals the journey's results, connecting personal growth to broader outcomes.

- Example: Julia's newfound confidence led her to apply for— and secure—a leadership role. Her team thrived under her guidance, delivering projects on time and earning client praise. Julia's success became a case study for the program, inspiring others to participate.

This act ties the story together, showing how learning creates meaningful, lasting change.

STRUGGLE   JOURNEY   TRANSFORMATION

⚡ YOUR TURN: IDENTIFY YOUR STORY ELEMENTS

Take time to outline an L&D story from your organization using the Struggle, Journey, Transformation framework:

1. Think of a successful L&D initiative you've been involved with. Map out the following:
   - o **Struggle:** What was the key challenge or pain point?
     - What specific problems were people facing?
     - What was at stake if nothing changed?
     - How did this impact individual or team performance?

- o **Journey:** What learning interventions or support were provided?
  - ▪ Which specific programs or resources made a difference?
  - ▪ What key moments led to breakthroughs or insights?
  - ▪ What obstacles were overcome during the learning process?
- o **Transformation:** What measurable changes occurred?
  - ▪ What specific metrics improved?
  - ▪ How did behaviors or performance change?
  - ▪ What broader impact did this have on the organization?

2. Draft a two- or three-sentence version of each element, focusing on specific details that make the story compelling.

3. Review your draft and circle the most impactful metrics or moments that could serve as "hooks" for different audiences.

TAILORING STORIES TO DIFFERENT AUDIENCES

Not all audiences care about the same aspects of a story. A compelling narrative for executives may focus on measurable outcomes, while employees might connect more with the personal growth journey. Tailoring your story ensures it resonates with the right stakeholders.

For Executives: Focus on Strategic Outcomes

- Highlight metrics, productivity gains, or client satisfaction improvements.
- Example: A leadership development program increased project completion rates by 20 percent, directly impacting revenue.

For Managers: **Emphasize Team Dynamics**

- Show how the learning initiative improved team collaboration, morale, or performance.

- Example: After empathy training, a team resolved conflicts more effectively, increasing engagement scores by 15 percent.

For Employees: **Highlight Personal Growth**

- Share relatable, human-centered stories of transformation.

- Example: An employee's new skills led to a promotion, boosting their confidence and career trajectory.

⚡ YOUR TURN: ADAPT YOUR STORY FOR DIFFERENT STAKEHOLDERS

Take your story from the previous exercise and practice tailoring it for three different audiences. Spend five minutes on each version:

1. **Executive Version**
   - o Lead with: A key business metric or strategic outcome
   - o Focus on: Revenue increase, productivity gains, or market impact
   - o End with: Future implications for business growth
   - o Keep it under two minutes

2. **Manager Version**
   - o Lead with: Team performance improvement
   - o Focus on: Collaboration, efficiency, or skill development

---

>   o   End with: Practical applications for other teams
>   o   Include specific examples of team dynamics
> 3. **Employee Version**
>   o   Lead with: Personal growth opportunity
>   o   Focus on: Skills gained and career development
>   o   End with: Actionable steps others can take
>   o   Highlight relatable challenges and solutions

⚡After completing both versions, identify:

- Which elements of your story resonated most with each audience?
- What metrics or moments did you emphasize differently?
- How did you adjust your language for each group?

Share your adapted stories with a colleague and get feedback on the most compelling elements for each audience.

> 🧭 **Remember:** The most effective L&D stories connect individual growth to organizational impact. Your goal is to make both visible and meaningful to each audience.

FROM STORIES TO EVIDENCE: BUILDING YOUR L&D IMPACT NARRATIVE

Storytelling frameworks and audience targeting are essential foundations, but they're only the beginning. The true power of L&D storytelling emerges when we combine compelling narratives with concrete evidence. Consider how Charity: Water evolved from sharing water crisis statistics to weaving Lethebo's journey with clear metrics about wells built and lives changed. This combination of story and data created an undeniable case for action.

You face a similar opportunity. When we integrate performance metrics, business outcomes, and human experiences into our narratives, we transform learning initiatives from "nice-to-have" programs into strategic drivers of organizational success. Each story becomes evidence of L&D's impact, speaking to your stakeholders' hearts and minds.

Building Evidence-Based Narratives

The most compelling L&D stories combine the art of storytelling with the science of data. They weave together quantitative evidence and qualitative experiences, creating credible and emotionally resonant narratives. To build these evidence-based narratives:

1. **Start with Data Patterns:**
   o Review metrics to identify trends worthy of deeper exploration.
   o Look for correlations between learning activities and business outcomes.
   o Track metrics over time to show sustained impact.

2. **Layer in Human Elements:**
   o Collect testimonials that explain the numbers.
   o Document specific examples of how learning led to improved performance.
   o Include quotes that bring the data to life.

3. **Build the Evidence Chain:**
   o Connect individual success to team improvement.
   o Link team improvements to organizational outcomes.
   o Show both immediate and long-term impact.

This approach transforms simple statistics into compelling stories about the power of L&D, creating narratives that resonate with hearts and minds.

⚡ **YOUR TURN: EVIDENCE CHAIN BUILDING**

Practice creating an evidence-based narrative for a learning program:

- Select a recent learning initiative from your organization.
- List the key data points/metrics you have available.
- Identify two or three compelling human stories or testimonials.
- Draft a brief narrative that connects individual success → team improvement → organizational impact.
- Identify what additional evidence would strengthen your story.

INNOVATIVE AND CREATIVE STORYTELLING METHODS

While a compelling data-driven narrative forms the foundation of any great story, how we deliver that story can transform its impact. In L&D, moving beyond traditional written reports and PowerPoint presentations opens powerful possibilities for engagement and retention. Let's explore four approaches to turn your impact stories into memorable experiences.

1. Data Visualization: Making Numbers Speak

Visuals are powerful allies in storytelling, transforming complex data into instantly digestible insights. When crafted thoughtfully, data visualizations can reveal patterns, highlight relationships, and make abstract concepts tangible.

Creating effective data visualizations requires strategic choices:

Choosing the Right Format

- Bar charts and line graphs excel at showing trends over time, perfect for tracking skill development progress.

- Heat maps reveal patterns across teams or departments, highlighting areas of impact.

- Infographics work well for complex learning journeys, breaking down multiple touchpoints.

- Dashboards provide real-time program impact visibility.

Best Practices

- Start with your key message; let it guide your visual choices.

- Focus each visualization on one main insight.

- Maintain consistent colors and branding.

- Provide clear labels and context.

- Ensure accessibility with alt text and descriptions.

- Test with different stakeholder groups for clarity.

Tool Selection

- Design: Canva or Adobe Creative Cloud for professional infographics
- Data: Tableau or PowerBI for interactive dashboards
- Timelines: Office Timeline for journey mapping
- Presentations: Prezi for dynamic storytelling

Choose tools based on your team's skill level and available resources. Many offer templates specifically designed for learning and development narratives.

2. Interactive Storytelling: Creating Dialogue

Interactive storytelling transforms passive audiences into active participants, deepening engagement and understanding. This approach creates two-way conversations that make your impact stories more personal and memorable.

Implementation Strategies

- Create clickable journey maps where stakeholders explore different learning paths.
- Design choose-your-own-adventure style case studies.
- Build interactive dashboards where users can explore data points.
- Develop digital storytelling experiences with branching scenarios.

Success Elements

- Keep interactions purposeful and intuitive.
- Provide clear navigation cues.

- Include meaningful choices that reveal different aspects of your story.
- Balance interaction with information delivery.

3. Multimedia Storytelling: Engaging Multiple Senses

By combining different media types—text, audio, video, and images—multimedia storytelling creates rich, layered experiences that resonate with diverse audience preferences and learning styles.

Key Components

- Short, focused videos (two to three minutes) capturing transformation stories
- Audio testimonials from participants and stakeholders
- Photo essays documenting learning journeys
- Mixed media presentations combining live narration with recorded elements

Best Practices

- Maintain consistent narrative threads across media types.
- Use each medium for its strengths.
- Keep technical requirements minimal.
- Ensure accessibility across platforms.
- Create standalone pieces that work together or independently.

4. Gamification: Making Stories Experiential

Gamification adds game-like elements to storytelling, creating engaging experiences that invite active participation while maintaining professional credibility.

Effective Elements

- Progress tracking through learning journey milestones
- Achievement systems tied to story discoveries
- Collaborative challenges that reveal impact stories
- Interactive scenarios based on real learning outcomes

Implementation Tips

- Align game elements with your story's purpose.
- Keep mechanics simple and intuitive.
- Focus on meaningful progression.
- Use competition thoughtfully.
- Ensure game elements enhance rather than overshadow your message.

Combining Methods for Maximum Impact

The most powerful storytelling often weaves together multiple approaches. Consider this example sequence:

1. Open with an interactive data visualization that lets stakeholders explore program impact.
2. Transition to a short video featuring participant testimonials.
3. Include a gamified element where audience members unlock additional success stories.
4. Close with a multimedia summary that ties everything together.

The key is choosing methods that serve your story rather than overshadowing it. Each approach should enhance understanding, deepen engagement, and strengthen your message's impact.

> ✏️ **Remember:** These innovative methods aren't about being flashy; they're about making your L&D impact stories more accessible, engaging, and memorable. Choose and combine approaches based on your audience, resources, and message to create experiences that resonate and inspire action.

CONNECTING BACK TO THE L&D MISSION

At its core, L&D's mission is to drive organizational success through people development. When you choose innovative storytelling methods, you share information and advance this mission by making learning's impact visible and compelling. Just as Lethebo's story inspired thousands to join *Charity: Water's* mission by making clean water access personal and urgent, creative storytelling in L&D can transform how our organizations view and value learning. Through thoughtful visualization, interaction, multimedia, and gamification, you create experiences that help employees, managers, and leaders see learning not as a program to complete but as a crucial driver of both personal and organizational success.

IDENTIFYING AND CAPTURING IMPACTFUL STORIES

Crafting compelling narratives begins with finding the right stories to tell. Not all stories carry the same weight, and the most impactful ones resonate deeply with your audience while demonstrating the tangible and intangible value of L&D. The key is to uncover narratives that highlight personal transformation, team successes, and organizational impact.

CHARACTERISTICS OF IMPACTFUL STORIES

1. Personal Transformation

The most memorable stories often focus on an individual's journey—how they overcame a challenge, learned a new skill, or achieved personal growth through L&D initiatives.

- **Example:** Rachelle, a sales representative who struggled with complex negotiations, often lost deals in the final stages. After attending an advanced negotiation skills workshop, she applied new techniques like anchoring and strategic concessions in her next deal. She closed a $2 million contract—her largest ever—and helped her peers adopt these techniques. Within six months, Rachelle became the go-to negotiation mentor for new hires, and her team's close rate improved by 35 percent. Her story is now featured in the company's sales onboarding program.

- **Why It Matters:** Personal stories are relatable and emotionally engaging, making it easier for others to see themselves in the narrative.

2. Team Success

Stories demonstrating collective growth and collaboration are powerful for illustrating how L&D drives team performance.

- **Example:** When a software company merged its UX and development teams, conflicting work styles led to missed deadlines and tension. The combined team participated in a two-day collaboration workshop followed by monthly coaching sessions. They learned to use agile ceremonies effectively and adopted shared vocabulary for technical discussions. Within three months, their project delivery time decreased by 30 percent, customer satisfaction scores rose by 25 percent, and team members reported significantly higher job satisfaction.

The team's success became a model for other departments undergoing similar integrations.

- **Why It Matters:** Team-level stories show the broader ripple effects of learning, appealing to managers and executives who prioritize operational efficiency.

3. Organizational Impact

At the highest level, impactful stories connect L&D initiatives to strategic outcomes like profitability, innovation, or customer satisfaction.

- **Example:** Facing an aging leadership population and high external hiring costs, a global manufacturing company launched a comprehensive leadership development program. They identified high-potential employees across departments and enrolled them in a year-long curriculum combining virtual learning, mentorship, and practical projects. Within two years, internal promotions increased by 40 percent, saving $3.2 million in recruitment costs. More importantly, these new leaders, already familiar with company culture, reduced their teams' time-to-productivity by half compared to external hires. The program became central to the company's five-year strategic plan, with the CEO regularly citing it as a key competitive advantage.

- **Why It Matters:** Organizational-level stories demonstrate L&D's role in driving business growth and resilience.

While these characteristics define powerful stories, the key to building a robust story library lies in systematic capture and curation. A methodical approach ensures you consistently identify and document the most impactful narratives across your organization.

TECHNIQUES FOR CAPTURING STORIES

Finding impactful stories requires a thoughtful approach to gathering insights from employees, managers, and stakeholders. Here are some techniques to help you capture meaningful narratives:

1. Conducting Interviews

Interviews are a direct way to uncover personal and team-level stories. Focus on open-ended questions that encourage individuals to share their experiences.

Key Interview Questions:

- **Identifying the Challenge:**
  - o What specific challenge prompted you to join the program?
  - o How was this challenge affecting your work or team performance?
  - o What had you tried previously to address this challenge?
- **Understanding the Learning Journey:**
  - o Which aspects of the training directly addressed your challenge?
  - o What key insights or skills did you gain?
  - o How did you apply what you learned?
- **Measuring Impact:**
  - o What tangible changes have occurred since completing the program?
  - o How has this affected your team or organization?
  - o What metrics or feedback demonstrate this impact?

Example: An interview with a manager might reveal how communication training improved their team's ability to navigate conflicts, leading to higher engagement scores.

2. Leveraging Surveys and Feedback

Surveys and feedback forms allow you to gather stories at scale, identifying trends and standout examples for deeper exploration.

- **How to Use:**
    - o Include open-ended questions like, "How has this program impacted your performance or career?"
    - o Use follow-up interviews to dive deeper into compelling responses.

Example: After a customer service training, survey responses highlighted several employees who credited the program with improving their client interactions. These individuals were then interviewed for more detailed stories.

3. Observing Behavioral Changes

Sometimes, stories reveal themselves through observation. Look for noticeable behavior, performance, or culture shifts following L&D interventions.

- **What to Observe:**
    - o Increased collaboration within teams
    - o Higher participation in learning programs
    - o Improved customer feedback tied to training outcomes

Example: A leadership team that started implementing conflict resolution techniques post-training saw a reduction in escalations and a more cohesive workplace environment.

4. Collecting Testimonials

Short testimonials can provide powerful snapshots of individual experiences. They're quick to gather and can add authenticity to broader narratives.

> **Example:** An employee shares, "After the data analytics course, I automated several reports, saving my team ten hours a week." This testimonial can become part of a larger story about operational efficiency.

Testimonials—the authentic *voice of learners* in the field—transform abstract metrics into compelling human stories. When learners share their victories, their words resonate far more deeply than any statistical report ever could.

⚡ YOUR TURN: STORY INTERVIEW PRACTICE

Put the interview techniques into practice by drafting a story capture plan:

- Select a recent learning program in your organization.
- Write three to five specific interview questions you would ask participants.
- Identify two or three key stakeholders you would interview.
- Create a simple template to document the stories you gather.

BALANCING PERSONAL AND ORGANIZATIONAL BENEFITS

The most impactful stories demonstrate a balance between individual success and organizational outcomes. This dual perspective reinforces L&D's value as a personal and strategic growth driver.

- **Personal Impact:** Highlight how an employee grew in their role, gained confidence, or advanced their career.

- **Organizational Impact:** Show how that individual's growth contributed to team productivity, client satisfaction, or business goals.

Example: A junior data analyst who developed advanced skills through training became a senior analyst leading high-impact projects. Their success improved team morale and helped the organization win new client contracts.

ALIGNING STORIES WITH THE VALUE CREATION COMPASS

Just as the Value Creation Compass guided your understanding of L&D's strategic impact in Chapter 4, it now offers you a powerful framework for organizing and capturing success stories. Each compass direction represents a distinct type of value creation, requiring its own narrative approach:

- **True North (Empowering People):** Stories of personal transformation that show how learning unlocks human potential. For example, how a first-time manager found their leadership voice through targeted development, transforming from an uncertain team lead to a confident decision-maker.

- **East (Driving Growth):** Stories that connect learning directly to business success. Such as how a sales team's advanced negotiation training led to winning three major accounts, directly impacting revenue growth.

- **South (Building Resilience):** Narratives that demonstrate organizational adaptation and strength. Like the story of how cross-functional training helped a team navigate a major market disruption, maintaining productivity while competitors struggled.

- **West (Customer Value):** Narratives showcasing how enhanced capabilities improve stakeholder experiences. For instance, how a customer service team's emotional intelligence training led to a 30 percent increase in satisfaction scores.

By intentionally gathering stories across all compass directions, you create a comprehensive narrative portfolio that demonstrates L&D's multifaceted impact. This balanced approach ensures your stories resonate with different stakeholders while reinforcing L&D's role in driving individual and organizational success.

⚡ YOUR TURN: VALUE CREATION STORY MAPPING

Practice categorizing stories using the Value Creation Compass:

- Think of a recent learning success in your organization.

- Map this story to one of the compass directions (north, south, east, or west).

- Identify what specific elements make it fit that direction.

- Brainstorm what additional data or details would strengthen its impact.

- Consider how you might adapt the story to resonate with different compass directions.

Sharing Stories Within the Organization

Once you've identified compelling narratives, the next step is sharing them in ways that inspire and engage your organization. While Chapter 8 will explore comprehensive strategies for amplifying L&D's impact through ambassador networks, recognition systems, and strategic communication, let's focus on the immediate practical aspects of story sharing that bring your narratives to life.

THE ART OF STORY DISTRIBUTION

Effective story-sharing is an art that combines timing, format, and channel selection. You must coordinate these elements like a skilled conductor leading an orchestra to create harmonious impact. The most powerful stories often falter not because of their content but because of how and when they're shared.

The timing of your story can dramatically affect its impact. Stories land with the greatest impact when they connect to moments that matter in your organization. A story about successful change management resonates more deeply during a major transformation initiative. A narrative about cross-functional collaboration carries extra weight when teams are beginning a new joint project. Some of the most effective moments to share include:

- During major organizational changes or initiatives
- When teams face challenges like those in your story
- Alongside learning program launches or milestones
- At natural business rhythm points (quarterly reviews, annual planning)
- In response to specific team or department needs

DIGITAL CHANNELS: THE BACKBONE OF STORY DISTRIBUTION

Digital platforms offer unique opportunities to share stories with depth and nuance. Each channel serves a distinct purpose and requires its own approach.

Intranet Articles

- Combine personal journeys with clear metrics.
- Include supporting visuals and infographics.
- Feature direct quotes from participants.
- Provide detailed examples of impact.
- Link to relevant resources or programs.

These longer-form pieces allow you to weave together an employee's transformation story with specific performance improvements, supporting your narrative with visuals, quotes, and data that bring the impact to life.

Email Updates

- Lead with compelling outcomes.
- Keep content brief and focused.
- Include clear calls to action.
- Link to more comprehensive resources.
- Use consistent, recognizable formatting.

In today's fast-paced work environment, these brief touchpoints must capture attention quickly. Structure these stories like news headlines; lead with a powerful outcome, then provide a path to the fuller story for those eager to learn more.

Collaboration Platforms

- Share ongoing narrative threads.
- Encourage team discussion and feedback.
- Feature quick wins and daily victories.
- Enable peer-to-peer story sharing.
- Build community through shared experiences.

Platforms like LinkedIn (external sharing) or Teams and Slack (internal sharing) create opportunities for dynamic, evolving narratives. Here, stories can unfold naturally, with team members adding their perspectives and building upon shared experiences. This creates a living document of learning impact that grows richer with each contribution.

THE POWER OF IN-PERSON STORYTELLING

While digital channels provide reach, in-person sharing creates intimacy and immediate impact. Team meetings become perfect venues for "learning moments"—brief but powerful stories that highlight specific applications of new skills or knowledge. Picture a project manager sharing how their newly acquired negotiation skills helped navigate a challenging client conversation, transforming a potential crisis into a breakthrough moment.

Training sessions offer natural opportunities to weave success stories into the learning experience. When participants hear how their peers applied similar knowledge to overcome real challenges, abstract concepts suddenly become concrete possibilities. These stories serve as bridges between theory and practice, helping learners envision their paths to success.

Lethebo's story reminds us of the profound connection between storytelling and action. It wasn't just the clean water statistics that inspired donors; it was the deeply personal, vividly told narrative of a young girl's transformation. Similarly, in L&D, storytelling has the power to turn abstract results into meaningful, memorable, and actionable messages.

Stories give life to the data and metrics we worked so hard to capture in the previous chapter. They transform percentages and performance metrics into human experiences that stakeholders can connect with emotionally. By integrating storytelling with measurement, we can prove our value and inspire others to advocate for it.

STORIES THAT STAND OUT

We create a powerful foundation for demonstrating L&D's impact by systematically connecting metrics to stories. This intentional bridge between measurement and meaning ensures our impact stories are engaging, credible, actionable, and directly tied to organizational success. As we move forward, remember that numbers tell only half the story; the combination of robust data and compelling narratives truly brings our impact to life.

However, even the most compelling stories need a strong platform to be heard. Like any powerful message, L&D's impact stories require intentional positioning to capture attention and drive action. In the next chapter, we'll explore how to build a distinctive L&D brand that ensures your stories don't just resonate but stand out, stick, and become part of your organization's natural conversation.

🔑 KEY LEARNINGS

- **The Power of Human Connection:** L&D measurement comes alive when data blends with authentic human stories, as shown in Charity: Water's approach with Lethebo's compelling journey. By combining statistics with personal narratives, we create evidence that resonates on both emotional and analytical levels.

- **Building Bridges of Understanding:** Stories transform metrics into meaningful evidence of learning's impact on individuals and organizations. Through carefully crafted narratives, we help stakeholders grasp the full scope of L&D's influence, from skill development to business outcomes.

- **The Hero's Journey:** Following Struggle-Journey-Transformation, these stories showcase personal growth and measurable results that resonate with stakeholders. This framework helps illustrate the challenges faced and victories achieved, making the learning journey relatable and inspiring.

- **Tailoring the Message:** Effective L&D narratives adapt to different audiences while maintaining their core truth, revealing unique value to each group. Whether speaking to executives about ROI or managers about team development, the story flexes while the evidence remains consistent.

- **Evidence That Inspires:** The fusion of metrics and stories creates compelling evidence that validates impact and motivates action, turning observers into champions. This powerful combination helps build organizational support and drive continued investment in learning initiatives.

7

THE PURPLE COW EFFECT: *BE UNFORGETTABLE*

"A brand is not what you say it is. It's what they say it is."

—*Marty Neumeier*

BE REMARKABLE

In 1994, Jeff Bezos was brainstorming a name for his new online business that would stand out in an increasingly growing digital marketplace. He initially considered "Cadabra," short for "abra-cadabra," to evoke a sense of magic and possibility. However, when someone misheard it as "Cadaver," Bezos knew it wasn't the right fit. While competitors chose names like Books.com and BookStacks.com that limited their scope, Bezos deliberately chose "Amazon," inspired by the world's largest river, because it represented something vast, powerful, and full of possibility—just like his vision for a company that would sell far more than books.

This principle of intentional distinctiveness was later dubbed "The Purple Cow Effect" by marketer Seth Godin. Seth argued that a purple cow in a field of black and white cows would be remarkable—worth remarking about. The lesson was about making deliberate choices in how you present yourself to the world, choices that make people take notice and remember.

For us in L&D, this challenge resonates deeply. Our work transforms organizations—developing leaders, building capabilities, and driving innovation—yet, like a black-and-white cow in the field, even excellent L&D work can blend into the organizational landscape. When a manager successfully leads their team through change, a new hire rapidly becomes productive, or a department significantly improves performance, these successes might not be naturally connected back to the L&D initiatives that enabled them. Creating a "purple cow" for L&D means being intentional about standing out— crafting a brand that ensures your contributions are visible and memorable. Just as Bezos chose a name that would stand out in a sea of book-related competitors, you must find ways to distinguish your work in the crowded organizational landscape.

This chapter focuses on the essential elements of building a distinctive L&D brand that captures attention, communicates value, and creates lasting impact. We'll explore how to craft a brand identity that resonates with stakeholders and helps demonstrate learning's strategic value across your organization.

Let's begin by understanding why branding matters for L&D and how to build a brand that stands out.

THE POWER OF BRAND IDENTITY

Every day, we encounter hundreds of brands competing for our attention. Yet only a handful stick in our minds and influence our decisions. What makes these brands stand out? They've mastered something essential: the ability to create meaningful connections through consistent experiences and delivered promises.

Consider how the most successful brands achieve this: Apple doesn't just sell technology; its clean design and intuitive interfaces whisper innovation in every interaction. Nike's "Just Do It" transcends athletic wear to become a call to action in our daily lives. When you walk into a Starbucks in Seattle or Singapore, you're not just buying coffee; you're stepping into a consistent experience where the familiar rhythm of coffee orders and quiet conversations creates a reliable backdrop to your day. These brands don't just occupy market space; they occupy mind space. They tell stories that resonate, make promises that matter, and consistently deliver on them.

What does this have to do with L&D?

Everything.

In the landscape of the corporate L&D function, we often find ourselves in a paradoxical position. We spend our days developing others' capabilities yet frequently struggle to articulate our narrative. We create transformative learning experiences, drive organizational change, and build the capabilities that power business success. Yet one of two scenarios inevitably unfolds: We let others define who we are and what we do—usually reducing us to "the training team"—or we remain our organization's best-kept secret, our true impact hidden behind a veil of modest silence.

This is why branding isn't just about logos or taglines; it's about taking control of your narrative. It's about clearly defining yourself and the value you provide before others do it for you. It's about refusing to let your impact remain hidden and ensuring your voice shapes how learning is perceived and valued in your organization.

The lack of a defined, mature L&D brand significantly affects how the learning function operates and is perceived. You find your function:

- **Undervalued:** Your value gets diminished to "the training team," while your broader impact on organizational success goes unrecognized.

- **Reactive:** You find yourself constantly fighting fires rather than preventing them, brought in to fix problems after they emerge.

- **Overlooked:** Strategic initiatives launch without learning considerations, limiting their potential impact and sustainability.

However, when a strong, mature brand exists, its positive influence becomes evident in key aspects of organizational life—particularly in how stakeholders engage with, perceive, and value learning. Consider how these key indicators evolve as your brand develops:

- **Program Engagement:** From programs being attended out of obligation to initiatives with waiting lists

- **Resource Discussions:** From constant budget scrutiny to strategic investment conversations

- **Innovation Reception:** From skepticism about new approaches to enthusiasm for fresh ideas

- **Stakeholder Interpretation:** From viewing learning as an interruption in work to seeing it as critical for success

Understanding both the consequences of an undefined brand and the benefits of a mature one makes it clear: We need to build our L&D brand with intention and purpose. But where do we begin? Like any solid structure, we start with the foundation.

⚲ **Remember:** Branding is defining who you are and the value you provide *before* others do it for you.

ARCHITECTURE FOUNDATION: YOUR L&D STORY

The foundation of a powerful L&D brand isn't just about visual design or catchy taglines; it's rooted in your story. As we explored in Chapter 6, storytelling is how you communicate impact, connect with stakeholders, and bring your value to life. This narrative forms the bedrock of everything that follows, from your visual identity to your program architecture. Before you begin sketching logos or choosing colors, you need to deeply understand and articulate why your L&D function exists, the story you want to tell, and how it transforms your organization.

Start by examining your purpose through essential questions that probe the heart of your function:

- What role does learning play in your organization's success?
- How does learning transform people and teams?
- What unique value does your L&D function provide?
- What do you want the L&D function to have achieved in five years?
- Why is your L&D function necessary?
- What do you want learners to feel about L&D?

Answering these questions isn't just a theoretical exercise; the answers are the practical foundations that will guide every decision you make about your brand. Take time to deeply consider each question, as your answers will shape every aspect of your L&D brand moving forward.

⚡ YOUR TURN: CREATE YOUR BRAND STORY ACTION PLAN

1. Schedule a two-hour Brand Story Session with your core team and key stakeholders.
2. Have participants answer these questions independently before the session.
3. During the session, identify common themes and draft your core narrative.
4. Create a one-page brand story document capturing who you are, why you exist, and how you transform the organization.

→ **Next Step:** Block time for your Brand Story Session within the next two weeks. Your brand story is the foundation upon which everything else will build.

YOUR BRAND PROMISE

With your brand story as your foundation, it's time to craft the promise to bring that story to life. Your brand promise transforms your narrative into a clear commitment to your stakeholders—one that will guide every learning initiative and interaction. While a mission statement describes your purpose, a brand promise declares the specific difference you'll make. The most memorable brand promises have shaped entire industries. Consider these examples:

Apple's "Think Different" began as a response to IBM's "Think" but evolved into something far more profound—a dual promise to create innovative products while inspiring customers to embrace creativity and innovation themselves.

Starbucks promises "To inspire and nurture the human spirit—one person, one cup, and one neighborhood at a time," positioning itself as a coffee company and a catalyst for human connection.

Nike declares its intention "To bring inspiration and innovation to every athlete in the world," notably avoiding any mention of products and instead focusing on its broader purpose of enabling human achievement.

These promises share their ability to transcend products and speak to deeper human aspirations. They're memorable not because of clever wordplay but because they tap into fundamental human desires for creativity, connection, and achievement.

Like these consumer brands, your L&D brand promise should be the cornerstone of your identity—a central commitment that shapes perceptions, drives trust, and defines your value. It must emerge from a deep understanding of your organizational needs and your L&D function's unique capabilities, ensuring it resonates with authenticity and delivers on expectations.

The most effective brand promises share three essential characteristics:

- **Business Alignment:** They directly connect to organizational goals and metrics.

- **Authentic Capability:** They build on demonstrated L&D strengths.

- **Sustainable Delivery:** They can be consistently fulfilled over time.

Let's examine three effective L&D brand promises and why they work:

1. **"Accelerating Performance Through Learning"**
   o This promise resonates particularly well in organizations focused on speed-to-market or rapid innovation. It creates a clear throughline from learning initiatives to business performance, emphasizing velocity and impact. Most importantly, it's measurable; you can track how quickly performance improves after learning interventions.

2. **"Building Tomorrow's Capabilities Today"**
   o Forward-thinking organizations in rapidly evolving industries find this promise compelling because it positions L&D as a strategic partner in future-preparing the organization. It speaks to proactive skill development and demonstrates foresight in capability building. The promise inherently justifies investment in learning as preparation for future challenges.

3. **"Transforming Potential into Excellence"**
   o Organizations with a strong talent development focus often embrace this promise because it speaks to individual growth and organizational impact. It creates a narrative arc from potential to excellence, supporting personal development and organizational success. The promise works because it aligns individual aspirations with organizational goals.

The key to these promises' success lies in their execution. For instance, when an organization promised "Development at the speed of business," they completely restructured their program development process, shifting from months-long creation cycles to agile, weeks-long sprints. Similarly, the promise of "Practical skills for real challenges" was brought to life by integrating actual work projects into every learning program.

These promises work because they're specific, meaningful, and demonstrable. They give stakeholders a clear picture of what to expect and provide the L&D team with a clear standard to meet.

⚡ YOUR TURN: CREATE YOUR BRAND PROMISE

Review your brand story responses, highlighting themes about:

1. How you uniquely drive business performance
   - o Where you consistently deliver value
   - o What stakeholders repeatedly praise

2. Draft two or three potential promises that:
   - o Connect to your organizational goals
   - o Build on your proven strengths
   - o Can be consistently delivered
   - o Feel authentic to your culture

3. Test your top promise by asking:
   - o Can we measure this?
   - o Can we deliver this consistently?
   - o Will this resonate with our stakeholders?

→ **Next Step:** This week, schedule thirty minutes with your team to craft your brand promise. Use the examples above as inspiration, but ensure your promise reflects your organization's unique culture and needs.

These promises are just the beginning, though. They need strong supporting elements to bring them to life in your organization's daily operations. Think of your next task as building the foundation that will help you consistently deliver on these promises.

DEFINE YOUR BRAND PILLARS

With your brand promise established as your cornerstone, you need foundational elements to help you deliver on that promise consistently and effectively. Think of your brand pillars as the load-bearing columns supporting and reinforcing your brand promise throughout your learning ecosystem.

Brand pillars need to meet four key requirements to be truly effective:

- **Actionable:** Your team should understand how to apply them daily.

- **Measurable:** You should be able to assess if you're living up to it.

- **Distinctive:** It should reflect what makes your L&D function unique.

- **Authentic:** It must align with your organizational culture and capabilities.

These characteristics ensure your brand pillars don't just sound good on paper but drive meaningful change in how your L&D function operates and delivers value. Let's examine five core pillars that exemplify these characteristics and have proven particularly powerful in transforming L&D functions I've worked with over the years:

1. **Business Impact**

   "*Driving measurable business results*" became a defining pillar at one organization where skepticism about learning's value ran deep. We transformed our approach by requiring every program to demonstrate clear connections to business metrics. This wasn't a superficial exercise. We developed rigorous impact maps linking learning objectives to specific business outcomes. Program sponsors had to identify and commit to measuring concrete results. This disciplined approach elevated learning from a nice-to-have into a strategic driver of business performance.

2. **Innovation**

   Another organization struggled with the perception that L&D lacked creativity in learning solutions. We established *"bringing fresh approaches to persistent challenges"* as our guiding pillar. This meant fundamentally rethinking how we approached innovation. We created a structured innovation pipeline, dedicating resources to exploring and testing new learning approaches. More importantly, we developed a framework for rapidly evaluating and implementing promising solutions by following the design thinking methodology. The result was a shift in perception; stakeholders began seeing L&D as a source of creative solutions to complex business challenges.

3. **Accessibility**

   The pillar of *"learning available anytime, anywhere, for everyone"* demanded a complete reimagining of how we delivered development opportunities. We rebuilt the entire learning ecosystem around this principle, fundamentally changing our program design and delivery approach. Every learning experience had to meet rigorous standards for accessibility and flexibility. This transformation dramatically increased engagement with learning across all levels of the organization.

4. **Community**

   In an environment where learning was viewed as primarily formal training, we established *"learning better together"* as a core pillar. This required reimagining our entire approach to development. We integrated cohort-based programs and peer learning networks throughout our program architecture, making collaborative learning a cornerstone of every major initiative. The transformation was profound: Knowledge sharing evolved from a structured activity into an organic part of daily work. Learning became less about formal programs and more about continuous development through meaningful connections.

5. **Excellence**

The pillar of "*maintaining the highest standards in content and delivery*" emerged from recognizing that credibility is earned through consistent quality. We established clear quality standards and review processes for all learning initiatives. More importantly, we built measurement systems to track satisfaction, behavior changes, and business impact. This rigorous approach to excellence helped establish learning as a trusted driver of organizational performance.

CHOOSING YOUR PILLARS

Your brand pillars should reflect both your current strengths and aspirational goals. Start by asking:

- What do we do exceptionally well?
- What do our stakeholders value most?
- What capabilities do we need to develop?
- How do we want to be known?

The key is choosing pillars that are both aspirational and achievable. They should stretch your team while remaining within reach. Most organizations find that three to five pillars provide enough structure without becoming unwieldy.

⚡ **YOUR TURN: DEFINE YOUR BRAND PILLARS**

1. Gather Input (one to two hours):
   - o Review stakeholder feedback from the past year.
   - o List your team's proven strengths.
   - o Note where you consistently receive praise.
   - o Identify gaps between the current and desired state.

2. Select Your Pillars:
   - o Choose three to five themes that emerged from your review.
   - o Test each against the four requirements: Actionable, Measurable, Distinctive, and Authentic.
   - o Draft clear statements for each pillar.
   - o Add one or two concrete examples of how each pillar guides daily work.

→ **Next Step:** Schedule a pillar definition workshop with your core team. Use the five examples above as inspiration, but ensure your pillars authentically reflect your function's unique strengths and aspirations.

🪁 **Remember:** Brand pillars aren't just statements on a wall; they're the principles that guide your daily decisions and shape how you deliver value to your organization.

YOUR VISUAL IDENTITY

When the golden arches of McDonald's appear on the horizon during a long road trip, they promise more than just food; they signal a consistent experience, a familiar comfort no matter where you are. Visual identity, at its best, isn't just recognition but an instant connection to meaning, values, and promises kept. In your organization, this same principle can transform L&D from a department into a trusted presence that signals opportunity and growth.

For L&D, visual identity is more than aesthetics. Every visual element should reinforce your learning philosophy and support your brand pillars while fitting seamlessly within your organizational culture. A well-designed L&D brand stands out enough to be recognizable but feels natural within your company's visual ecosystem.

The master brand elements should work together to tell your story:

- **Name:** Your overarching learning brand that captures your purpose and promise
- **Logo:** Visual representation of your learning philosophy that works at any size
- **Colors:** Palette that reflects your brand pillars and resonates with your culture
- **Typography:** Fonts that balance readability with personality across all platforms
- **Design System:** Guidelines for consistent application across all learning materials

---

⚡ YOUR TURN: BUILD YOUR VISUAL IDENTITY

1. Research and Requirements (Week One):
   - Review your organization's brand guidelines.
   - Study successful internal brands (e.g., Employee Resource Groups, company initiatives).
   - Note what visual elements resonate in your culture.
   - Document your must-haves and constraints.

2. Design Process (Weeks Two–Three):

o Draft a creative brief that captures your brand story and pillars.

o Create three distinct visual concepts.

o Test each concept in real applications:

o Learning platform interface

o Program materials

o Communications

o Presentation templates

3. Stakeholder Input (Week Four):

o Share concepts with key stakeholders, including:

- Learning team

- Marketing/brand team

- Sample of target audience

o Gather feedback on what resonates.

o Refine based on input.

→ **Next Step:** Set up a meeting with your marketing or brand team to understand your organization's visual guidelines and constraints. Their expertise will help ensure your L&D brand stands out and fits in.

With a compelling visual identity in place, we now need to ensure that identity serves a clear purpose in effectively organizing and presenting your learning offerings.

PROGRAM ARCHITECTURE

While a strong visual identity helps your brand get noticed, the true test of its effectiveness lies in how it helps learners navigate and engage with your programs. Now that we've established how your brand looks, let's explore how to structure your learning programs to make them accessible and impactful.

Just as city planners consider how people live, work, and move through spaces, your program architecture should reflect how people learn, develop, and grow in your organization. Like a city map that helps visitors navigate confidently, your architecture should make it easy for employees to find the right development opportunities at the right time.

Create clear pathways through your learning offerings:

- **Core Programs:** Fundamental development offerings that every employee needs, like a city's essential services

- **Specialized Tracks:** Role or skill-specific development, like specialized districts serving specific needs

- **Leadership Development:** Management and executive programs that serve as your city's strategic centers

- **Performance Support:** Just-in-time learning resources, functioning like convenient corner stores

- **Quick-Skill Programs:** Boost sessions that act as rapid transit between larger development destinations

---

⚡ YOUR TURN: DESIGN YOUR LEARNING ARCHITECTURE

1. Audit Current State:
   o Map all existing programs.
   o Identify gaps and overlaps.
   o Note which pathways are clear vs. confusing.
   o Review usage patterns.

2. Create Your Blueprint:
   o Organize offerings into clear categories.
   o Design intuitive navigation paths.
   o Define connections between programs.
   o Plan for future growth.

→ **Next Step:** Create a visual map of your current learning offerings. Understanding where you are is the first step to building where you want to go.

A well-designed program architecture is essential, but even the most elegant structure needs to become part of your organization's daily reality. The next challenge is ensuring your brand becomes deeply embedded in your organization's DNA.

MAKING YOUR BRAND STICK

Disney has mastered the art of creating lasting brand impressions. From theme park cast members who stay perfectly in character to themed trash cans that match each land's aesthetic to the carefully selected scents pumped onto Main Street—every detail reinforces their promise of magical experiences. Whether you've visited Disney's theme park or not, you likely know that Disney's attention to brand experience has become legendary in the business world.

While most L&D teams can craft compelling brand elements, the greater challenge lies in making them stick. Many L&D brands remain superficial—living in logos and taglines rather than becoming part of the organizational conversation. Just as Disney ensures every detail of their parks reinforces their promise of magical experiences, you must make your L&D brand come alive through consistent, meaningful touchpoints. Let's explore how to transform your brand from concept to cultural cornerstone.

CREATING MEMORABLE MOMENTS

Imagine walking into an Apple Store. Before anyone speaks to you, the space itself tells you exactly what the brand promises: simplicity, innovation, and accessibility. Now, think about your learning programs—do they create that same level of immediate recognition and emotional connection? Brand integration in L&D requires more than repetition; memorable moments reinforce your message. Consider these approaches:

Signature Experiences

Create distinctive elements that people associate with your learning brand. At BDO Canada, one leadership program orchestrates every detail of the participant experience: A warm welcome email arrives a week before. Custom breakfast orders await on arrival. Personalized name cards mark each seat, and carefully selected music creates an atmosphere throughout the day. Like Disney's attention to detail, these thoughtful touches show participants they're entering a space where everything has been considered with their experience in mind. At another organization, every program begins with a "Connection Circle" where participants stand together and share what brought them there; each adds a word to create a collective intention for their learning journey. This zero-cost ritual has become so powerful that teams now spontaneously form Connection Circles before tackling major challenges, taking a moment to ground themselves in learning and purpose.

Visual Anchors

Your visual identity should show up in unexpected but meaningful ways. One L&D team created "growth zones"—designated areas in their offices marked with their logo where people could engage in informal learning conversations. These spaces became powerful physical reminders of their learning brand. Another organization partnered with IT and communications to roll out a custom laptop background during their annual learning festival month—turning every computer into a daily touchpoint for their learning message. Whether in physical or digital spaces, these visual anchors serve as constant reminders of your organization's commitment to development. Consider integrating your brand promise into high-traffic areas, using digital displays to showcase learning moments, or creating branded learning spaces within your workplace that invite collaboration and development.

Language Patterns

Develop a consistent way of talking about learning that reflects your brand. This goes beyond taglines to include how you describe programs, frame outcomes, and discuss development. When your language becomes part of how people naturally talk about learning, your brand has truly stuck. Transform "soft skills" into "power skills," shift from "training sessions" to "learning experiences," and replace "mandatory courses" with "growth opportunities."

The Power of Intentional Integration

Brand sustainability requires more than initial launch momentum; it needs systematic integration into organizational life. This integration happens across multiple dimensions:

- **Physical Integration:** Design learning spaces and materials that consistently reflect your brand elements.
- **Cultural Integration:** Embed learning discussions into regular team meetings and business reviews.
- **Behavioral Integration:** Recognize and reward learning behaviors that align with your brand promise.
- **Strategic Integration:** Connect learning goals to business planning and performance discussions.

The key is consistency across all touchpoints—from digital platforms to physical spaces, casual conversations, and formal presentations. Every interaction should reinforce your learning brand's core message and promise.

⚡ YOUR TURN: BUILD YOUR BRAND

Identify three signature moments in your current learning programs that could become distinctive brand experiences. Test different approaches to make these moments more memorable and aligned with your brand promise.

The journey to brand strength requires patience and persistence. Brand building takes time, but it transforms how your organization views and values learning when done right. Your brand becomes the bridge between L&D's capabilities and organizational perception, positioning learning as a crucial driver of business success.

FROM HIDDEN TO STRATEGIC PARTNER: BDO CANADA'S LEARNING BRAND JOURNEY

When I joined BDO Canada, I found a talented L&D team quietly delivering valuable programs across the organization. Like many L&D functions, we were doing important work that often went unrecognized; we had the capability but lacked a unified identity. While pockets of the organization knew about specific programs, many employees weren't aware of the full scope of learning opportunities available to them. Our ability to drive strategic impact was limited without a clear brand presence.

We saw an opportunity to transform learning from a behind-the-scenes support function into a recognized catalyst for growth and innovation. This wasn't just about increasing visibility; it required a fundamental shift in how we positioned learning within BDO. We needed to create an identity to help employees instantly recognize, value, and engage with learning opportunities.

OUR BRAND STORY

We began where all strong brands begin—with our story. As discussed in the previous chapter, storytelling isn't just about conveying information; it's about creating an emotional connection that resonates with your audience and builds trust. To craft our L&D brand, we engaged stakeholders across BDO to uncover how learning could best support our organization's evolution toward becoming top-tier. Through thoughtful discussion and reflection, we explored essential questions about our purpose:

- What role should learning play in organizational success?
- How could we differentiate our learning approach?
- What promises could we make and consistently deliver on?
- How would we measure and communicate our impact?
- What would make our learning brand uniquely BDO?

These discussions revealed our core story: BDO's success depends on our ability to continuously develop new capabilities and adapt to changing client needs in a rapidly evolving professional services landscape. Learning isn't just about skill development; it's about creating a culture where every employee feels empowered to grow, innovate, and deliver exceptional value to our clients. We are the engine that powers BDO's journey to the top tier by developing our greatest asset: our people.

This story became our compass, guiding every aspect of our brand development from mission to visual identity.

OUR BRAND PROMISE

These conversations led us to craft a mission that clearly signaled our strategic intent: "To establish learning and development as a strategic differentiator at BDO—setting the industry standard for excellence, empowering top talent through continuous growth opportunities, and driving organizational success by transforming L&D into a service that delivers measurable business value."

OUR BRAND PILLARS

To deliver on this promise, we built our brand on clear pillars that would guide our decisions and actions. Each pillar became a catalyst for specific changes in how we approached learning at BDO:

Excellence in Delivery transformed our approach to program design. We established a rigorous quality assurance process where each learning experience was evaluated against specific excellence criteria before launch. This meant:

- Creating detailed facilitator guides ensuring consistent delivery
- Building pre- and post-session measurements into relevant programs
- Providing learning sustainment following each program
- Implementing post-program feedback loops and measuring learning transfer for continuous improvement

Business Impact reshaped how we developed new programs. Every learning initiative now requires:

- Clear alignment with BDO's strategic priorities
- Specific, measurable business outcomes
- Regular impact reporting to stakeholders

Community-Driven Development became a reality through:

- Establishing practice communities across service lines
- Creating peer learning networks
- Recognizing and rewarding knowledge contributors

These pillars didn't just guide our decisions; they fundamentally changed how learning happened at BDO. When a partner recently commented, "Learning used to be something we did to people; now it's something we do together," we knew our brand pillars were coming to life.

OUR VISUAL IDENTITY

In crafting our visual identity, we knew we needed a symbol that could carry the weight of our ambitions while remaining elegantly simple. The answer emerged in the form of a mountain—a powerful metaphor that resonated deeply with our purpose. This wasn't a decorative choice; it was a strategic decision to embed meaning into every visual touchpoint of our brand.

The mountain symbolizes the essence of learning and development at BDO. At its most basic level, it represented achievement—the climb toward excellence that every professional undertakes. However, its symbolism ran deeper. Like learning itself, mountains offer different perspectives at each new height. What seems insurmountable from the base becomes a milestone on your journey when viewed from higher up. Each ascent builds capability and confidence, transforming challenges into stepping stones toward greater achievement.

We designed our mountain logo with intentional sophistication, ensuring it would resonate across all applications—from digital learning platforms to physical learning spaces. Its clean lines and upward trajectory spoke to progress and aspiration, while its layered peaks suggested the multiple pathways to growth available within BDO.

Most importantly, our mountain symbol connected emotionally with our people. When they saw it, they didn't just see a logo; they saw their professional journeys reflected back at them. It became a reminder that every small step contributes to larger achievements, that the view gets better as you climb, and that there's always another peak to strive for. The mountain became more than our visual signature; it became a symbol of possibility, promising both the challenge of the climb and the reward of reaching new heights.

To complement our visual symbol, we needed words that would be equally powerful yet simple—a rallying cry that would inspire action. "Never. Stop. Learning." emerged as our tagline, chosen for its directness and emotional resonance. Unlike our comprehensive brand promise, which detailed our strategic commitment to the organization, this tagline spoke directly to the heart of every BDO professional. Its simplicity made it memorable; its action orientation made it motivating, and its universal relevance made it personal to everyone, regardless of their role or level.

Our mountain symbol and "Never. Stop. Learning." tagline created a powerful visual and verbal signature. The mountain logo and those three words clearly represented people's professional journeys. They became a reminder that every small step contributes to larger achievements, that the view gets better as you climb, and that there's always another peak to strive for. The combination became more than our visual signature; it became a symbol of possibility, promising both the challenge of the climb and the reward of reaching new heights.

PROGRAM ARCHITECTURE: STRUCTURING DEVELOPMENT FOR IMPACT

At BDO Canada, we recognized that to truly live our brand promise, we needed a clear, intuitive, and equitable program structure—one that would make learning not just available, but embedded in how our people grow, lead, and drive impact. Our approach to program architecture was built on three core principles:

1. **Learning for All** – Development shouldn't be limited to a select few; it must be accessible to everyone, at every stage of their career.

2. **Guided Growth** – Learning should be structured in a way that guides employees through their development journey, offering clear pathways and progression.

3. **Strategic Alignment** – Every learning initiative must map back to our competency model and firm-wide priorities, ensuring it contributes to BDO's long-term success.

A Multi-Tiered Approach: The Leadership Development Journey

To ensure learning was structured for growth at every level, we developed the Leadership Development Journey, a three-tiered model designed to support professionals throughout their career:

1. **Leadership Development for All** – Steering away from traditional, nomination-based development to a more equitable approach, ensuring every employee has access to learning.

2. **Path to Partner** – For those nominated into the partner pipeline, structured development helps them prepare for the next stage of leadership.

3. **Partner Development** – Even senior leaders need continued growth to navigate complex challenges and lead with excellence. This track ensures that partners continue evolving in their leadership.

Learning isn't just about climbing the corporate ladder—it's about building capability at every level. By structuring development this way, we eliminated ambiguity and ensured that no matter where someone is in their career, they know exactly where to focus their growth.

Branded Learning Experiences: Reinforcing Growth Through Identity

Beyond leadership development, we branded our learning ecosystem to reinforce our identity and create an intuitive navigation system—one that makes it easy for employees to engage with learning in a meaningful way.

- **Business Growth Academy (BGA)** – Because business development is a core priority, we launched BGA to build firm-wide sales capabilities. The tiers of BGA mirror the mountain metaphor, reinforcing growth as a continuous journey:
  - Essentials (foundational for all)
  - Elevate (managers and senior managers)
  - Ascend (partners)
  - Summit (top sales leaders)
- **SkillUP Summit** – Our flagship, firm-wide virtual learning event designed to align with three core strategic priorities:

Gen AI, Leadership, and Business Growth. Held over three half-days, it ensures that learning is accessible, engaging, and directly connected to firm-wide success.

- **Power Skills Series** – Recognizing that soft skills are power skills, we launched a quarterly instructor-led training series focusing on essential capabilities like emotional intelligence, self-leadership, and coaching. These sessions are open-enrollment and first-come, first-serve, ensuring wide accessibility.

- **Digital Self-Paced Learning Hub** – To complement our live programs, we built a self-directed learning platform with clear development pathways, giving employees the ability to learn anytime, anywhere.

A strong learning brand isn't just about looking good—it's about making engagement effortless. By structuring our programs with branded, recognizable tiers and experiences, we made learning instantly identifiable and easy to navigate.

Tying It All Together: Alignment & Execution

To ensure sustainability and impact, every learning initiative is designed with:

- **Direct alignment to our competency model** – Programs are mapped to the firm's core competencies and strategic priorities. This ensures that learning isn't just nice to have—it's directly fueling business success.

- **Tiered Learning Levels** – No one starts as an expert. Our tiered approach allows for progressive development, guiding employees from foundational skills to advanced mastery.

- **Instructor-Led and Self-Paced Options** – By balancing structured, instructor-led training with flexible, self-paced learning, we ensure that development is both engaging and accessible.

- **Cultural Reinforcement** – Every learning program sits under the SkillUP brand, tied to our firm-wide mantra: Never. Stop. Learning. This ensures that learning isn't just something employees do—it's part of who we are.

The Bottom Line: A Learning Architecture That Drives Action

A well-structured learning ecosystem isn't just about offering courses—it's about guiding employees through a journey. By creating a tiered, branded, and strategically aligned learning structure, we ensured that learning at BDO isn't random or reactive—it's intentional, accessible, and designed for long-term success.

When learning is easy to navigate, employees engage. When employees engage, they grow. And when they grow, the organization thrives.

MAKING OUR BRAND STICK

The true test of any brand is how it lives in the organization. We implemented our brand through:

Consistent Integration

- Every learning session is closed with the phrase "Never Stop Learning."
- All presentations included our visual identity.
- Communications maintained consistent messaging and tone.
- Learning spaces reflected our brand elements.

Cultural Integration

- Leaders were equipped to speak about the importance of learning.
- Learning Ambassadors were identified and empowered.
- Success stories were regularly shared and celebrated.
- Brand elements were made easily accessible.

Behavioral Integration

- Learning principles were incorporated into performance discussions.
- Recognition programs highlighted continuous learning.
- Leaders modeled learning behaviors.
- Teams incorporated learning goals into their planning.

THE TIPPING POINT

The real magic happened about a year into this consistent practice. We began hearing our brand language used naturally in conversations across the organization. "Never Stop Learning" wasn't just a tagline anymore; it had become part of BDO's cultural vocabulary. The impact of the SkillUP Summit lingered long after the event concluded, with participants enthusiastically sharing their experiences and key takeaways with colleagues. This organic advocacy sparked a chain reaction: People began proactively reaching out to ask about participating in more learning programs, eager to continue their development journey. When we launched the Power Skills Series, the first three classes were completely full in under 30 minutes, prompting us to add an additional 20 sessions to meet the demand. In meetings, hallway conversations, and team discussions, our learning brand had become so embedded that people naturally referenced it—clear evidence that it had truly become part of our organizational DNA.

LESSONS FOR OTHER ORGANIZATIONS

While every organization's journey will be different, several principles from our transformation are universally applicable:

Step	Key Actions
1. Start with Clear Intent	- Know what you want your L&D brand to accomplish - Align with the organizational strategy - Build for the future you want to create
2. Make it Meaningful	- Ensure every brand element has a purpose - Connect it to organizational values - Support business objectives
3. Build for Integration	- Make it easy to adopt and share - Create tools and resources - Enable organic growth
4. Be Patient and Persistent	- Recognize that brand building takes time - Prioritize consistency over perfection - Focus on small wins to build momentum

The transformation from hidden function to strategic partner requires dedication, but the rewards are worth the effort. Through intentional brand building and consistent execution, you can emerge as a recognized, visible driver of organizational value.

However, even the strongest brands must evolve to stay relevant. As your organization changes and grows, your L&D brand needs to adapt while maintaining its core strength.

EVOLUTION AND ADAPTATION: WHEN YOUR BRAND NEEDS TO TRANSFORM

THE CATALYST FOR CHANGE

Just as successful companies like Apple and Nike have evolved their brands over time while maintaining their essential promise, L&D brands must navigate change thoughtfully. However, sometimes evolution isn't enough; you need a revolution. At General Motors, we faced this exact challenge. Despite having a capable L&D team delivering solid programs, we had an intractable problem: Stakeholders saw us as conventional. Whenever we proposed innovative learning solutions, we met skepticism and resistance. Our suggestions were often dismissed before they were even fully heard. Our capabilities weren't the issue; historical perceptions were holding us back.

STRATEGIC REINVENTION

We realized that tweaking our existing L&D brand wouldn't break through these entrenched perceptions. We needed to create an entirely new space where innovation could thrive. The solution emerged as the *Innovation Garage*—a completely distinct brand with its own identity and a clear promise: "Committed to Innovations that Drive Business Results."

This wasn't just a rebranding exercise. Like a startup operating within GM, the Innovation Garage had different operating principles. We transformed a physical space into a creative learning environment, established new ways of working with stakeholders, and approached problems with design thinking methodology. Most importantly, we changed how we presented ourselves to the organization.

The impact was immediate and profound. The same innovative solutions that had previously met resistance were now welcomed with enthusiasm when presented under the Innovation Garage banner. Stakeholders who had been skeptical began actively seeking our involvement in their initiatives. Teams started coming to us with their challenges, eager to partner on innovative solutions. The Innovation Garage became known as the place where traditional training barriers didn't apply—where new approaches weren't just accepted but expected.

This transformation taught us a valuable lesson: Sometimes, the most effective way to evolve your brand is to create a new one that can exist alongside it, giving you the freedom to break from historical constraints while maintaining your core strengths.

RECOGNIZING THE NEED FOR EVOLUTION

How do you know when it's time to evolve your brand? Look for these signals:

Misalignment with Strategy

When your organization's direction shifts significantly, your learning brand might need to follow. At one company, their L&D brand focused heavily on classroom excellence, just as the organization was moving toward digital-first operations. They needed to evolve their brand to reflect this new reality.

Stakeholder Feedback

Listen for disconnects between your brand promise and stakeholder perceptions. Are you hearing consistent feedback that doesn't align with your intended brand identity? This might signal the need for evolution.

Market Changes

External factors can necessitate brand evolution. The rapid shift to virtual learning during global disruptions forced many L&D brands to reposition themselves around digital delivery and remote engagement.

APPROACHES TO BRAND EVOLUTION

The Fresh Start

Sometimes, like with our Innovation Garage, you must create something entirely new. This approach works when:

- Current perceptions are strongly entrenched
- You need to signal a decisive break from the past
- You're entering completely new territory

The Gradual Shift

Other times, evolution can be more subtle. One organization gradually shifted its brand from "Training Excellence" to "Performance Partnership" over two years, maintaining its visual identity while transforming its positioning.

The Brand Extension

Adding new elements to your brand can help it evolve while maintaining established equity. Consider how one L&D function added a "Digital Academy" sub-brand to its portfolio, signaling innovation while preserving its core identity.

MANAGING THE TRANSFORMATION

Stakeholder Engagement

Involve key stakeholders in the evolution process. Their input improves the result and builds buy-in for the change. Share early concepts, gather feedback, and let them see the evolution in progress.

Communication Strategy

Create a clear narrative around why and how your brand is evolving. Help people understand the connection between the change and better learning outcomes. Be transparent about what's changing and what remains constant.

Phased Implementation

Consider a staged approach to brand evolution:

1. Introduce the need for change.
2. Preview new elements.
3. Phase in new brand components.
4. Gradually retire old branding.
5. Reinforce the new identity.

Brand evolution is not a sign of failure; it's a sign of vitality. The most enduring L&D brands know when to adapt and how to do it while staying true to their core purpose. Whether creating something entirely new like the Innovation Garage at GM or thoughtfully evolving an existing brand like BDO Academy, success lies in intentional change that aligns with organizational needs.

Your L&D brand serves as a bridge between learning's impact and organizational success. When that bridge needs reinforcement or reconstruction, have the courage to act. Sometimes, that means building something entirely new; other times, it means strengthening what already works. The key is recognizing which path will best serve your organization's future and having the conviction to pursue it.

YOUR BRAND, YOUR LEGACY: BUILDING FOR THE FUTURE

A strong L&D brand is more than visual identity or clever taglines; it's the bridge between your team's capabilities and your organization's perception of them. When built thoughtfully and maintained consistently, it becomes the catalyst for cultural transformation.

The most successful L&D brands share common characteristics:

- They tell a clear, compelling story about learning's value.

- They make specific promises and consistently deliver on them.

- They thoughtfully evolve while maintaining core principles.

- They become part of the organization's natural vocabulary.

However, perhaps most importantly, they transform how organizations think about learning. When your brand is strong, learning isn't seen as an interruption to work; it becomes an integral part of how work gets done.

Your Next Steps

As you begin or continue your brand journey, remember:

- **Start with Purpose:** Let your why guide every brand decision.

- **Build for Impact:** Create brand elements that enhance learning effectiveness.

- **Stay Patient and Persistent:** Look for small wins and celebrate progress.

Your L&D brand has the potential to transform how your organization views and values learning. It can turn skeptics into advocates, transform training from a requirement into an opportunity, and position learning as a crucial driver of business success.

Whether you're starting from scratch or evolving an existing brand, the principles we've explored provide a roadmap for success.

The journey may be challenging, but the destination—a learning culture that drives organizational success—is worth every step.

STANDING OUT IN THE FIELD

Great brands don't just occupy market space; they occupy mind space. When Steve Jobs returned to Apple in 1997, he didn't just change a logo; he ignited a revolution that transformed how we think about technology. When Phil Knight built Nike, he wasn't selling shoes; he was selling the promise of athletic greatness. When Howard Schultz expanded Starbucks, he wasn't scaling coffee shops but creating a "third place" between work and home.

Now, it's your turn.

The tools we've explored—brand pillars, visual systems, and program architecture—aren't just organizational frameworks. They're the building blocks of a revolution in how organizations perceive, value, and embrace learning. BDO's mountain doesn't just symbolize growth; it challenges every employee to see their career as a continuous climb toward excellence. GM's Innovation Garage isn't just a rebranding; it's a bold declaration that learning can transform even the most traditional institutions.

Like Amazon's deliberate choice to stand out in a sea of book-related competitors, L&D must be intentionally positioned to capture attention in today's complex organizational landscape. No matter how transformative, your contributions won't naturally catch attention without strategic branding. Just as a Purple Cow stands out in a field of ordinary cattle, you must deliberately distinguish yourself—not through gimmicks or self-promotion but through a clear demonstration of strategic impact.

Your brand isn't just a logo or tagline; it's the culmination of every principle we've explored. It's the story people tell about L&D when you're not in the room. It's how learning becomes embedded in your organization's DNA. Through thoughtful brand building, evolution, and consistent execution, you can transform L&D from a support function into a strategic catalyst for organizational success.

Make it remarkable. Make it matter, and like that Purple Cow, make it impossible to ignore.

What story will your brand tell?

🔑 KEY LEARNINGS

- **Strategic Positioning:** Like Amazon's deliberate name choice, L&D branding requires positioning that elevates your function from a support role to a strategic priority. This intentional approach ensures learning becomes fundamental to organizational success.

- **Beyond Surface Elements:** A compelling L&D brand transcends visual elements to become embedded in organizational DNA, transforming learning's perception from optional to essential. This integration shapes how the business operates.

- **Experience Orchestration:** Following Disney's meticulous approach, successful L&D brands carefully craft every interaction to reinforce their promise. This consistent attention across touchpoints builds lasting trust.

- **Foundation of Brand Pillars:** Strong L&D brands are built on clear, guiding principles that inform decisions and shape experiences. These pillars ensure initiatives align with organizational needs and deliver on brand promises.

- **Adaptive Evolution:** Like successful consumer brands, L&D functions must evolve their identity while maintaining core strengths. Whether through gradual shifts or strategic reinvention, this thoughtful adaptation ensures the brand remains relevant and impactful as organizational needs change.

8

BREAKFAST REVOLUTION: *AMPLIFYING IMPACT*

"Marketing is a contest for people's attention."

—*Seth Godin*

THE BACON BLUEPRINT

In the 1920s, Edward Bernays faced an intriguing challenge: convincing Americans that bacon and eggs should be the cornerstone of breakfast. Most Americans started their day simply at the time—toast, coffee, perhaps a piece of fruit. However, Bernays, hired by a bacon company looking to boost sales, understood that changing behavior required more than clever advertising. It demanded a complete reimagining of Americans' view of breakfast—a true culture shift.

His strategy was brilliant in its simplicity. He sought out the most trusted voices of the time—physicians. Approaching a respected doctor, Bernays asked, "Would a heavier breakfast be healthier for the average American?" When the physician confirmed the benefits of a substantial morning meal, including lasting energy, Bernays didn't stop there. He sent the physician's endorsement to thousands of other physicians, creating a coalition of medical advocates who endorsed the idea.

The results were transformative. Bacon and eggs became more than a meal; they were positioned as a doctor-approved cornerstone of American health. Bernays elevated his campaign far beyond simple product promotion by linking bacon to health—a topic with universal appeal and authority. (Sure, we now know bacon isn't exactly a superfood—unless you consider salt and fat their own food groups—but back then, this narrative was revolutionary.) What began as a marketing initiative evolved into a cultural movement that would define American breakfast habits for generations.

Bernays' campaign highlights a timeless truth: the power of strategic amplification. A message amplified through trusted voices and deliberate systems can transform behavior and drive culture change.

Today's leaders face a similar challenge: How do we transform learning from a corporate initiative into an organizational movement? Like Bernays, we know that great programs alone aren't enough. We need strategic amplification to ensure our initiatives resonate, thrive, and embed themselves into the fabric of organizational culture.

In this chapter, we'll explore four key strategies for amplifying your impact:

1. **Cultivating learning ambassadors**
2. **Building recognition systems**
3. **Establishing external credibility**
4. **Communicating success internally**

These four strategies provide the foundation for amplifying your impact, transforming L&D from a supportive function into a visible and influential driver of organizational growth. By applying these principles, you're promoting programs and embedding learning into the fabric of your organization's culture and success.

CULTIVATING YOUR AMBASSADOR NETWORK

I stumbled into the power of learning advocates by accident. Our team had been pushing out carefully crafted communications about a new technical training program for months, with mediocre results. Then, I noticed something: In certain departments, enrollment was suddenly spiking—not because of our marketing but because of people like Marcus in IT.

Marcus wasn't special because he completed the training (although I was happy he did). He was special because he kept finding organic ways to mention what he'd learned when helping colleagues troubleshoot problems—no formal presentations, no forced enthusiasm, just natural moments of "Oh yeah, I learned this trick in that training last month." Within weeks, his entire department was asking about the program.

This wasn't a dramatic transformation story. It was more like planting seeds—small, unassuming moments that quietly took root and spread through casual conversations. While we were focused on pushing our message out, the real impact grew organically in the quiet exchanges between colleagues, where curiosity and knowledge flourished naturally.

Even the most thoughtfully designed brand needs advocates to bring it to life. Just look at the rise of social media influencers—those modern-day tastemakers who convince us we need yet another kitchen gadget or that life isn't complete without a matcha latte. While we may not be asking our Learning Ambassadors (also known as influencers) to go viral on TikTok, the principle is the same: People trust people.

Our L&D teams can create innovative programs and dynamic resources, but people like Marcus and Learning Ambassadors at every level breathe life into these initiatives. They're the ones who normalize learning in daily operations, influence their peers through example, and drive sustained engagement long after the workshop ends. These ambassadors transform learning from a department initiative into an organizational movement.

THE SECRET TO FINDING YOUR LEARNING AMBASSADORS

Contrary to popular belief, the best ambassadors aren't always those with fancy titles or corner offices. The most impactful advocates are the ones whose voices are respected, regardless of rank—those informal leaders who naturally foster trust, encourage growth, and inspire action among their peers.

When building your network, look for individuals who embody these characteristics:

- **Natural Teachers:** They instinctively share knowledge, offer guidance, and support others' development.

- **Credible Voices:** Their opinions carry weight, and their influence extends across teams and levels.

- **Growth Mindset:** They actively seek learning opportunities, embrace change, and model adaptability.

- **Results Focus:** They understand the connection between learning and performance and can advocate for its tangible benefits.

The goal isn't to create a committee; it's to find genuine champions of growth—people whose passion for learning is contagious.

FIND FIVE "FRIENDS OF LEARNING"

Your ambassador network starts with finding five key individuals— your friends of learning. These are the people who already align with the values of your L&D initiatives and have the reach and credibility to influence others. Think of them as the founding members of your learning community. If you and everyone on your L&D team put your heads together and each identify five friends of learning, you are on your way.

HOW TO START

1. **Identify Your Ambassadors:** Start with the natural teachers and mentors you already know—those colleagues who light up when sharing knowledge, who others naturally turn to for guidance, or who consistently champion others' growth.

Often, your most impactful ambassadors are already in your network, quietly demonstrating your desired qualities. Then, expand your search through surveys, manager recommendations, and informal conversations to identify others who embody these ambassador qualities.

2. **Diverse Representation:** Ensure your five reflect different levels, departments, and perspectives to maximize their collective influence and ensure learning resonates across all corners of your organization.

3. **Invite Them to Join:** Frame this as an opportunity to shape your organization's future, not another task on their plate. When inviting potential ambassadors, share specific examples of how you've seen them influence others' growth. Position this as joining a community of like-minded advocates who will help transform how your organization approaches learning and development. Be clear about the impact they'll have while keeping the commitment manageable.

QUARTERLY AMBASSADOR FORUMS

Once you've identified your five friends of learning, the key is to keep the momentum going. Establish quarterly ambassador forums, which serve as check-in and community-building opportunities.

In these forums:

- **Share Success Stories:** Ambassadors can showcase how learning has impacted their areas, inspiring others to follow suit.

- **Solve Challenges Together:** Create a safe space for ambassadors to discuss obstacles they've encountered in embedding learning into their teams and brainstorm solutions.

- **Foster Growth:** Offer micro-trainings to develop advocacy skills, helping them become even more effective champions.

- **Identify New Learning Opportunities:** Listen for their input on skill or program gaps that may exist.

These gatherings are more than just meetings; they're a cornerstone of your learning community. They provide ambassadors with the structure and support they need to sustain enthusiasm, deepen their influence, and amplify the impact of your L&D initiatives.

EMPOWERING YOUR AMBASSADORS

While regular forums provide structure, true impact requires giving your ambassadors the tools to thrive. Enthusiasm alone isn't enough; effective ambassadors need practical resources, clear guidance, and meaningful recognition to advocate confidently and consistently.

Start by creating a digital ambassador toolkit, a living resource that evolves with your network. This shouldn't just be a folder of generic documents; it should include dynamic tools like:

- **Impact Reports:** Summarize the measurable outcomes of learning programs to build credibility.

- **Success Story Templates:** Help ambassadors craft and share compelling narratives.

- **Conversation Guides:** Provide talking points and strategies for advocating learning's value in team meetings or one-on-one interactions.

Empowerment isn't just about tools; it's about partnerships. The most successful ambassador programs position members not as messengers but as problem-solvers, integral to shaping the organization's learning culture.

THE HEALTHCARE SYSTEM TRANSFORMATION: ILLUSTRATIVE EXAMPLE

A powerful example of this approach emerged in a major healthcare system facing significant change. The L&D team identified twenty-five potential learning ambassadors across five hospitals—from nurse managers to IT specialists to HR partners. Instead of asking these ambassadors to simply promote learning programs, they engaged them as true partners in solving organizational challenges.

During their first ambassador forum, these advocates highlighted a critical gap: new medical technology training wasn't reaching night shift workers effectively. The traditional nine-to-five training schedule left night shift workers scrambling to attend sessions during their off-hours, leading to low completion rates and growing frustration.

The L&D team saw this as an opportunity to demonstrate the power of their ambassador network. They formed three cross-functional teams, each led by ambassadors from different hospitals, to reimagine the training approach. Night shift nurses worked alongside IT specialists to identify pain points, while HR partners provided insights on scheduling constraints and compliance requirements.

Over six weeks, these teams prototyped different solutions. They tested various combinations of delivery methods, ultimately landing on an innovative hybrid approach. The final design included:

- Self-paced virtual modules that could be completed during quieter night shift periods
- Peer-led practice sessions scheduled across all shifts
- Mobile-friendly microlearning segments for just-in-time support
- Virtual office hours with trainers spanning all shifts
- A buddy system pairing experienced users with new learners

The ambassadors' deep understanding of their colleagues' needs made this solution particularly effective. They knew, for instance, that night shift workers preferred shorter, more frequent learning sessions rather than long blocks of training. They also recognized the importance of building in practice time during actual night shifts, when the workflow and challenges were most relevant.

The impact demonstrated the power of engaged ambassadors:

- Training completion rates rose from 65 percent to 92 percent.

- Employee satisfaction with learning accessibility increased by 27 percent.

- New hire time-to-proficiency decreased by three weeks.

- Incident reports related to technology use dropped by 45 percent.

- Night shift retention rates improved by 18 percent.

Most importantly, this success created a blueprint for future initiatives. The ambassadors had evolved from program promoters to true partners in organizational transformation. They continued to identify challenges, co-create solutions, and drive change across all five hospitals, establishing a new standard for how learning initiatives could be developed and deployed.

This case underscores that when ambassadors are equipped and empowered, they support learning and drive transformation. Their intimate knowledge of day-to-day operations and their passion for improvement create solutions that stick.

SUSTAINING AMBASSADOR ENGAGEMENT

Keeping your ambassadors engaged is an ongoing commitment to fostering their enthusiasm and ensuring they feel valued. The best ambassadors thrive when supported, recognized, and given opportunities to make meaningful contributions. After all, advocacy is most effective when it's tied to purpose and impact.

OPPORTUNITIES FOR ADVOCACY

To sustain momentum, provide structured ways for ambassadors to actively contribute to your learning culture:

- **Learning Spotlights:** Invite ambassadors to share quick success stories or learning moments during team meetings. These five-minute highlights can inspire peers and demonstrate the real-world value of development initiatives.

- **Success Stories:** Feature ambassadors in internal communications, celebrating the initiatives they've led and the results they've achieved. A story about a new onboarding process that improved retention can serve as a powerful example for others.

- **Mentor Connections:** Pair ambassadors with colleagues seeking guidance in their learning journeys. These mentorship opportunities elevate the ambassadors' influence and build deeper connections across the organization.

These activities amplify the impact of your ambassadors and position them as thought leaders within their teams.

RECOGNITION MATTERS

Never underestimate the power of acknowledgment. Formal recognition strengthens engagement and reinforces the importance of the ambassador role:

- **Performance Reviews:** Include ambassador contributions as a formal part of their performance evaluation, linking their advocacy efforts to career growth.

- **High-Visibility Opportunities:** Provide ambassadors with chances to lead major projects, present at company-wide meetings, or represent L&D in cross-functional initiatives.

- **Appreciation from Leadership:** Ensure learning leaders regularly thank ambassadors, publicly and privately, for their contributions. A personal note or shout-out during a meeting can go a long way in building loyalty.

Sustaining engagement isn't just about keeping ambassadors involved; it's about making them feel their role is indispensable.

Measuring Ambassador Impact

What gets measured gets improved. To truly understand the value of your ambassador network, you need both quantitative data and qualitative insights that reveal how learning is taking root across the organization.

Key Metrics to Watch

While basic metrics like program enrollment and completion rates provide a starting point, a thriving ambassador network reveals deeper cultural shifts. Look for:

- **Proactive Learning Requests:** Increased demand for learning resources and support from teams influenced by ambassadors.

- **Higher Engagement Scores:** Teams with active ambassadors often report stronger engagement and satisfaction in employee surveys.

- **Learning as a Cultural Norm:** When business leaders and employees naturally reference learning in discussions—whether during project planning or performance reviews—you know your culture is changing.

- **Ambassador-Led Initiatives:** Track the number and success of projects initiated by ambassadors, from peer-led workshops to innovative solutions for team challenges.

LOOKING AHEAD

"They" say it takes a village—and in L&D, our village is built by our friends of learning. Your ambassador network isn't just a helpful extension of your team; it's a force multiplier that amplifies your reach and embeds learning into the heart of your organization.

Ambassadors don't just promote programs; they transform learning into a way of working. They create new connections, challenge old mindsets, and inspire teams to view development as essential to success. With their support, L&D moves from a department initiative to an organizational movement.

As you continue to build and nurture your ambassador network, remember that your goal isn't just to create program promoters. You're cultivating partners who will help shape the future of learning in your organization. By giving them the support, tools, and recognition they need, you empower them to lead a cultural transformation—one conversation, connection, and initiative at a time.

While ambassadors create the momentum for learning, their impact multiplies when paired with systematic recognition. Just as Bernays didn't simply spread his message but created a framework for doctors to champion it, we need to build systems that consistently celebrate and reinforce the value of learning.

Recognition in organizations is usually a mess. We've all sat through those awkward quarterly awards ceremonies where someone reads generic accomplishments off a slide—or we've received one of those automated "Great job!" emails that somehow make you feel worse than being ignored.

However, occasionally, you catch glimpses of what real recognition looks like. It's in the way a team naturally starts sharing their learning moments during sprint reviews or how a manager casually mentions their direct report's growth during a stakeholder update. These aren't structured recognition programs; they're moments where learning becomes part of the natural conversation.

The challenge is figuring out how to make these organic moments happen more often without turning them into another corporate checkbox exercise.

⚡ YOUR TURN: IDENTIFY YOUR AMBASSADORS

Commit to identifying your five friends of learning in the next two weeks. Have your colleagues do the same. Then, commit to having your first ambassador forum within the next three months.

CREATING RECOGNITION SYSTEMS

THE POWER OF BEING SEEN

Think back to a moment when someone truly saw your growth. Maybe it was a mentor acknowledging how far you've come, a peer celebrating your innovative solution, or a leader highlighting your impact in front of the team. That feeling—of being seen, valued, understood—creates an energy and motivation that propels us forward. It's more than just a feel-good moment; it fuels continued growth.

In today's workplace, where much of our development happens in the shadows—between Zoom calls or through late-night problem-solving—recognition becomes our bridge to engagement. When we celebrate learning systematically, we do more than boost morale. We shape organizational DNA, signaling that growth isn't just a nice-to-have; it's who we are.

BUILDING SYSTEMATIC RECOGNITION

Think of recognition as compound interest. Small, consistent deposits create exponential returns over time. When we layer recognition across individual, team, and organizational levels, we create a multiplier effect that transforms isolated achievements into cultural momentum. The key is building systems that capture and amplify these moments without draining them of their authenticity.

Let's explore how this works at each level, the technology that enables it, and how these layers build upon each other to create lasting impact.

Individual Level: From Moments to Momentum

At the individual level, effective recognition connects personal achievement to career growth. However, the real power comes from making recognition a natural part of work rhythms:

- **Daily Moments:** Micro-recognition in team channels that spotlight skill application

- **Weekly Rhythms:** Learning reflection prompts in one-on-ones, moving beyond "What did you accomplish?" to "What did you learn?"

- **Monthly Progress:** Portfolio building that captures not just what someone learned but how they've applied it

- **Quarterly Impact:** Career conversations that explicitly connect learning achievements to advancement opportunities

Technology enables this through:

- Digital badges aligned with key capabilities
- Personal growth portfolios in your learning platform
- Integration with performance management systems
- Automated prompts for reflection and documentation

The goal isn't just to acknowledge completion; it's to help individuals see their growth trajectory and inspire others through their journey.

Team Level: Creating Collective Energy

Teams amplify recognition's impact through collective celebration. When we spotlight cross-functional collaborations and shared learning milestones, we reinforce that growth is a team sport. These moments create positive peer pressure that elevates everyone's game.

Effective team recognition includes:

- **Daily Practice:** Learning spotlights in stand-ups and team channels

- **Sprint Rhythms:** Project retrospectives that celebrate learning alongside delivery

- **Monthly Momentum:** Team challenges that encourage collective skill-building

- **Quarterly Wins:** Cross-training initiatives that highlight complementary strengths

Supporting infrastructure might include:

- Team dashboards visualizing collective learning progress
- Collaborative spaces for knowledge sharing
- Recognition templates for team achievements
- Integration with project management tools

The key is creating spaces where teams can naturally surface and celebrate learning without it feeling forced or administrative. When teams spontaneously share their growth moments, you know you're on the right track.

Organizational Level: Scaling Impact

At the organizational level, we connect these individual and team victories to a larger purpose. These moments aren't just ceremonies but cultural rituals that embed learning into our organizational identity.
Key components include:

- **Monthly Showcases:** Teams demonstrating new capabilities through work examples
- **Quarterly Festivals:** Learning celebrations that connect skills to outcomes
- **Ongoing Channels:** Dedicated spaces for sharing learning journeys
- **Annual Impact:** Reports highlighting learning's organizational transformation

Technology amplifies this through:

- Company-wide recognition platforms
- Analytics dashboards showing learning impact
- Integration with communication systems
- Automated impact tracking and reporting

The most effective organizational recognition doesn't just celebrate the completion of learning programs; it spotlights how learning has fundamentally changed how work gets done. This might mean showcasing how a team's new data visualization skills transformed their quarterly business reviews or how improved coaching capabilities led to measurable improvements in team performance.

SYSTEMS TRANSFORMATION

COMMON PITFALLS AND SOLUTIONS

Even well-designed recognition systems can stumble. Here are typical challenges and how to address them:

1. **The Authenticity Challenge**
   - o Pitfall: Recognition feels forced or administrative
   - o Solution: Start with natural moments of celebration and build a structure around them

2. **The Consistency Challenge**
   - o Pitfall: Initial enthusiasm fades over time
   - o Solution: Embed recognition into existing workflows and meetings

3. **The Technology Trap**
   - o Pitfall: Over-relying on tools without human connection
   - o Solution: Use technology to enable, not replace, personal recognition

4. **The Measurement Mistake**
   - o Pitfall: Focusing only on the quantity of recognition
   - o Solution: Balance metrics with quality and impact measures

The key at every level is authenticity and connection. Recognition should feel less like a corporate program and more like a natural celebration of growth. These layered recognition approaches create a virtuous cycle where learning becomes increasingly visible, valued, and vital to organizational success.

BUILDING YOUR RECOGNITION ENGINE

Here's your blueprint for creating a recognition system that sustains itself:

1. **Start with Monthly Rituals**
   - Launch "learning impact moments" in team meetings.
   - Create a simple template for sharing growth stories.
   - Establish a rhythm of peer recognition.
   - Designate a time for celebrating skill application.
2. **Build Recognition Infrastructure**
   - Design digital badges aligned with key capabilities.
   - Create a success story template and sharing process.
   - Establish clear criteria for different recognition levels.
   - Develop a recognition toolkit for managers.
3. **Empower Recognition Champions**
   - Identify and train department recognition leaders.
   - Provide templates and prompts for recognition moments.
   - Create easy-to-use platforms for peer acknowledgment.
   - Reward and highlight active recognizers.

MAKING IT STICK

When I consulted with a global technology firm, their recognition system was purely transactional: certificates for course completion and generic "good job" emails, the kind of recognition that feels more like a checkbox than a celebration.

We started small, introducing "learning impact moments" in weekly team meetings. Instead of generic praise, leaders shared specific examples: "Jianu applied her new data visualization skills to transform our client presentation, leading to a contract renewal." These stories created a ripple effect that convinced us to invest in making recognition more systematic.

Our next step was creating a digital home for these stories. We carved out a dedicated space on the company's existing Microsoft Teams platform, creating a channel called "growth stories." We kept it simple: A standard template asked people to share what they learned, how they applied it, and its impact—no fancy technology, just a straightforward way to document and celebrate growth.

The key was making it easy. We created a simple format:

- What did you learn?
- Where did you apply it?
- What was the impact?
- Who helped you along the way?

We also established "recognition guides" in each department— people who were naturally good at spotting and celebrating others' growth. We didn't give them fancy titles or complicated responsibilities. Instead, we equipped them with weekly prompts and examples of great recognition moments. Their enthusiasm was contagious.

The transformation was gradual but profound. By month three, peers were spontaneously recognizing each other. What accelerated adoption was connecting these recognition moments to career development. During quarterly reviews, managers would pull up team members' growth stories, using them to discuss impact and progression. This created a virtuous cycle—people began documenting their learning journey for recognition and as a portfolio of their growth.

The metrics told a compelling story:

- Active participation grew to 47 percent of employees.

- Learning satisfaction rose by 18 percent.

- Previously invisible informal learning became measurable.

- 57 percent of employees had shared or been mentioned in a growth story.

- Performance reviews became richer with concrete examples.

However, the real transformation was cultural. Learning stopped being something that happened in training sessions and became something people actively looked for and celebrated in daily work. Team meetings naturally included sharing of learning moments. People began reaching out across departments to learn from colleagues they'd read about in growth stories.

One manager summed it up perfectly: "We've always had great learning programs, but now we have a way to see and celebrate how that learning comes to life in our work. It's changed how we think about development. It's not just about completing courses anymore; it's about the impact we create with what we learn."

MEASURING WHAT MATTERS

To gauge your recognition system's effectiveness, track immediate indicators and cultural signals:

1. **Track the Quantifiable**
   o Recognition frequency
   o Program enrollment trends
   o Participation rates across departments
   o Time between recognition moments

2. **Monitor Cultural Shifts**
   o Spontaneous peer celebrations
   o Learning references in everyday conversations

- o Employee-initiated recognition moments
- o Stories of impact being shared

⚡ YOUR TURN: BUILD YOUR RECOGNITION ENGINE

1. **This Week:** Identify three opportunities for recognition in your next team meeting. Start small, but be specific.

2. **This Month:** Create a simple recognition ritual—maybe it's learning impact moments or growth stories—and test it with your team.

3. **This Quarter:** Build your recognition infrastructure—templates, platforms, and processes that make celebration systematic.

4. **This Year:** Scale your recognition system across departments, measuring impact and adjusting based on feedback.

Remember, effective recognition isn't about grand gestures. It's about consistent, authentic appreciation that transforms learning from an event into a cultural cornerstone. When we get it right, recognition becomes more than a program; it becomes a self-sustaining force that drives continuous growth and development.

With internal recognition systems driving engagement, the next step is to amplify your impact beyond your organization's walls. Like ripples expanding in a pond, your learning initiatives can create waves of influence that extend far beyond their original scope—but only if you strategically position them for external visibility.

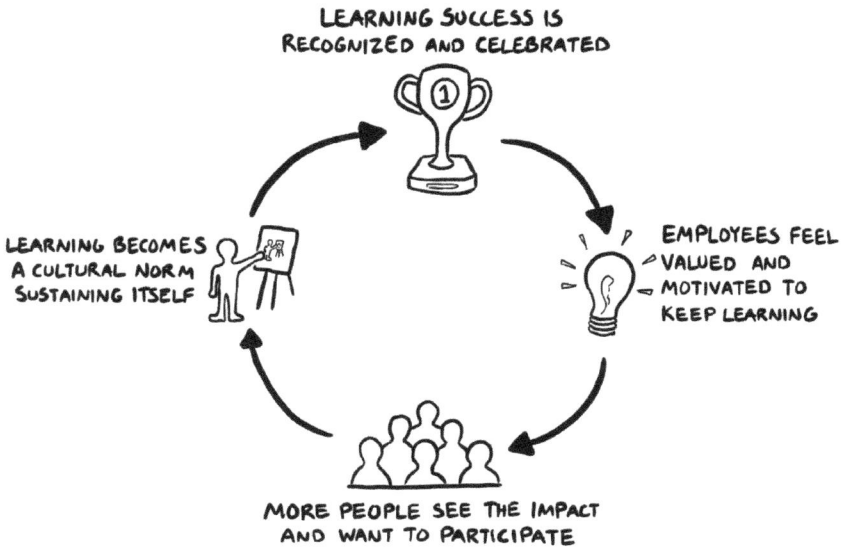

LEARNING SUCCESS IS RECOGNIZED AND CELEBRATED

EMPLOYEES FEEL VALUED AND MOTIVATED TO KEEP LEARNING

MORE PEOPLE SEE THE IMPACT AND WANT TO PARTICIPATE

LEARNING BECOMES A CULTURAL NORM SUSTAINING ITSELF

DEMONSTRATING EXTERNAL EXCELLENCE: THE STRATEGIC POWER OF INDUSTRY RECOGNITION

Picture this: Your team pours months of effort into designing a groundbreaking L&D initiative. The results are tangible, and the impact is palpable, but within the organization, it's just *another* win on the long list of what L&D quietly delivers. Now, picture that same initiative is recognized externally, earning an industry award and setting a new standard for excellence. Suddenly, it's not just your success; it's the organization's success! External validation transforms quiet wins into bold statements, shifting perceptions and amplifying your influence.

In the competitive landscape of corporate learning, validation comes in many forms. Internal metrics show impact. Employee feedback demonstrates value. However, a unique alchemy happens when external recognition enters the equation. It transforms good programs into industry standards, learning teams into thought leaders, and organizations into talent magnets.

It makes sense when you think about it. In a business world where every function must demonstrate value, external recognition validates what we already know: Thoughtful, strategic learning initiatives drive organizational success. It transforms learning from a necessary investment into a competitive advantage—not because the award changed the program but because it confirms what strong L&D teams have always understood: Exceptional learning design and delivery deserve recognition as business drivers.

Many view industry awards as the finish line—recognition for work well done. However, most strategic leaders understand that awards are both the finish line and the starting blocks. They're frameworks for designing excellence, catalysts for organizational influence, and powerful signals to the market about an organization's commitment to talent development.

BUILDING A STRATEGIC AWARDS PORTFOLIO

The journey to winning an award doesn't start with the submission. It starts with understanding the requirements. Award applications are more than forms to fill out; they're strategic roadmaps for designing impactful programs. Downloading and reviewing award criteria upfront allows you to "start with the end in mind," reverse-engineering your program design to align with the measurable outcomes and key elements required for recognition.

This approach works in two ways:

1. **Strategic Program Design:** Use the criteria to shape your initiative from the beginning, ensuring it meets high standards for innovation, measurable impact, and alignment with business goals.

2. **Demonstrating Impact:** Frame your program with the specific metrics, narratives, and stakeholder endorsements that awards require, creating a built-in validation process as you execute.

Key industry awards to consider include:

- **Brandon Hall Excellence Awards:** Often called the "Academy Awards" of HCM, these awards recognize achievements in learning, talent management, and human capital development.

- **Chief Learning Officer LearningElite Awards:** Honors organizations with exemplary workforce strategies that deliver measurable business results.

- **ATD BEST Awards:** Acknowledges enterprise-wide talent development success and organizations excelling in building learning cultures.

- **Learning Technologies Awards:** Celebrates innovative learning technologies and solutions that enhance effectiveness and engagement.

When choosing awards to pursue, focus on those that align with your organization's strategic priorities. Submissions that stand out share these traits:

- **Clear Business Alignment:** Directly tie your program to organizational goals.

- **Measurable Impact:** Showcase quantifiable outcomes that validate success.

- **Innovation:** Highlight creative solutions to challenges.

- **Stakeholder Support:** Include endorsements from across the organization for added credibility.

Award submissions serve as powerful frameworks for developing impactful learning programs. By treating award criteria as your blueprint, you align every aspect of your initiative—from goal setting to measurement—with proven standards of excellence. The result? Programs intentionally built to deliver and demonstrate measurable business value.

However, winning awards is just the beginning of building industry influence. The real opportunity lies in leveraging these achievements to establish your organization as a thought leader in the learning space. This requires a broader strategy that combines award recognition with authentic industry engagement and knowledge sharing.

BUILDING INDUSTRY PRESENCE: BEYOND THE AWARDS

What if your next big success isn't about what you've achieved but about what you've learned? Every learning organization has moments worth sharing—breakthroughs that could help others, failures that could prevent missteps, and lessons that could accelerate industry growth. However, impact happens only when these stories leave your walls. The question isn't whether your experiences have value; it's how to share them in ways that advance both your organization and the profession.

THE POWER OF LEARNING OUT LOUD

Sharing your organization's successes isn't just about building your brand; it's about advancing the profession as a whole. When you put your ideas into the world, you're contributing to a collective effort that drives innovation, sets new standards, and creates lasting impact beyond your walls.

However, in an era of polished LinkedIn posts and carefully curated case studies, the real impact often comes from sharing the messy truth of organizational learning. Success stories inspire, but honest accounts of challenges and failures transform. When General Electric implemented a reverse mentoring program to foster fresh perspectives, they discovered early on that reluctance to teach or learn—particularly across generational divides—required intentional strategies to build trust and ensure clear outcomes. Similarly, companies like Heineken have revealed the importance of aligning mentoring goals with practical realities like work styles and schedules, sparking important conversations about the nuanced design of such programs.

These candid reflections mirror broader challenges in leadership development. Research highlights that overemphasizing theoretical content at the expense of application can limit a program's impact, as seen in common pitfalls identified by organizations like PeopleThriver. By sharing these struggles openly, companies inspire meaningful conversations about how to align leadership initiatives with real-world demands, helping others refine their approaches for lasting success.

These "learning out loud" moments do more than help others; they build deeper credibility than any success story could. They show that your organization is mature enough to learn from setbacks and confident enough to share those lessons. They demonstrate the kind of authentic leadership that builds lasting influence.

Consider balancing your industry contributions this way:

- Share one lesson learned for every success story.
- Include "what we'd do differently" in your case studies.
- Present conference sessions on "productive failures."
- Write about your current challenges and how you're approaching them.

⚡ **Remember:** The learning profession is built on the belief that we grow through reflection and honest assessment. When you share successes and setbacks, you don't diminish your expertise; you prove it.

Authentic storytelling lays the foundation for industry influence. However, even the best story needs a platform. By strategically choosing where and how to share your insights, you can amplify your impact and build a significant presence.

EFFECTIVE INDUSTRY PRESENCE STRATEGIES

Your journey to industry influence should be strategic and sustainable. Here are key platforms that have high visibility and impact:

- **Industry Publications:** Start by sharing insights through respected journals like the *Chief Learning Officer* or *Training Industry Magazine*. Focus on practical wisdom backed by real results.

- **Conference Presentations:** Major industry events like ATD, Learning Technologies, and DevLearn seek fresh perspectives backed by concrete outcomes. Choose venues where your insights will resonate most strongly.

- **Research Participation:** Engage in industry studies that align with your expertise. Your data enriches the profession's understanding while positioning your organization as a source of insights.

CRAFTING YOUR CONTENT STRATEGY: AUTHENTIC STORIES AND REAL IMPACT

Start with one story that truly matters. Don't feel the need to share everything at once; instead, focus on an initiative that stands out for its complexity, results, or ability to challenge the status quo. Choose an initiative that:

- Taught you something unexpected
- Challenged your assumptions
- Required significant adaptation
- Produced measurable results

Document both the victories and the stumbles. Highlight the pivotal moments that forced you to pivot, the feedback that led to a breakthrough, and the surprises—good or bad—that reshaped the path forward. Authenticity isn't just about sharing successes; it's about offering a transparent look at the messy, imperfect journey that led to meaningful outcomes.

Ask yourself:

- What assumptions did we have to abandon along the way?

- Where did we face resistance, and how did we overcome it?

- What unexpected insights emerged during the implementation?

By focusing on these elements, you're not just sharing a story; you're creating a narrative that inspires, teaches, and builds credibility.

⚡ YOUR TURN: BUILD YOUR INDUSTRY PRESENCE STRATEGY

1. **Establish Your Foundation** (This Month)

   - Identify two strategic initiatives currently in progress.

   - Find an industry award that aligns with these initiatives.

   - Download and analyze award submission guidelines.

   - Create your signature story with key learnings and metrics.

2. **Build Your Framework** (This Quarter)

   - Use award criteria to shape program design and measurement.

   - Draft your first industry article or case study.

   - Share with trusted peers for feedback.

   - Set submission timeline for both awards and content.

---

3. **Expand Your Influence** (This Year)
   - Submit to one industry award and one publication platform.
   - Join two professional communities.
   - Document new stories and lessons learned.
   - Create a calendar for sharing insights throughout the year.

Your experiences—both successes and setbacks—hold valuable lessons for the learning community. Each story you share contributes to the profession's collective wisdom. Each failure you describe helps others avoid similar pitfalls. Each insight you offer moves our industry forward.

📌 **Remember:** Keep award criteria visible during program planning to ensure alignment between implementation and recognition requirements. Remember that each piece of content or submission should serve multiple purposes—from award recognition to thought leadership development.

Start small, but start now. Choose one story. Share it authentically. Watch how your honest account of both success and struggle resonates with others. Your insights and experience matter. Start sharing them today.

CONVERTING EXTERNAL SUCCESS TO INTERNAL INFLUENCE

External recognition feels great, but its true power lies in what happens next. Industry awards and accolades aren't endpoints; they're catalysts to ignite conversations, influence decisions, and drive momentum within your organization. They transform conversations from "Should we invest in learning?" to "How can we scale our award-winning approach?" It's not about the trophy but the doors it opens to amplify your impact. However, this shift doesn't happen automatically. It requires a deliberate strategy to translate external validation into internal influence. Let's explore how to craft messages that resonate with every stakeholder in your organization.

STRATEGIC COMMUNICATION: AMPLIFYING RECOGNITION AND LEARNING VALUE

While tailoring recognition messages to different stakeholders is crucial, it's just one piece of a larger communication puzzle. In today's attention economy, even transformative learning programs— award-winning or otherwise—can fade into obscurity without deliberate, strategic communication. The key is building a comprehensive approach that amplifies both major achievements and day-to-day successes.

SPEAKING THEIR LANGUAGE: A STAKEHOLDER-FOCUSED APPROACH

Each stakeholder group requires a unique communication approach that speaks to their priorities and preferences:

Executive Engagement

Executives need clear lines between learning and business performance. Every conversation should showcase ROI, market advantage, and risk mitigation. Frame external recognition as market validation of the organization's talent strategy. Key focuses include:

- Industry benchmarking data and competitive positioning
- Market visibility and employer brand impact
- Clear metrics: "Our leadership program delivered 18 percent productivity gains and reduced turnover costs by $2.3 million."

- Strategic alignment: "Digital skills training accelerated our cloud transformation, reducing time-to-market by 40 percent."

Manager Impact

Managers need practical tools and visible results. Connect validation to their day-to-day challenges:

- Performance metrics: "Team A reduced errors by 30 percent after technical training."
- Best practices validated by industry experts
- Monthly toolkits with quick-reference guides and talking points
- "Manager Minutes"—bite-sized updates linking learning to team outcomes
- Ready-to-use development conversation templates

Employee Growth

For employees, make development tangible and achievement visible:

- Individual contributions that led to recognition
- Peer transformation stories: "How Sarah leveraged our UX pathway to redesign our top product"
- Clear career progression examples
- Immediate application opportunities
- Recognition and celebration of learning milestones

BUILDING YOUR COMMUNICATION ARCHITECTURE

Mastering stakeholder language is just the start. Success requires a robust communication architecture that turns individual messages into sustained momentum. Here's how to build it:

1. **Map Your Communication Ecosystem**
   - Identify where your stakeholders spend their time.
   - Assess existing communication platforms.
   - Match message types to platform strengths.
   - Leverage existing channels—don't create new ones.
   - Meet stakeholders where they are (e.g., Salesforce for sales teams, Slack for tech teams).

2. **Create Strategic Rhythms**

   Build a consistent drumbeat of communication through:
   - **Weekly Pulse:** Quick-hit success stories and metrics embedded in team meetings
   - **Monthly Impact:** Detailed program updates with clear business outcomes
   - **Quarterly Reviews:** Strategic analysis connecting learning initiatives to business performance
   - **Annual Impact Report:** Comprehensive review linking learning investment to organizational transformation

   Start planning your communication strategy before major moments like award announcements. Build a calendar of opportunities to reinforce your message throughout the year. Consider how each piece of external validation and daily success can support your next big initiative or strategic priority.

3. **Leverage Internal Partnerships**

   Your Communications and Marketing teams are essential allies in elevating both recognition moments and ongoing learning visibility. They bring expertise in:
   - Channel optimization
   - Message crafting
   - Audience engagement
   - Brand alignment

Partner early and often to:

- Shape the narrative of learning success
- Integrate learning stories into company communications
- Maximize the impact of recognition moments
- Build learning's reputation as a business driver

CREATING SUSTAINABLE MOMENTUM

When executed well, this strategic approach creates a virtuous cycle:

- Learning initiatives drive measurable business impact.
- Impact stories fuel executive investment.
- Investment accelerates program innovation.
- Innovation delivers greater value.

Your role is to keep this cycle turning—tracking metrics, telling stories, and celebrating wins that transform L&D from support function to strategic driver. Through consistent, strategic communication that resonates with every stakeholder, you make learning's value impossible to ignore.

⭐ **Remember:** In today's talent economy, learning isn't just about development; it's about competitive advantage. Make that value impossible to ignore through communication that speaks to every stakeholder in their language.

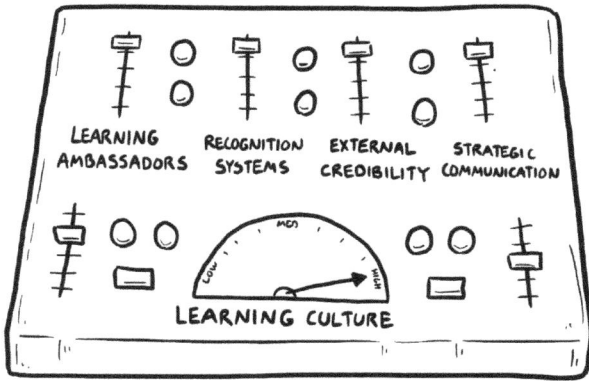

BUILDING YOUR LEGACY

Amplification isn't just about making learning visible; it's about creating lasting transformation. When you build a network of passionate advocates, implement systematic recognition, and communicate strategically, you create an unstoppable force for organizational change. These aren't just tactics; they're the foundation of a learning culture that sustains itself and grows stronger with each success story shared, each milestone celebrated, and each barrier overcome.

Your journey begins with those crucial first steps: identifying your five advocates, establishing your first recognition ritual, and sharing that initial success story. Each small action creates ripples that, when combined with others, generate waves of cultural transformation. This is how learning moves from an event to a way of being, from a program to a movement.

The strategies we've explored—from building ambassador networks to earning industry recognition—provide powerful tools for amplifying learning's impact. Yet even the most carefully crafted amplification strategy can face obstacles.

This brings us to our next frontier: How do we address the barriers that can prevent even the most powerful learning initiatives from reaching their full potential? In Chapter 9, we'll explore the eight critical barriers that often prevent learning initiatives from delivering their full value and, more importantly, how to transform these challenges into catalysts for innovative impact. Just as we've learned to amplify our successes through strategic influence and systematic recognition, we'll discover how to transform barriers into bridges for organizational growth.

🔑 KEY LEARNINGS

- **Strategic Amplification:** Like Bernays' breakfast revolution, powerful L&D initiatives become movements through strategic influence networks. This transformation turns individual success stories into catalysts for organizational change.

- **Ambassador Impact:** A network of passionate learning ambassadors multiplies L&D's reach through authentic advocacy. These trusted voices help shift learning from a departmental service into a cultural movement.

- **External Recognition:** Industry acknowledgment strengthens internal credibility, converting external validation into organizational influence. This dynamic elevates L&D's strategic position and drives investment in development.

- **Targeted Communication:** Speaking distinct languages—from executive metrics to employee experiences—enhances L&D's visibility and value. This tailored messaging connects learning's impact to each organizational level.

- **Culture of Achievement:** Strategic recognition systems create momentum by celebrating both individual growth and business success. This alignment weaves learning achievements into the fabric of company culture.

9

BRIDGE BUILDER'S HANDBOOK: *CONQUERING OBSTACLES*

"A smooth sea never made a skilled sailor."

—Unknown

THE BRIDGE THAT ALMOST WASN'T

"It can't be done."

That's what experts told chief engineer Joseph Strauss in 1930 when he proposed building a bridge across San Francisco's Golden Gate strait. Engineers cited impossible winds and treacherous currents. City officials pointed to the economic constraints. Critics dismissed it as an expensive vanity project—a waste of resources better spent elsewhere. The consensus was clear: Some barriers aren't meant to be crossed.

Strauss saw something different. Where others saw insurmountable barriers, he recognized opportunities hiding in plain sight. Fierce winds became a catalyst for innovative engineering. Budget constraints sparked creative financing solutions. Public skepticism fueled his determination to prove lasting value.

Strauss and his team didn't allow obstacles to define the project's fate. They refined their designs and approached barriers one by one. Today, millions cross the Golden Gate Bridge without a second thought. Few remember the chorus of impossibilities that nearly prevented its existence. Yet this engineering marvel stands as more than a bridge; it's a monument to the power of human ingenuity, resilience, and reframing barriers as opportunities.

In L&D, we face Golden Gate moments daily. Our barriers aren't made of steel and concrete, but they can feel equally insurmountable. Stakeholder skepticism echoes the voices of critics from 1930. Resource constraints mirror the Great Depression's financial pressures. Resistance to change reflects the same human tendency to doubt what's never been done before.

Yet, like Strauss, we have a choice. We can view these barriers as roadblocks or see them as catalysts for innovation—opportunities to rethink, realign, and reimagine what's possible. This chapter explores eight key barriers to value creation in L&D. More importantly, it shows how each obstacle, approached thoughtfully, can become a practical pathway to building more effective learning programs.

At the center of these challenges lies a critical truth: Just as the Golden Gate Bridge required a clear vision before the first cable could be strung, L&D initiatives demand absolute clarity of purpose. Without this foundation—this unwavering alignment between learning objectives and organizational priorities—even the most ambitious programs risk becoming monuments to missed opportunities rather than catalysts for transformation.

BARRIER 1: LACK OF CLARITY

Learning programs often emerge in organizational silos, divorced from strategic goals and business realities. Success metrics become vague and poorly defined when initiatives lack clear connections to organizational objectives. The impact grows harder to measure, harder to communicate, and ultimately harder to defend. Stakeholders begin viewing L&D as a "nice-to-have" function rather than a critical driver of organizational success.

This misalignment can manifest in multiple ways:

- Programs that don't address the organization's pressing challenges
- Resources diverted to initiatives with limited or unclear value
- Frustration from both L&D teams and business leaders due to unmet expectations

Without alignment, even the most well-designed initiatives risk falling short of their potential.

Why This Happens:

- **Reactive Approach:** Many L&D teams operate in "order-taker" mode, responding to ad hoc requests without understanding the broader business context. This reactive approach limits their ability to design impactful programs.
- **Stakeholder Disconnect:** Business leaders often fail to articulate their needs clearly or tie them to overarching strategic objectives, leaving L&D teams guessing about priorities.
- **Pressure to Deliver Quickly:** Tight timelines and competing demands can lead L&D teams to skip the crucial alignment phase, prioritizing speed over strategic fit.

These issues create a cycle of misalignment where L&D struggles to demonstrate its value, further perpetuating its marginalization within the organization.

Solutions:

Overcoming this barrier requires a proactive and strategic approach to ensure L&D initiatives are purposefully aligned with organizational goals. Here's how:

1. **Build Strategic Partnerships:** Establish regular dialogue with business leaders to understand their challenges, priorities, and vision for success. Create a shared understanding of how L&D can drive business outcomes through targeted learning initiatives.

   - **Actionable Tip:** Schedule quarterly strategic alignment sessions with key stakeholders using the Value Creation Compass to map learning initiatives to business priorities.

2. **Create Clear Success Metrics:** Develop comprehensive measurement frameworks that link learning outcomes to business results. Focus on metrics that matter to stakeholders and demonstrate tangible impact.

   - **Actionable Tip:** Build a measurement dashboard that tracks both leading indicators (participation, satisfaction) and lagging indicators (behavior change, business impact) for each major initiative.

3. **Implement Strategic Governance:** Establish a clear process for evaluating and prioritizing learning initiatives based on strategic alignment and potential business impact.

   - **Actionable Tip:** Create a simple decision matrix that scores potential initiatives on strategic alignment, resource requirements, and expected impact.

Illustrative Example in Action:

A global technology company was facing a leadership crisis. Their $2 million leadership development program was underperforming: Participation was low, and business leaders dismissed it as a distraction from "real work." Recognizing the need for a new approach, the L&D team paused the program and spent a month interviewing executives about their most pressing challenges.

These conversations uncovered a critical issue: 40 percent of senior leaders were approaching retirement, but only 15 percent of key roles had clear successors. Armed with this insight, the team redesigned the program with succession planning at its core. They developed focused learning paths aligned with essential leadership capabilities, implemented mentoring partnerships, and introduced metrics like succession readiness scores to track progress.

Within eighteen months, the program achieved transformative results: successor readiness increased to 85 percent, participant engagement rose from 23 percent to 92 percent, and successors were identified and developed for twenty-eight key positions. What had once been dismissed as a costly distraction became a cornerstone of business continuity, ensuring the organization's leadership pipeline was ready for the future.

BARRIER 2: STAKEHOLDER INDIFFERENCE

Even exceptional learning programs can wither on the vine without stakeholder support. When business leaders view L&D as optional rather than essential, the impact cascades through the organization. Budgets evaporate. Teams deprioritize participation. Momentum stalls. The most thoughtfully designed initiatives collect dust while pressing business challenges go unaddressed. Like a bridge without a proper foundation, programs without stakeholder support inevitably collapse under their weight, leaving behind a legacy of missed opportunities and eroded credibility.

Why This Happens:

1. **Unclear Role of L&D:** Stakeholders often don't see how L&D contributes to achieving business goals. Misalignment with organizational priorities can make programs seem irrelevant or tangential.

2. **Communication Gaps:** L&D teams frequently fail to communicate in the language of leadership—business outcomes, ROI, and measurable results. This disconnect can foster misunderstandings about the purpose and potential of L&D initiatives.

3. **Erosion of Trust:** Past initiatives that didn't deliver visible results—or a lack of transparency about outcomes—can make stakeholders wary of investing time or resources in L&D efforts.

Solutions:

1. **Create Stakeholder Ownership:** Transform stakeholders from observers into architects of learning initiatives. Involve them in program design, success metrics, and ongoing governance to create shared accountability for outcomes.

   - **Actionable Tip:** Establish a learning advisory board with key stakeholders that meets quarterly to review the program's impact and shape future initiatives.

2. **Translate Learning into Business Impact:** Master the language of business value. Move beyond learning metrics to demonstrate clear connections between L&D initiatives and business priorities.

   - **Actionable Tip:** Create one-page program briefs showing direct links between learning objectives and business KPIs, with projected ROI calculations.

3. **Build an Evidence-Based Partnership:** Develop a systematic approach to collecting, analyzing, and sharing program impact data with stakeholders.

   - **Actionable Tip:** Implement monthly stakeholder dashboards combining leading indicators (participation, satisfaction) with lagging indicators (behavior change, business results).

Illustrative Example in Action:

Consider a global manufacturing company with a $5 million leadership development program teetering on the edge of budget cuts after years of waning executive support. Enter a newly appointed L&D director who decided to take a bold, collaborative approach. Instead of defending the existing program, she invited skeptical executives to join the redesign process.

Through a series of focused working sessions, these once-critical stakeholders uncovered key capability gaps that were costing the company $12 million annually in project delays and talent attrition. With this insight, the program was entirely refocused to address these gaps. The same executives who had doubted the program became its strongest advocates, teaching sessions, mentoring participants, and championing its success.

Within a year, the impact was undeniable: Project delays decreased, talent retention improved by 25 percent, and executives began competing to have their teams participate. The program's budget increased, and what had once been viewed as a liability transformed into a powerful competitive advantage—all because stakeholders shifted from critics to co-owners of the program.

STAKEHOLDERS   L + D

WITHOUT CLEAR BUSINESS IMPACT

WITH CLEAR BUSINESS IMPACT

BARRIER 3: THE RESOURCE TRAP

The pattern is painfully familiar: Tight budgets. Stretched schedules. Limited headcount. When organizations view L&D as a cost center rather than a value creator, they trap themselves in a cycle of under-investment. Teams resort to quick fixes rather than transformative solutions. Programs get stripped to their essentials. Quality suffers. Impact diminishes, and the resulting disappointment only reinforces the perception that L&D isn't worth the investment.

Why This Happens:

1. **Perception of L&D as a Cost Center:** Leadership may view learning initiatives as expenses rather than strategic investments, deprioritizing L&D when budgets tighten.

2. **Competing Priorities:** Employees who are already managing demanding workloads may view training as an additional burden rather than an opportunity, leading to lower participation rates.

3. **Inefficient Delivery Methods:** Reliance on outdated or labor-intensive approaches can drain resources without scaling effectively, making L&D efforts seem inefficient or unsustainable.

Solutions:

1. **Prove Value *Before* Seeking Resources:** Build a compelling business case using pilot programs and quick wins. Demonstrate how targeted investments in learning directly impact business metrics that matter to decision-makers.

   - **Actionable Tip:** Create a "value scorecard" tracking program costs against measurable business outcomes like reduced errors, improved sales, or faster onboarding.

2. **Design for Scale from the Start:** Architect learning solutions that can grow without proportional cost increases. Focus on

approaches that maximize impact while minimizing resource drain.

- **Actionable Tip:** Develop a "scale-ready checklist" assessing each initiative's potential for efficient growth across automation, content reuse, and peer-to-peer learning.

3. **Transform Constraints into Catalysts:** Use resource limitations to drive innovation in program design and delivery. Challenge traditional assumptions about what effective learning requires.

- **Actionable Tip:** Hold monthly "innovation sprints" where teams redesign existing programs to deliver the same or better outcomes with fewer resources.

Illustrative Example in Action:

A mid-sized non-profit healthcare organization faced a daunting challenge: training three thousand staff members on updated patient safety protocols with no additional budget and minimal disruption to the critical care they provide. Traditional classroom training was estimated to cost $1.2 million and require twelve thousand hours of staff time—time they couldn't afford to take away from serving patients in need.

The L&D team embraced the challenge with creativity and innovation. They developed micro-learning videos filmed during actual care scenarios, created a peer mentor network made up of experienced team leaders, and incorporated quick learning checkpoints into regular team meetings. The outcomes were remarkable: Training costs dropped by 63 percent, and staff completed the program seamlessly during natural breaks in their workflow. Most importantly, patient safety incidents decreased by 45 percent within three months.

By transforming budget constraints into opportunities for innovation, the organization improved safety and efficiency and set a precedent for future training initiatives that align with their mission and resource realities.

BARRIER 4: THE HUMAN FACTOR

Change feels like a threat before it becomes an opportunity. Employees and managers often retreat to the familiar when faced with new learning initiatives, viewing innovation as disruption and learning as risk. This instinctive resistance creates a paradox: The people who benefit most from learning become its biggest barriers. The cost isn't just in failed programs; it's in lost potential, stagnant capabilities, and diminishing organizational resilience.

Why This Happens:

1. **Clinging to the Status Quo:** Many employees and managers fear new methods might disrupt established workflows or lead to mistakes, especially if the perceived risks outweigh the benefits.

2. **Lack of Psychological Safety:** Without an environment that encourages open dialogue and supports experimentation, employees are less likely to engage with new initiatives or feel safe to speak up.

3. **Past Failures Breed Skepticism:** A history of poorly implemented or ineffective programs can erode trust in L&D, making future initiatives harder to adopt.

Solutions:

1. **Create Psychological Safety:** Address resistance by building an environment where experimentation is encouraged, and mistakes are viewed as learning opportunities. Make it safe to try new approaches and speak up without fear of repercussion.

   • **Actionable Tip:** Implement monthly "learning from failure" sessions where teams share setbacks and lessons learned, focusing on how these insights led to meaningful improvements.

2. **Break the Status Quo Mindset:** Help employees see beyond established patterns by demonstrating the concrete benefits of new approaches while acknowledging and addressing their legitimate concerns.

   • **Actionable Tip:** Create pilot programs where teams can experiment with new methods in a low-risk environment, with clear checkpoints to measure and showcase improvements.

3. **Rebuild Trust Through Early Wins:** Overcome skepticism from past failures by designing highly focused initiatives with clear, achievable outcomes that demonstrate immediate value.

   • **Actionable Tip:** Launch targeted micro-initiatives to solve specific pain points identified by skeptical teams and track success metrics they help define.

Illustrative Example in Action:

Picture a manufacturing plant struggling with a deteriorating safety record. Despite repeated training attempts, compliance was low, injuries were rising, and workers dismissed new safety protocols as "corporate interference." The breakthrough came when the L&D team took an unconventional approach: They invited the most vocal critics—seasoned floor workers—to co-create a new safety program.

These skeptics became the program's driving force. They designed peer-led safety workshops, developed training based on real-world scenarios, and launched a safety innovation council. Within eight months, safety compliance soared from 65 percent to 98 percent; workplace injuries dropped by 70 percent, and retention improved as workers cited the program as a reason to stay, even when competitors tried to recruit them.

The program's impact extended beyond safer operations; it demonstrated the power of turning resistance into ownership. By empowering employees to lead change, the organization improved outcomes and fostered a culture of collaboration and accountability.

BARRIER 5: THE DIGITAL DIVIDE

In today's digital workplace, learning technology can amplify or inhibit success. Outdated systems create friction. Poor integration fragments the learning experience. Limited access widens skill gaps. When organizations treat learning technology as an afterthought rather than a strategic enabler, they don't just frustrate learners; they create a digital divide that threatens engagement and equity.

Why This Happens:

1. **Underinvestment in Technology:** Organizations often hesitate to allocate budgets for updating learning management systems (LMS) or adopting advanced tools, viewing them as non-essential expenses rather than strategic enablers.

2. **Poor Integration:** Even when technology is available, systems may not integrate seamlessly, leading to inefficiencies and frustration for learners and administrators.

3. **Skill Gaps in Technology Use:** Employees and managers may lack the training to effectively use available tools, further diminishing their utility.

Solutions:

1. **Build a Learning Tech Ecosystem:** Move beyond single-point solutions to create an integrated learning environment that supports diverse learning needs and workflows.

   • **Actionable Tip:** Create a learning technology roadmap that prioritizes integration, accessibility, and scalability, with clear milestones for implementation.

2. **Democratize Access:** Ensure learning technology reaches every corner of your organization, regardless of role, location, or technical proficiency.

- **Actionable Tip:** Implement a "tech equity audit" to identify and address access gaps, particularly for frontline, remote, or deskless workers.

3. **Focus on User Experience:** Make learning technology intuitive and engaging, reducing friction and increasing voluntary adoption.

   - **Actionable Tip:** Create a "learning tech council" with representatives from different user groups to provide ongoing feedback and guide improvements.

Illustrative Example in Action:

Imagine a regional food and beverage company grappling with the challenges of modernizing its operations. While office staff leveraged advanced systems for inventory management and quality assurance, production workers relied on outdated paper manuals and sporadic training sessions. The result was a growing skills gap of 35 percent between production teams and corporate employees, leading to increased quality control issues and inefficiencies on the production line.

The L&D team proposed a transformative solution: implement mobile-first learning to empower production workers. They equipped four thousand team members with rugged tablets loaded with an offline-capable learning platform. The app gamified topics like food safety protocols, machine maintenance, and quality assurance standards. Shift supervisors were given tools to record and share best practices directly from the production floor, creating a more immediate and relatable learning experience.

Within six months, the skill gap narrowed to 12 percent. Quality issues dropped by 38 percent, and production workers created over five hundred peer-to-peer training videos, sharing innovative tips and solutions. What started as a digital transformation effort became a movement of grassroots learning and collaboration, transforming the workplace culture and setting the company apart in a competitive industry.

BARRIER 6: MEASUREMENT MIRAGE

The value of learning is real, but it often feels just out of reach—like chasing a mirage. Traditional metrics miss the mark. Satisfaction scores and completion rates tell an incomplete story. ROI calculations oversimplify complex transformations. Without the ability to capture and communicate true impact, L&D teams find themselves in a frustrating paradox: Their most meaningful work often appears the least valuable on paper.

Why This Happens:

1. **Lack of Clear Metrics:** Many organizations fail to define program success criteria, leaving impact evaluation vague or inconsistent.

2. **Data Collection Challenges:** Gathering reliable, relevant data across diverse teams and geographies can be time-consuming and logistically complex.

3. **Overemphasis on ROI:** Traditional return-on-investment (ROI) models often fail to capture learning programs' nuanced, long-term benefits.

Solutions:

1. **Master the Value Creation Compass:** Move beyond traditional metrics to capture the full spectrum of learning impact, from individual growth to organizational transformation.

   - **Actionable Tip:** Build a multi-layer measurement framework that tracks immediate learning outcomes, behavior change, business impact, and long-term organizational capabilities.

2. **Make Impact Visible:** Transform data into compelling narratives that resonate with stakeholders and illuminate the connection between learning and business success.

264

- **Actionable Tip:** Create an "impact visualization library" combining quantitative metrics, qualitative stories, and visual data representations for each major initiative.

3. **Measure What Matters:** Focus on metrics directly connected to business priorities and stakeholder concerns rather than traditional learning measures.

- **Actionable Tip:** Develop a "strategic impact dashboard" that aligns learning metrics with key business KPIs and updates automatically.

Illustrative Example in Action:

Imagine a mid-sized nonprofit organization focused on housing assistance programs struggling to justify its $2 million annual investment in volunteer training. Traditional metrics—satisfaction surveys and participation rates—failed to convince stakeholders of the program's value. The connection between training initiatives and tangible community impact seemed unclear. Leadership began considering a drastic budget reduction.

The training team decided to rethink their approach to measurement. Instead of focusing solely on participation metrics, they tracked how specific training initiatives influenced key outcomes: successful housing placements, client satisfaction, and volunteer retention. They gathered testimonials from volunteers who navigated complex cases thanks to their training and mapped correlations between training engagement and program success rates.

The results told a powerful story: Trained volunteers achieved 45 percent faster placement rates for clients, increased housing retention by 32 percent, and improved client satisfaction scores by 38 percent. Volunteer turnover dropped by 25 percent, saving the organization $400,000 annually in recruitment and onboarding costs. Armed with this evidence, leadership reversed their budget-cutting plans and doubled their investment in training programs.

The takeaway? Often, the value of learning isn't missing; it's hidden in places we haven't measured yet.

BARRIER 7: THE INERTIA EFFECT

Newton's first law of motion haunts L&D: Programs at rest tend to stay at rest. The decay is inevitable when organizations treat learning as a fixed asset rather than a dynamic force. Content ossifies. Methods stagnate. Engagement withers. What began as a cutting-edge initiative gradually calcifies into organizational dead weight, consuming resources while delivering diminishing returns. Like a wheel that's stopped spinning, the energy required to restart motion grows with each passing day of stillness.

Why This Happens:

1. **Ignored Feedback Loops:** Many organizations collect feedback from learners but fail to act on it, allowing programs to stagnate.

2. **Lack of a Structured Review Process:** Without clear accountability for program evaluation, content and delivery methods often fall behind best practices.

3. **Resource Allocation Challenges:** Limited time and budget are often funneled into developing new programs rather than improving existing ones.

Solutions:

1. **Generate Perpetual Motion:** Design learning initiatives that create momentum through built-in feedback loops and continuous adaptation cycles.

   - **Actionable Tip:** Implement a "motion metrics" dashboard-tracking program for vitality indicators, such as content updates, participant engagement, and real-world application rates.

2. **Build Momentum Through Small Wins:** Create a system of incremental improvements that compound over time, making evolution feel natural rather than forced.

- **Actionable Tip:** Establish monthly "momentum meetings" where teams identify and implement one small but meaningful program enhancement.

3. **Convert Friction into Force:** Transform resistance points into energy sources for positive change, using challenges as catalysts for innovation.

   - **Actionable Tip:** Create a "friction log" where participants document pain points, then convert top issues into improvement opportunities during quarterly sprints.

Illustrative Example in Action:

Imagine a global technology firm facing a leadership development dilemma. Their flagship program, once celebrated for its impact, had stalled. Participation dropped 30 percent over two years, and frustrated business units started creating competing initiatives. The program that had once fueled leadership growth was now falling behind as the business raced ahead.

Instead of scrapping the program, the L&D team took an innovative approach, embracing the concept of continuous motion. They established a "leadership lab" where program graduates became co-creators, prototyping new modules and testing fresh approaches based on real-world leadership challenges. This shifted the program from a static curriculum to a dynamic ecosystem that evolved monthly to address emerging needs.

The results were transformative. Participation rebounded, surging 45 percent, and business units dismantled their alternative programs to rejoin the main initiative. Beyond engagement, the program began identifying and addressing leadership challenges before they impacted the broader organization—anticipating issues months in advance. The program didn't just regain momentum; it became a proactive driver of leadership excellence.

In learning, as in physics, overcoming inertia isn't about applying brute force; it's about creating systems that sustain motion and momentum over time.

BARRIER 8: THE MIRROR

After examining these seven barriers, we arrive at a profound revelation: The most formidable obstacle in L&D isn't found in organizational charts or budget sheets; it's reflected in our own mirror. While external barriers demand strategic solutions, the key to unlocking L&D's hidden value lies within ourselves. The final barrier isn't about resources, technology, or stakeholder buy-in but about our courage to reimagine what's possible.

The Familiar Path

Every year, thousands of hikers flock to Mount Monadnock in New Hampshire. Its well-worn trails, marked by years of footsteps, offer familiarity and ease. Yet those who venture off these paths discover something extraordinary: quieter trails, hidden overlooks, and untouched natural beauty. The less-traveled routes may be harder, but they reveal treasures the main trails never could.

For L&D, the well-worn paths of our industry are equally familiar. We rely on attendance sheets, satisfaction surveys, and basic ROI calculations—not because they tell the whole story but because they're comfortable. These metrics, rooted in tradition, feel safe. They are recognizable, quick to produce, and easy to explain. The comfortable path beckons:

- Measuring completion rates instead of business impact
- Designing programs around content rather than outcomes
- Accepting our role as order-takers rather than strategic partners
- Staying silent when we should be challenging assumptions
- Copying best practices instead of creating next practices

These familiar trails feel safe, but they lead to predictable destinations. True transformation requires venturing into uncharted territory.

The Price of Comfort

The cost of comfort isn't just measured in missed opportunities. It's calculated in:

- Innovations never attempted
- Solutions never discovered
- Value never created
- Transformations never realized
- Potential never reached

Every time we choose the familiar over the possible, we fortify our barriers—building walls that are more restrictive than any budget constraint, more limiting than any stakeholder skepticism, and more damaging than any resource shortage. Staying on these well-trodden trails, we risk missing the deeper insights that demonstrate the transformative power of learning.

Breaking away from the familiar requires curiosity, courage, and a willingness to embrace discomfort. It challenges us to rethink not just how we measure value but why we measure at all. Though this shift can be unsettling, the rewards—greater credibility, alignment with strategic goals, and amplified impact—are undeniable.

The allure of the familiar lies in its simplicity and acceptance. Satisfaction surveys and completion rates may not resonate deeply with stakeholders, but they provide a sense of accomplishment. They are easy to present, require little explanation, and offer a veneer of success.

However, comfort can be a trap. The metrics we've relied on for so long may no longer meet the needs of today's organizations. In a world demanding more sophisticated evidence of value, clinging to outdated methods limits our ability to prove L&D's strategic relevance.

Breaking the Mold

Overcoming this final barrier demands more than strategy; it requires courage. Here's how to begin:

1. **Embrace the Unknown:** Start each initiative by asking not "What have others done?" but "What could be possible?" Challenge yourself to propose solutions that make you slightly uncomfortable; they often have the greatest potential.

2. **Redefine Your Role:** Stop seeing yourself as a program designer and think like a value architect. Your canvas isn't limited to learning experiences; it extends to business transformation.

3. **Choose Courage Over Comfort:** When faced with a choice between the familiar and the transformative, pause. Ask yourself: "Am I choosing this path because it's right or because it's comfortable?"

4. **Lead from Any Level:** You don't need a title to lead transformation. Team members can challenge assumptions, propose bold solutions, and champion new approaches.

THE BRIDGE BUILDER'S CHOICE

We all face a choice like Joseph Strauss at the Golden Gate. We can accept the barriers before us as immutable facts or see them as opportunities waiting to be transformed. The difference lies not in our resources or authority but in our courage to envision and pursue something greater.

As you close this chapter, ask yourself:

- What bridges am I not building because they seem too difficult?
- Where am I accepting barriers that could be transformed into opportunities?
- What could be possible if I approached my work with the audacity of a bridge builder?

The final barrier isn't external; it's the boundary between who we are and who we could become. Like the Golden Gate Bridge, our greatest achievements often lie on the other side of our comfort zone, waiting to be built one courageous decision at a time.

📌 **Remember:** Every transformative bridge in history was once considered impossible—until someone had the courage to build it.

Today's L&D landscape is your Golden Gate strait. Your next initiative could be that bridge that others say can't be built. Will you be the one who proves them wrong?

🔑 KEY LEARNINGS

- **Breaking the Mirror Barrier:** The most critical obstacle in L&D isn't external; it's our tendency to choose familiar, comfortable approaches over transformative ones. When we move beyond traditional metrics and conventional programs, we discover opportunities for impact that our comfort zone kept hidden.

- **Conquering Stakeholder Indifference:** Successful L&D teams transform skeptical stakeholders into program champions by involving them in design, showing clear business impact, and speaking their language. True stakeholder engagement comes from shifting them from observers to architects of learning initiatives.

- **Bridging the Digital Divide:** Technology gaps don't just frustrate learners; they create inequity in skill development. By democratizing access through mobile solutions, offline capabilities, and user-centered design, L&D can transform technology from a barrier to an accelerator of organizational learning.

- **Moving Beyond the Measurement Mirage:** Effective measurement isn't about satisfaction scores or completion rates; it's about capturing real business impact. When L&D teams focus on metrics that matter to stakeholders and directly connect to business priorities, they transform learning from cost center to strategic asset.

- **Defeating the Inertia Effect:** Static programs decay over time, but building continuous feedback loops and improvement cycles creates self-sustaining momentum. Programs stay relevant and impactful by designing learning initiatives that generate momentum through built-in adaptation cycles.

CONCLUSION
THE WATER BEARER'S JOURNEY: *MAKING HIDDEN VALUE VISIBLE*

"Do not follow where the path may lead.
Go instead where there is no path and leave a trail."

—*Muriel Strode*

In a quiet, sun-drenched village in India, a water bearer begins his daily journey. Each morning, he hoists a wooden yoke across his shoulders, its two clay pots gently swaying as he makes his way to the stream. One pot is perfect, delivering water without a drop lost. The other pot has a hairline crack running down its side. With each homeward journey, the cracked pot watches helplessly as half its water seeps away.

One morning, consumed with shame, the cracked pot breaks its silence. "I am broken, flawed," it whispers. "Every day, I fail you. Why keep a pot that can't fulfill its purpose?"

The water bearer's eyes soften, and a gentle smile playing on his lips holds a secret. "Tomorrow," he says, "pay attention to the path as we walk to the stream."

The next morning, they begin their familiar journey as the sun rises. However, this time, the cracked pot sees something it has never seen before: a ribbon of color threading along their path. Marigolds dance in golden clusters, while violets paint the earth in brilliant hues—all blooming precisely where its daily drips had fallen.

"Do you see those flowers?" the water bearer asks, reading the pot's wonder. "I planted seeds along this path, knowing your unique gift would nurture them. Your 'flaw' transformed this dusty path into a garden of joy. You weren't failing; you were creating beauty in ways the perfect pot never could. You simply weren't seeing it."

This story strikes at the heart of our work. Like the cracked pot, we focus on our perceived shortcomings: the engagement scores that don't tell the whole story, the ROI that defies neat measurement, and the countless moments of transformation that slip between the cracks of our dashboards. However, here's what we often miss: While we're busy measuring the water in our pot, we're cultivating entire ecosystems of growth. Every conversation sparks a chain reaction of insight. Every workshop plants seeds of possibility. Every learning moment—even the ones that feel incomplete or imperfect—waters the soil of future breakthroughs.

Think about it: That leadership workshop you ran last month? It might have triggered a conversation that inspired a manager to completely reimagine their team's culture. The digital skills training that felt too basic? It could be the very foundation that enables someone to pioneer innovation in your organization years from now. Our impact isn't just hidden; it's exponential, rippling outward in ways we may never fully grasp but that fundamentally reshape the landscape of possibility for individuals, teams, and entire organizations.

A CHAPTER-BY-CHAPTER REFLECTION

CHAPTER 1: THE HIDDEN NETWORK – *HOW LEARNING POWERS EVERYTHING*

Like the invisible mycelium network that nourishes an entire forest, learning forms the foundation of organizational vitality. This chapter reveals how L&D operates as an essential but often unseen force, connecting and strengthening every aspect of organizational life. Through personal stories and compelling examples, we discover that while the immediate results of learning initiatives might not always be visible, their impact ripples through the organization in profound ways: fostering resilience, enabling collaboration, and catalyzing innovation. Just as a forest's health depends on its underground network, organizational success relies on the learning infrastructure we build and nurture.

⚡ *Ask Yourself:* Where do I see the "mycelium network" of learning quietly at work in my organization? What connections am I not yet nurturing? When was the last time I helped someone unlock their potential? What did I see in them that others missed?

CHAPTER 2: THE DIAMOND'S BRILLIANCE – *THE ART OF VALUE*

Like a perfectly cut diamond, value reveals different facets of brilliance depending on who's looking at it and how they're looking at it. This chapter unveils that value, like a gem, is fundamentally multifaceted and shaped by the perspectives and priorities of those evaluating it. Through research with CFOs and real-world examples, we discover how L&D's impact manifests across three crucial dimensions: economic value (measurable business outcomes), personal value (individual transformation), and societal value (broader community impact). While traditional ROI metrics matter, they only capture one facet of learning's true worth—just as viewing a diamond from only one angle misses much of its beauty. By understanding and articulating value in all its dimensions and considering the unique perspectives of our stakeholders, we can create compelling cases for learning investments and drive more meaningful organizational change.

⚡ *Ask Yourself:* What business metrics matter to my CFO that I haven't yet connected to learning? Which dimensions of value might I be overlooking? Where in my organization is transformation happening that I haven't yet connected back to learning?

CHAPTER 3: THE TREASURE HUNTER'S GUIDE – *SEEKING VALUE*

The most legendary treasure hunters don't wait for X to mark the spot; they read the terrain others overlook, finding gold where others see only sand. This chapter ignites us to adopt this same proactive mindset, embedding value-seeking as the critical foundation for all impact. The Four Cs framework—curiosity, connection, context, and courage—becomes our compass, transforming us from reactive problem-solvers into strategic opportunity seekers. Like skilled treasure hunters who spot diamonds in rough stone, we master the art of systematically uncovering untapped potential and weaving it into organizational needs. Most importantly, the chapter equips us with practical tools to transform from order-takers into proactive seekers of impact.

⚡ *Ask Yourself*: Which of the Four Cs (curiosity, connection, context, courage) is my team's strongest asset? What opportunities am I missing because of an underdeveloped C?

CHAPTER 4: THE VALUE ARCHITECT – *CREATING WHAT MATTERS*

Like a compass guiding explorers through uncharted territory, this chapter introduces the Value Creation Compass—a strategic framework that fundamentally transforms how we create and demonstrate organizational impact. The Compass empowers us to create value across four critical dimensions: empowering people, building organizational resilience, driving business growth, and delivering exceptional customer value. Each direction provides a unique lens through which we can uncover hidden potential, ensure alignment with organizational priorities, and measure impact in tangible ways. Through Alan Gray's transformation of the Darien Library, we witness how this strategic approach can revolutionize programs and entire organizations. By integrating the Compass into our planning and execution, we elevate L&D from a support function to a strategic driver of organizational success, capable of both meeting immediate learning needs and creating lasting competitive advantage.

⚡*Ask Yourself*: What would I do differently tomorrow if I were to completely reimagine my role as a value creator? Which compass direction is the most underdeveloped in my practice?

CHAPTER 5: HIDDEN TRACKS – *MEASURING WHAT MATTERS*

Like those paleontologists who uncovered ancient footprints in Wyoming, this chapter reveals the art and science of measuring learning's true impact. Through exploring foundational frameworks, we discover that effective measurement requires precision and perspective. The chapter challenges us to move beyond simple metrics to capture the full spectrum of learning's value across the four Value

Creation Compass dimensions. We learn to measure immediate outcomes and deeper transformations through practical frameworks and real-world examples, from individual skill development to organizational capability building. Measuring impact reveals the ways learning reshapes individual potential and organizational success. Combining quantitative metrics with qualitative insights creates a more complete picture of learning's strategic value.

⚡ *Ask Yourself:* What's the most powerful impact of my work that I have not been able to measure? What metrics do I track out of habit rather than value? How could aligning my measurement approach with the Value Creation Compass help tell a more complete story of your impact?

CHAPTER 6: STORYTELLING – *COMMUNICATING THE TRUE IMPACT*

Numbers alone rarely inspire action; the stories we tell transform data into meaning and metrics into motivation. This chapter illuminates how narrative transforms measurement into understanding, making learning's impact visible and unforgettable. Through frameworks like the three-part story structure and audience-specific storytelling techniques, we discover how to craft narratives that resonate with different stakeholders while maintaining authenticity and organizational alignment. The chapter reveals that the most powerful L&D stories combine robust data with compelling human experiences, creating evidence-based narratives that drive both emotional connection and meaningful outcomes.

⚡ *Ask Yourself:* What learner transformation stories would surprise my CEO? How could sharing these narratives change perceptions of L&D's value? How can I incorporate storytelling into my L&D strategy?

CHAPTER 7: THE PURPLE COW EFFECT –
BE UNFORGETTABLE

Your brand isn't just your logo or tagline; it's the story people tell about you when you're not in the room. This chapter demonstrates how those stories take shape through every touchpoint, conversation, and experience we create. Through examples like BDO's mountain metaphor and GM's Innovation Garage, we discover how intentional brand building shapes these narratives—from visual identity to program architecture to stakeholder experiences. Remarkable L&D brands aren't built by accident; they're crafted through deliberate choices about how we show up, the promises we make, and the impact we deliver. In a field of ordinary, be the Purple Cow—not by being different but by being transformative in ways that make others stop, take notice, and spread your story.

⚡ *Ask Yourself:* What story is my organization telling about L&D when I'm not in the room? What's the one word I wish people used to describe the learning team? How could thoughtful brand building help close that gap?

CHAPTER 8: THE RIPPLE MAKERS –
AMPLIFYING IMPACT

Like Edward Bernays transforming American breakfast habits, this chapter shows how great ideas need strategic amplification to create lasting change. Through four key strategies—cultivating learning ambassadors, building recognition systems, establishing external credibility, and communicating success internally—we discover how to create sustainable momentum for learning initiatives. However, the chapter's deeper insight reveals that amplification isn't about making noise; it's about orchestrating the conditions where small victories cascade into organizational transformation. Creating lasting impact isn't about having the loudest voice but about empowering others to become our advocates.

⚡ *Ask Yourself:* Who are the natural amplifiers in my organization whose voices could elevate my impact? Which skeptic's endorsement would most transform my team's credibility? What recent success, if widely known, would change how stakeholders perceive my team?

CHAPTER 9: BRIDGE BUILDER'S HANDBOOK – *CONQUERING OBSTACLES*

Barriers to value creation are often seen as immovable obstacles, but this chapter reframes them as launchpads for innovation and transformation. Drawing inspiration from the construction of the Golden Gate Bridge, the narrative emphasizes that overcoming challenges requires creativity, persistence, and strategic alignment. Through examining eight core challenges—from stakeholder skepticism to resource constraints—we discover that every barrier presents a chance to demonstrate L&D's strategic value. The chapter's power lay not just in its solutions but in its fundamental message: The greatest bridges in history were all once considered impossible until someone had the courage to build them. The most powerful lesson is that our biggest obstacle isn't external; it's our tendency to choose comfortable, familiar approaches instead of pursuing bold new possibilities.

⚡ *Ask Yourself:* What "impossible" learning challenge would transform my organization if solved? Which barrier have I accepted as permanent that might be my biggest opportunity? What's stopping me from taking the first step toward that solution today?

THE WATER BEARER'S LESSON

Like the water bearer who saw beyond a crack to recognize the beauty created, your impact often manifests unexpectedly. You might track metrics and monitor dashboards, but your true value blooms in the confidence of a newly promoted leader, the innovation of a cross-functional team, or the resilience of an organization navigating change.

Each morning brings a choice: Will you simply carry water or cultivate gardens along your path? Will you design another program or architect transformation? Will you measure what's convenient or reveal what truly matters?

⚡ YOUR TURN: MAKE THE HIDDEN VISIBLE

As you close this book, I invite you to reimagine your role—not just as a water bearer of learning but as an architect of transformation who helps others see the extraordinary in the everyday.

1. **Plant Your Seeds:** What initiatives could you start today that might bloom into something beautiful tomorrow? Maybe it's a peer learning program that could grow into a culture of continuous development or a mentorship network where employees teach their specialized expertise to colleagues.

2. **Notice Your Flowers:** Look for the unexpected impact of your work. That new hire who's thriving because of your onboarding redesign—that's your flower. The team that navigated change successfully because of your resilience workshop—that's your garden growing.

3. **Share Your Path:** Don't keep your garden hidden. Use the tools and frameworks we've explored to help others see the beauty you're creating. Document the growth, tell the stories, and invite stakeholders to celebrate the successes and organizational impact.

The Bridge to Tomorrow

When Joseph Strauss first gazed across the Golden Gate strait, others saw insurmountable challenges—treacherous currents, unforgiving winds, impossible distances. However, where they saw barriers, he saw possibility. Where they saw risk, he saw transformation waiting to unfold.

This book's tools, frameworks, and strategies aren't just about making your value visible; they're your blueprint for building bridges between potential and achievement, between the present and future, and between the ordinary and the extraordinary.

Value exists in every corner of your organization. Your role is to reveal it. Like the water bearer who helped the cracked pot see its worth, you now have the tools to illuminate the impact others might miss—to make the threads that connect learning to innovation, growth, and possibility visible.

The true value of L&D isn't hidden anymore; it's written in the stories of transformation you create every day—just waiting for you to look down on your path.

Now, take these tools and reveal your value so others can't help but see.

REFERENCES

INTRODUCTION CHAPTER

1. Attributed to Buddha. (n.d.). *What we think, we become. What we feel, we attract. What we imagine, we create.* (Original source unknown).

2. Author(s) unknown. (n.d.). *What JFK learned about leadership from a NASA janitor.* Big Think. Retrieved January 26, 2025, from https://bigthink.com/business/what-jfk-learned-about-leadership-from-a-nasa-janitor

3. EarthDay.org. (n.d.). *Fact sheet: Bees.* Retrieved November 27, 2024, from https://www.earthday.org/fact-sheet-bees/

4. The White House. (2014, June 20). *Fact sheet: The economic challenge posed by declining pollinator populations.* Obama White House Archives. Retrieved December 26, 2024, from https://obamawhitehouse.archives.gov/the-press-office/2014/06/20/fact-sheet-economic-challenge-posed-declining-pollinator-populations

5. Vuori, T., & Huy, Q. (2016). Distributed Attention and Shared Emotions in the Innovation Process: How Nokia Lost the Smartphone Battle. *Administrative Science Quarterly*, 61(1), 9–51. https://doi.org/10.1177/0001839215606951

6. Wahba, P. (2017, October 23). How Sears Went from Gilded-Age Boom to Modern-Day Bust. *Fortune.* Retrieved from https://fortune.com/2017/10/23/sears-roebuck-history-decline/

7. Thomas, L., & Hirsch, L. (2017, September 19). Toys R Us files for bankruptcy as Amazon exerts influence. *CNBC*. Retrieved from https://www.cnbc.com/2017/09/18/toys-r-us-files-for-bankruptcy.html

8. McCracken, H. (2018, September 26). How Microsoft has transformed its culture. *Fast Company*. Retrieved from https://www.fastcompany.com/90243484/how-microsoft-has-transformed-its-culture

9. Stone, B. (2013). *The Everything Store: Jeff Bezos and the Age of Amazon*. New York, NY: Little, Brown and Company.

10. Seetharaman, D., & Cutter, C. (2020, April 10). How the Coronavirus Is Ushering in a New Era of Telemedicine. *The Wall Street Journal*. Retrieved from https://www.wsj.com/articles/how-the-coronavirus-is-ushering-in-a-new-era-of-telemedicine-11586530001

CHAPTER 1

1. Seuss, D. (1978). *I can read with my eyes shut!* New York, NY: Random House.

2. Bandura, A. (1997). *Self-efficacy: The exercise of control*. New York, NY: W.H. Freeman.

3. Brookings Institution. (2016). *Thirteen Economic Facts about Social Mobility and the Role of Education*. Retrieved from https://www.brookings.edu/wp-content/uploads/2016/06/THP_13EconFacts_FINAL.pdf

4. UNESCO. (n.d.). *Her Education, Our Future: Factsheet on Gender Equality in Education*. Retrieved from https://www.unesco.org/sdg4education2030/en/knowledge-hub/hereducationourfuture-factsheet-latest-facts-gender-equality-education

5. Organisation for Economic Co-operation and Development (OECD). (n.d.). *Education: Economic and Social Outcomes*. Retrieved from https://www.oecd.org/en/topics/education-economic-and-social-outcomes.html

6. World Bank. (n.d.). *Education Overview.* Retrieved from https://www.worldbank.org/en/topic/education/overview

7. Nadella, S., & Shaw, G. (2017). *Hit refresh: The quest to rediscover Microsoft's soul and imagine a better future for everyone.* New York, NY: Harper Business.

8. Business Insider. (2024). *Microsoft's valuation surpasses $3 trillion under Nadella.* Retrieved January 26, 2025, from https://www.businessinsider.com/satya-nadella-microsoft-powerhouse-ai-investment-openai-2024-7.

9. Benzinga. (2023). *Steve Ballmer vs. Satya Nadella: Leadership comparison.* Retrieved January 26, 2025, from https://www.benzinga.com/trading-ideas/long-ideas/23/11/35912780.

10. United Nations Development Programme (UNDP). (n.d.). *The Transformative Power of Education in the Fight Against Poverty.* Retrieved from https://www.undp.org/blog/transformative-power-education-fight-against-poverty

11. Khan Academy. (2023). *Khanmigo: AI-powered tutor and teaching assistant.* Retrieved January 26, 2025, from https://khanmigo.ai

CHAPTER 2

1. Buffett, W. (2008). *Letter to Shareholders.* Berkshire Hathaway Inc.

2. Maslow, A. H. (1954). *Motivation and personality.* Harper & Row.

3. Generation. (n.d.). *Digital customer service program.* Generation. Retrieved December 31, 2024, from https://kenya.generation.org/digital-customer-service/

4. Keating, K. F. (2022). Exploring the beliefs about training in organizations: A perspective from chief financial officers [Doctoral dissertation, University of Pennsylvania]. ProQuest Dissertations & Theses Global. https://www.proquest.com/ope

nview/80ddb93d1935a4a0085d89596f80a766/1?cbl=18750&
diss=y&pq-origsite=gscholar

CHAPTER 3

1. Bruckheimer, J. (Producer), & Verbinski, G. (Director).
   (2003). *Pirates of the Caribbean: The Curse of the Black Pearl*
   [Film]. Walt Disney Pictures.

2. Morgan, T. (2018, August 9). *The 'American Pickers' find the
   Aerosmith van that started it all*. HISTORY. https://www.
   history.com/news/american-pickers-aerosmith-van

3. TigerConnect. (n.d.). *Avita Home Health & Hospice*.
   TigerConnect. Retrieved October 26, 2024, from
   https://tigerconnect.com/resources/case-studies/
   case-study-avita-home-health-amp-hospice-lp/

4. Parker, S., & Chandrasekhar, R. (2014). *Intrapreneurship
   at Alcatel-Lucent* (Case No. W14642). Ivey Publishing.
   Retrieved from https://www.hbsp.harvard.edu/product/
   W14642-PDF-ENG

5. MDA Leadership. (n.d.). *Otter Tail Corporation: Building
   a Strong Leadership Pipeline*. Retrieved from https://
   mdaleadership.com/wp-content/uploads/2024/04/MDA_
   Otter-Tail-Case-Study.pdf

6. Six Seconds. (2014, January 14). *Case Study: Emotional
   Intelligence Improves Leadership at FedEx*. Six Seconds. Retrieved
   from https://www.6seconds.org/2014/01/14/case-study-
   emotional-intelligence-people-first-leadership-fedex-express/

CHAPTER 4

1. Einstein quote - Miller, W. (1955, May 2). Death of a genius: His
   fourth dimension, time, overtakes Einstein. *LIFE*, 38(18), 64

2. Darien Library. (n.d.). *About the library*. Darien Library.
   Retrieved December 31, 2024, from https://www.
   darienlibrary.org/about

3. Hepworth, M., & Lainson, P. (2015). Collaborative, creative, participative: The changing role of public libraries in the 21st century. *Public Library Quarterly*, 34(3), 210-225. https://doi.org/10.1080/01616846.2015.1062676

4. Wiseman, L. (2017). *Multipliers: How the best leaders make everyone smarter* (Rev. ed.). Harper Business.

CHAPTER 5

1. University of Oxford. (2025, January 2). *Major new footprint discoveries on Britain's "dinosaur highway."* Retrieved from https://www.ox.ac.uk/news/2025-01-02-major-new-footprint-discoveries-britain-s-dinosaur-highway

2. Deloitte. (2023). *Learning analytics to drive business impact.* Retrieved from https://www2.deloitte.com/us/en/blog/human-capital-blog/2023/learning-analytics-to-drive-business-impact.html

3. Mind Tools for Business. (2024). *Unlocking excellence: The importance of L&D alignment with business strategy.* Retrieved from https://www.mindtools.com/thought-leadership/reports/unlocking-excellence

4. Training Industry, Inc. (2024). *Executive perspectives on the business impact of L&D.* Retrieved from https://trainingindustry.com/research-report-executive-perspectives-on-the-business-impact-of-ld

5. McKinsey Global Institute. (2025). *The data-driven enterprise of 2025: Building the right foundations for a data-driven future.* Retrieved from https://www.mckinsey.com/~/media/mckinsey/business%20functions/mckinsey%20analytics/our%20insights/the%20data%20driven%20enterprise%20of%202025/the-data-driven-enterprise-of-2025-final.pdf

6. Brandon Hall Group. (2020). *Learning measurement study highlights.* Retrieved from https://brandonhall.com/brandon-hall-group-research-highlights-october-17-23-2020

7. Watershed. (2024). *Measure your L&D impact: A data-driven approach*. Retrieved from https://www.watershedlrs.com/resources/research/measure-your-l-and-d-impact-a-data-driven-approach

8. Kirkpatrick, D. L., & Kirkpatrick, J. D. (2006). *Evaluating training programs: The four levels* (3rd ed.). Berrett-Koehler Publishers.

9. Phillips, J. J., & Phillips, P. P. (2002). *The ROI fieldbook: Strategies for implementing ROI in HR and training*. Butterworth-Heinemann.

10. Brinkerhoff, R. O. (2003). *The success case method: Find out quickly what's working and what's not*. Berrett-Koehler Publishers.

11. Thalheimer, W. (2018). *The learning-transfer evaluation model: Sending messages to enable learning effectiveness*. Retrieved from https://www.worklearning.com

12. Morris, H. (2024, May 11). *The golden age of airplane food: How airlines once made meals a selling point*. CNN. Retrieved from https://www.cnn.com/2024/05/11/business/airplane-food-travel/index.html

Chapter 6

1. Harrison, S. (2018). *Thirst: A story of redemption, compassion, and a mission to bring clean water to the world*. Currency.

Chapter 7

1. Stone, B. (2013). *The everything store: Jeff Bezos and the age of Amazon*. Little, Brown and Company.

2. Godin, S. (2003). *Purple cow: Transform your business by being remarkable*. Portfolio.

CHAPTER 8

1. Tye, L. (1998). *The father of spin: Edward L. Bernays and the birth of public relations.* Crown Publishers

2. Verywell Mind. (n.d.). *Reverse mentoring: Benefits, challenges, and tips.* Retrieved from https://www.verywellmind.com/reverse-mentoring-8634501

3. PeopleThriver. (n.d.). *Why leadership development programs fail and how to fix them.* Retrieved from https://peoplethriver.com/why-leadership-development-programs-fail/

CHAPTER 9

1. Schwartz, E. (2000). *The Golden Gate Bridge: Report of the Chief Engineer, 1931–1937.* Golden Gate Bridge Highway & Transportation District.

CHAPTER 10

1. Strode, M. (1903). *Wind-Wafted Wild Flowers.* G.P. Putnam's Sons.

APPENDIX

BRINGING THE COMPASS TO LIFE: PRACTICAL TOOLS FOR MEASUREMENT AND ACTION

In Chapter 4, we introduced the Value Creation Compass—a multidimensional framework for uncovering and amplifying learning's true impact. In Chapter 5, we explored how the Compass can guide better measurement strategies that resonate with stakeholders.

This appendix serves as a practical field guide for putting the Compass into action. It provides tactical tools, detailed frameworks, and simple strategies to help you design, measure, and communicate learning's hidden value with precision.

Before we dive into the full tactical breakdown, we'll introduce one additional tool—the Value Matrix—to complement and strengthen your application of the Compass.

THE VALUE MATRIX: A COMPANION LENS FOR USING THE COMPASS

As you prepare to operationalize the Value Creation Compass, the Value Matrix offers an additional, complementary perspective.

While the Compass orients you toward four strategic areas of value—Empowering People, Driving Business Growth, Building Organizational Resilience, and Delivering Customer Value—the Value Matrix helps you think more tactically across two critical dimensions:

- **Time Horizon** (Short-Term vs. Long-Term)
- **Nature of Impact** (Tangible vs. Intangible)

This simple yet powerful matrix encourages you to consider where your initiatives create value today and where they will create lasting impact tomorrow.

It also ensures you balance measurable outcomes with harder-to-capture, transformational shifts.

By using the Value Matrix alongside the Compass, you create a more comprehensive value story—one that satisfies immediate business needs while building future capability."

THE VALUE MATRIX: A FRAMEWORK FOR UNDERSTANDING IMPACT

In the complex landscape of organizational learning, value isn't one-dimensional; it exists across multiple timeframes and takes both tangible and intangible forms. The Value Matrix provides a comprehensive framework for understanding, designing, and measuring learning's full impact. Like a map that reveals both immediate landmarks and distant horizons, this matrix helps us navigate the complete terrain of value creation.

The Four Quadrants of Value

The Value Matrix organizes learning's impact across two critical dimensions: time horizon (short-term versus long-term) and nature of impact (tangible versus intangible). This creates four distinct quadrants, each capturing different aspects of learning's value.

		Time Horizon	
Impact Type		**Short-Term**	**Long-Term**
Tangible		• Revenue increase • Cost reduction • Error rate decrease • Time saved • Compliance scores	• Market share growth • Industry position • Talent retention • Innovation pipeline
Intangible		• Employee engagement • Team collaboration • Knowledge sharing • Client satisfaction • Workplace trust	• Organizational resilience • Cultural transformation • Brand strength • Learning maturity

(Left axis label: Nature of Impact)

Value Matrix

Understanding Each Quadrant

- *Tangible Short-Term (Immediate Results):* The most visible and easily measured forms of value appear here. These outcomes typically manifest within weeks or months and can be quantified in traditional business metrics. While essential for demonstrating immediate impact, focusing solely on this quadrant misses the deeper value learning creates.

- *Tangible Long-Term (Strategic Outcomes):* This quadrant captures the measurable business results that emerge over time. These outcomes often represent the compound effect of multiple learning initiatives working together. While harder to attribute to specific programs, these results often matter most to senior stakeholders.

- *Intangible Short-Term (Cultural Indicators):* The human side of learning appears here—behavior, engagement, and collaboration shifts that emerge quickly but resist simple measurement. These outcomes, while harder to quantify, often predict future tangible results.

- *Intangible Long-Term (Transformative Impact):* This quadrant manifests the deepest and most lasting forms of value. These outcomes represent fundamental shifts in organizational capability and culture. While the most challenging to measure, they often create the most sustainable competitive advantage.

Understanding these dimensions helps you:

- Design more comprehensive measurement strategies
- Communicate value to different stakeholders effectively
- Balance short-term wins with long-term transformation
- Create more impactful learning initiatives

Consider how a leadership development program might create value across all quadrants:

Tangible Short-Term:

- 20 percent faster project completion rates
- 15 percent reduction in decision-making delays
- 25 percent improvement in team productivity metrics

Tangible Long-Term:

- 40 percent increase in internal promotion rates
- 30 percent reduction in recruitment costs
- 50 percent improvement in succession readiness

Intangible Short-Term:

- Higher team engagement scores
- Improved cross-functional collaboration
- Enhanced psychological safety

Intangible Long-Term:

- Stronger leadership pipeline
- More innovative organizational culture
- Greater change resilience

Using the Matrix for Program Design

The Value Matrix isn't just a measurement tool; it's a design framework that helps ensure learning initiatives create a comprehensive impact. When planning new programs, consider:

1. **Balance Across Quadrants**
   o How does the initiative create value in each quadrant?
   o Are we overemphasizing one type of value at the expense of others?
   o What additional elements could we add to create a more balanced impact?

2. **Stakeholder Alignment**
   o Which quadrants matter most to different stakeholders?
   o How can we communicate value in ways that resonate with each audience?
   o What evidence will different stakeholders find most compelling?

3. **Measurement Planning**
   o What metrics will capture value in each quadrant?
   o How will we track both immediate and long-term impact?
   o What qualitative data will help tell our value story?

Making the Matrix Work for You

To leverage the Value Matrix effectively:

1. Start with the end in mind.

   o Map desired outcomes across all quadrants before designing.

   o Consider both immediate wins and lasting transformation.

   o Align measurement strategies with value-creation goals.

2. Communicate strategically.

   o Highlight different quadrants for different audiences.

   o Connect short-term wins to long-term vision.

   o Use both data and stories to illustrate impact.

3. Design for sustainability.

   o Build feedback loops that span all quadrants.

   o Create mechanisms for capturing emerging value.

   o Plan for both immediate and future measurements.

The Value Matrix transforms how we think about, design for, and measure learning's impact. By understanding value across these dimensions, we move beyond simple metrics to create initiatives that drive both immediate results and lasting transformation.

Remember: The most powerful learning initiatives don't just deliver value in one quadrant; they create ripple effects that touch all four, building immediate credibility while laying the foundations for future success.

With this complementary lens in mind, we now turn to detailed tactical applications of the Value Creation Compass itself—providing measurement frameworks, tools, and strategies for each of its four strategic directions.

THE VALUE CREATION COMPASS

Our journey reveals a crucial truth: Learning creates value through multiple pathways that no single metric can capture. The Value Creation Compass offers a solution by pointing toward four essential directions of impact. This framework helps us move beyond isolated metrics to reveal the interconnected ways learning initiatives strengthen organizational capability. When we align our measurement strategy with these strategic directions, we ensure our evidence resonates with stakeholders' priorities while capturing learning's full contribution to organizational success.

With these measurement principles established, let's explore how they apply to each dimension of learning's impact.

TRUE NORTH: EMPOWERING PEOPLE

The foundation of organizational value lies in human potential. When we develop our people, every other business outcome becomes possible. True north measurement reveals this transformation of individual capability into organizational strength, tracking skill acquisition and the deeper changes that create lasting impact.

1. Strategic Skill Development

Strategic skill development forms the cornerstone of organizational capability. We prepare employees for current challenges and future opportunities through targeted learning initiatives. This dual focus—addressing immediate needs while building future capability—creates a sustainable competitive advantage.

297

Measuring Impact

Domain	Tangible Indicators	Intangible Indicators
Capability Building	• Number of employees certified in new skills • Assessment scores	• Employee confidence in applying new skills • Self-reported readiness
Performance	• Task completion speed improvements (percentage change) • Error rate reductions (percentage change)	• Manager observations of improved performance • Team feedback on skill application
Business Impact	• Efficiency cost savings • Productivity gains	• Process innovation suggestions • Knowledge sharing within teams

Key Measurement Approaches

- **Pre- and Post-Competency Assessments:** Assess baseline proficiency and post-training skill levels using validated tools.

- **Task Accuracy and Speed Metrics:** Monitor improvements in completing tasks faster or with fewer errors.

- **Manager and Peer Feedback:** Conduct structured feedback sessions or surveys to evaluate observable changes in performance.

- **Error Rates:** Track reductions in errors or defects linked to skill gaps addressed by training.

Tools: Skills gap analysis tools like Skillsoft, LMS platforms like LinkedIn Learning, and performance tracking software like Workday.

2. Leadership Development

Leadership development represents one of our most powerful leverage points for organizational transformation. When we strengthen leadership capabilities across all levels, we enable:

- Accelerated innovation
- Enhanced team effectiveness
- Stronger organizational alignment
- Improved decision-making

Measurement Framework

Domain	Tangible Indicators	Intangible Indicators
Leadership Capability	• Promotion rates • Assessment scores	• Confidence ratings • Peer feedback
Team Impact	• Performance improvements (percentage change) • Retention rates under trained leaders	• Engagement scores • Collaboration quality
Organizational Effect	• Project success rates under trained leaders • Cost savings	• Cultural alignment • Cross-functional work

Key Measurement Approaches

- **360-Degree Feedback:** Gather feedback from employees, peers, and senior leadership.

- **Team Performance Metrics:** Track changes in team productivity, satisfaction scores, and collaboration effectiveness.

- **Succession Plan Metrics:** Measure readiness and promotion rates for leadership program participants and development pipeline strength.

- **Leadership Effectiveness Scores:** Use tools like Gallup or customized surveys to track increases in competency areas such as emotional intelligence, decision-making, or communication.

Tools: Hogan and Korn Ferry assessment platforms, team analytics tools like Microsoft Viva Insights, and pulse survey systems.

3. Employee Engagement and Retention

Learning aligned with personal growth and organizational needs creates powerful bonds that strengthen commitment, loyalty, and performance.

Measurement Framework

Domain	Tangible Indicators	Intangible Indicators
Engagement	• Survey scores • Participation rates	• Belonging metrics • Work satisfaction
Retention	• Employee turnover rates (percentage change) • Time-to-fill positions	• Exit interview feedback • Career growth satisfaction
Performance	• Productivity levels • Absenteeism rates	• Discretionary effort • Team morale

Key Measurement Approaches

- **Time to Proficiency:** Measure how quickly new hires achieve full productivity by defining key milestones for proficiency in their roles and tracking their progress. Compare averages across departments or roles to identify trends or areas for improvement.

- **Participation Rates in Development Programs:** Monitor registration, attendance, and completion rates to assess employee interest in growth opportunities.

- **Career Progression Metrics:** Track the number of employees moving into more advanced roles following development initiatives.

- **Retention Rates:** Analyze voluntary turnover rates of employees within their first year, particularly concerning those who participated in onboarding programs versus those who did not. Track retention trends for employees who engage in learning and development initiatives throughout their tenure.

- **Engagement Survey Data:** Use tools like Gallup Q12 or Peakon to gauge engagement levels annually.

- **Onboarding Feedback:** Implement post-onboarding surveys to collect feedback on the effectiveness of the onboarding experience. Focus on areas such as the perceived value of training, adequacy of resources provided, and clarity of role requirements.

Tools: HR systems like BambooHR, Workday, or SAP SuccessFactors to track time to proficiency, alongside performance tracking tools and employee feedback systems like Culture Amp for qualitative insights. Gallup Q12 or Peakon for engagement insights.

When we empower people through learning, we create the foundation for organizational excellence. Strategic skill development closes immediate performance gaps while building future capability. Leadership development catalyzes innovation and strengthens team effectiveness. Engagement and retention programs ensure these capabilities translate into sustained high performance. Together, these elements create a virtuous cycle of individual and organizational growth.

While individual capability forms the foundation, success requires weaving these capabilities into the organizational fabric. As we turn east, we'll explore how personal growth transforms into collective strength, enabling organizations to adapt and thrive amid constant change.

EAST: DRIVING BUSINESS GROWTH

Learning initiatives serve as catalysts for organizational growth and market success. By developing key capabilities in sales effectiveness, market expansion, innovation, and technology adoption, we create direct pathways to increased profitability and market leadership. When we connect learning to strategic business objectives, we transform from a support function into a key driver of competitive advantage.

1. Profitability and Revenue Growth

Learning directly influences financial performance by strengthening crucial business capabilities. From improving sales effectiveness to enhancing negotiation skills and financial decision-making, targeted development programs create clear pathways to revenue growth and improved profitability.

Measurement Framework

Domain	Tangible Indicators	Intangible Indicators
Revenue	• Revenue per trained employee • Sales growth rates	• Sales team confidence • Customer relationship quality
Profitability	• Margin improvements • Cost reduction rates	• Decision-making effectiveness • Strategic thinking capability
Performance	• Deal win rates • Average deal size growth	• Team collaboration quality • Sales process mastery

Key Measurement Approaches

- **Revenue per Employee:** Track the revenue generated by employees who have participated in targeted sales or negotiation training.

- **Deal Closing Rates:** Monitor improvements in the number and quality of deals closed after interventions.

- **Margin Growth:** Assess how profitability improves following financial literacy or pricing strategy training programs.

Tools: Sales enablement platforms like Salesforce, CRM tools, and financial analytics systems.

2. Market Expansion

Successful market expansion requires more than strategic planning; it demands building new capabilities throughout the organization. Learning initiatives prepare employees to:

- Navigate different cultural contexts
- Adapting to local business practices
- Develop market-specific engagement approaches
- Build international relationships

Measurement Framework

Domain	Tangible Indicators	Intangible Indicators
Market Entry	• New market revenue growth • Market share gains	• Market understanding • Team expansion readiness
Customer Acquisition	• New customer growth rates • Acquisition costs	• Cultural adaptation • Customer engagement
Capability	• Partnership success rates • Time-to-market	• Cross-cultural competency • Global mindset

Key Measurement Approaches

- **Customer Acquisition Metrics:** Track increases in new customer growth in regions targeted by market expansion training.
- **Localization Success Rates:** Measure how well employees adapt products or services to meet the needs of new markets.
- **Cross-Cultural Competency Tests:** Evaluate readiness for navigating cultural differences in new regions.

Tools: Cross-cultural training platforms, language training tools like Rosetta Stone, and analytics software for tracking regional performance.

3. Innovation and Creativity

Innovation capability drives sustained competitive advantage. Through learning initiatives, we develop:

- Creative mindsets
- Problem-solving capabilities
- Experimentation comfort
- Implementation capability

Measurement Framework

Domain	Tangible Indicators	Intangible Indicators
Innovation Output	• Product launch rates • Revenue contribution	• Creative confidence • Innovation mindset
Process	• Time-to-market success rates	• Experimentation willingness • Risk tolerance
Impact	• Revenue from solutions • Market share gains	• Customer reception • Team innovation capability

Key Measurement Approaches

- **Idea Submission Rates:** Track increases in the number of ideas submitted post-innovation training.

- **Implementation Success Rates:** Measure the percentage of submitted ideas turned into actionable outcomes.

- **Revenue from New Products or Services:** Analyze the financial contribution of innovations generated by creative thinking programs.

Tools: Collaboration platforms like Miro or Mural and innovation tracking systems.

4. Technology Adoption

In our digital age, effective technology adoption drives organizational success. Learning initiatives help employees:

- Embrace new tools
- Transform work processes
- Enhance outcomes
- Drive digital transformation

Measurement Framework

Domain	Tangible Indicators	Intangible Indicators
Adoption	• Utilization rates • Feature adoption	• Digital confidence • Change readiness
Efficiency	• Productivity gains • Automation rates	• User satisfaction • Workplace comfort
Value Creation	• Cost savings • Digital revenue	• Transformation readiness • Innovation capability

Key Measurement Approaches

- **Adoption Rates:** Use system logs to monitor the number of employees actively using new tools post-training.

- **Error Rate Reductions:** Track decreases in mistakes caused by misuse or underuse of technology.

- **Time-to-Proficiency Metrics:** Assess how quickly employees become proficient in using new systems.

Tools: Digital adoption platforms like WalkMe or Whatfix, analytics platforms, and performance monitoring tools.

The Growth Engine

Business growth emerges from the synchronized development of four key capabilities:

1. **Revenue Generation**
   o Sales effectiveness
   o Margin improvement
   o Performance excellence

2. **Market Leadership**
   o Cultural adaptation
   o Global mindset
   o Local success

3. **Innovation Drive**
   o Creative capability
   o Implementation success
   o Market impact

4. **Digital Excellence**
   o Technology comfort
   o Process transformation
   o Value creation

When these elements work together, organizations don't just grow—they thrive and lead.

While business growth provides clear evidence of learning's impact, sustainable growth ultimately depends on our ability to create exceptional customer value. As we turn south to examine customer value metrics, we'll explore how learning initiatives strengthen our ability to understand, serve, and delight customers. This closing dimension reveals how all our previous measures - people capability, organizational resilience, and business growth - ultimately converge in the customer experience.

BUILDING ORGANIZATIONAL RESILIENCE

BUILDING
ORGANIZATIONAL
RESILIENCE

In today's dynamic business environment, organizational resilience isn't just an advantage—it's a necessity for survival. Through focused learning initiatives, we build this resilience by strengthening four key pillars: operational excellence, cultural alignment, workforce well-being, and organizational agility.

1. Operational Excellence

Excellence in operations grows through systematic learning and development. Investing in operational capabilities enables organizations to achieve and sustain peak performance while building the knowledge base for continuous improvement.

Measurement Framework

Domain	Tangible Indicators	Intangible Indicators
Process Efficiency	• Cycle time reductions • Resource utilization rates	• Process understanding • Workflow confidence
Quality Impact	• Defect reduction rates • First-time-right percentage	• Quality mindset • Problem-solving effectiveness
Business Outcomes	• Cost savings • Productivity gains	• Continuous improvement suggestions • Employee satisfaction

Key Measurement Approaches

- **Process Improvement Metrics:** Track reductions in cycle time, throughput increases, or elimination of bottlenecks in workflows.

- **Error Reduction Tracking:** Measure the frequency and severity of errors before and after training or process changes.

- **Cost-Benefit Assessment:** Calculate time, resources, or materials savings achieved through process improvement efforts and measure efficiency gains.

Tools: Process improvement tools like Six Sigma software, Lean training trackers, and project management tools such as Asana or Trello.

2. Cultural Alignment

Cultural alignment represents one of learning's most profound contributions to organizational resilience. Through targeted development initiatives, we help employees:

- Understand organizational values
- Build collaborative capabilities
- Create high-performing cultures
- Support organizational goals

Measurement Framework

Domain	Tangible Indicators	Intangible Indicators
Value Integration	• Values-based behaviors • Program participation	• Value internalization • Ambassador effectiveness
Collaboration	• Cross-functional success • Team effectiveness	• Collaboration quality • Team cohesion
Organizational	• Employee retention • Productivity gains	• Commitment levels • Cultural satisfaction

Key Measurement Approaches

- **Culture Assessment Surveys:** Conduct pre- and post-training surveys to gauge alignment with company values and cultural expectations.

- **Behavioral Observation Logs:** Track observable behaviors that reflect cultural values, such as collaboration, inclusivity, or accountability.
- **Internal Communication Metrics:** Monitor employee engagement with cultural initiatives or internal campaigns promoting values and goals.

Tools: Platforms like Culture Amp or Glint for tracking cultural alignment and engagement metrics.

3. Workforce Well-Being

Employee well-being has emerged as a crucial driver of organizational resilience. Through targeted initiatives, we help employees build the physical, mental, and emotional capabilities needed to thrive amid increasing workplace demands. This investment in human sustainability creates compound returns through:

- Enhanced performance
- Reduced burnout
- Stronger commitment
- Sustainable growth

Measurement Framework

Domain	Tangible Indicators	Intangible Indicators
Health and Wellness	• Absenteeism rate • Healthcare costs	• Stress indicators • Work-life satisfaction
Engagement	• Productivity levels • Wellness program participation	• Energy levels • Workplace satisfaction
Organizational	• Turnover costs • Healthcare savings	• Team resilience • Organizational climate

Key Measurement Approaches

- **Absenteeism and Presenteeism Rates:** Track changes in attendance patterns before and after implementing well-being initiatives.

- **Employee Well-Being Surveys:** Use targeted surveys to measure shifts in stress levels, work-life balance, and overall resilience.

- **Healthcare Cost Trends:** Analyze reductions in claims related to stress or burnout following well-being programs.

Tools: Well-being platforms like Limeade or Calm for Business and HR analytics tools for tracking health-related metrics.

4. Organizational Agility

Agility has become essential for organizational survival and success. Learning initiatives play a critical role in developing this agility, equipping employees and teams with the capabilities needed to navigate and respond to change effectively. Through targeted development, we help organizations:

- Navigate change effectively

- Seize opportunities quickly

- Overcome challenges confidently

- Drive continuous adaptation

Measurement Framework

Domain	Tangible Indicators	Intangible Indicators
Change Response	• Implementation speed • Adaption success	• Change readiness • Team flexibility
Innovation	• New idea implementation • Time-to-market	• Innovation mindset • Creative confidence
Performance	• Market responsiveness • Competitive advantage	• Agility ratings • Adaptability score

Key Measurement Approaches

- **Change Management Success Rates:** Track how effectively teams complete projects or adapt to change after training.

- **Employee Feedback on Agility:** Conduct surveys to measure employee confidence and readiness to navigate change.

- **Decision-Making Speed Metrics:** Assess how quickly teams pivot strategies or make decisions after agility-building programs.

Tools: Platforms like Prosci Change Management, agile training systems, and collaboration tools like Slack.

When the four pillars of organizational resilience work in harmony, operational excellence, cultural alignment, employee well-being, and organizational agility, they transform challenges into opportunities for growth.

A resilient organization creates the perfect platform for sustainable growth. As we turn west, we'll explore how organizational resilience enables bolder market moves, faster innovation, and stronger financial performance.

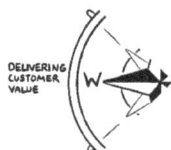

WEST: DELIVERING CUSTOMER VALUE

Customer experience has emerged as the ultimate differentiator in today's market. Through targeted learning initiatives, we develop the capabilities to consistently deliver exceptional customer value. By building customer insight, service excellence, and relationship management capabilities, we enable organizations to strengthen loyalty and enhance market position.

1. Customer Experience Excellence

Creating consistently exceptional customer experiences requires more than just service scripts or procedures. It demands deep customer understanding, genuine empathy, and sophisticated problem-solving capabilities. Learning initiatives help develop these necessary skills while building the confidence to handle complex customer situations effectively.

Measurement Framework

Domain	Tangible Indicators	Intangible Indicators
Satisfaction	• Customer satisfaction scores (CSAT) • Net promoter scores (NPS)	• Service confidence • Quality feedback
Service Delivery	• Resolution time • First contact resolution	• Service quality ratings • Employee empowerment
Impact	• Customer retention • Service costs	• Relationship strength • Service culture

Key Measurement Approaches

- **Customer Satisfaction Scores (CSAT):** Use surveys to track improvements in customer satisfaction following training programs.

- **Net Promoter Score (NPS):** Measure changes in customer loyalty through pre- and post-training surveys.

- **Customer Retention Metrics:** Analyze repeat customer rates before and after service-focused learning initiatives.

Tools: CRM platforms like Salesforce, customer survey tools like SurveyMonkey, and analytics dashboards.

2. Brand Strengthening

A brand lives or dies through customer experience. Through learning initiatives, we help employees:

- Understand brand values
- Deliver brand promises

- Become brand ambassadors
- Create competitive advantage

Measurement Framework

Domain	Tangible Indicators	Intangible Indicators
Brand Perception	• Awareness scores • Preference ratings	• Value alignment • Employee advocacy
Market Impact	• Market share growth • Brand premium	• Trust indicators • Loyalty depth
Engagement	• Customer engagement • Brand interaction	• Relationship quality • Advocacy strength

Key Measurement Approaches

- **Internal Brand Surveys:** Assess employees' understanding and alignment with brand values through targeted surveys.

- **External Perception Metrics:** Track changes in customer advocacy or loyalty metrics after brand-focused training.

- **Engagement Analysis:** Monitor the evolving quality of customer interactions through multiple touchpoints, measuring how brand training influences relationship depth, and evaluating the development of organic brand advocacy among customers.

Tools: Brand tracking platforms such as Brandwatch, analytics tools like PowerBI, and customer feedback systems like Qualtrics XM.

3. Building Customer Trust and Loyalty

Customer trust and loyalty emerge from consistent excellence over time. Learning initiatives help employees:

- Build strong relationships
- Demonstrate integrity

- Create lasting value
- Earn customer confidence

Measurement Framework

Domain	Tangible Indicators	Intangible Indicators
Trust Building	• Trust index scores • Resolution rates	• Relationship strength • Customer confidence
Loyalty Impact	• Customer lifetime value • Repeat purchase	• Emotional connection • Partnership quality
Value Creation	• Share of wallet growth • Customer profitability	• Value alignment • Strategic depth

Key Measurement Approaches

- **Trust Indicators:** Collect qualitative data from customer testimonials highlighting trust and reliability in interactions.

- **Customer Retention Trends:** Monitor repeat business trends following trust-building initiatives and track relationship length.

- **Value Evaluation:** Track how customer relationships deepen over time by measuring wallet share expansion, analyzing profitability trends, and assessing the evolution of strategic partnership opportunities.

Tools: Feedback systems integrated into CRM tools and customer sentiment analysis platforms.

The Customer Value Chain

Creating sustainable customer value emerges from three interconnected capabilities:

1. **Experience Excellence**
   o   Consistent delivery
   o   Problem-solving mastery
   o   Service culture

2. **Brand Strength**
   o   Value alignment
   o   Promise fulfillment
   o   Ambassador development

3. **Trust Leadership**
   o   Relationship depth
   o   Partnership growth
   o   Strategic value

When these elements work in harmony, organizations don't just satisfy customers; they create advocates and partners.

ABOUT THE AUTHOR

Dr. Keith Keating is a globally recognized practitioner, keynote speaker, and author in the field of Learning and Talent Development. As a Chief Learning and Talent Officer, he equips today's talent to thrive in an ever-evolving business landscape. He is the award-winning author of *The Trusted Learning Advisor* and *Hidden Value: How to Reveal the Impact of Organizational Learning*, both guides for elevating the L&D profession.

From high school dropout to doctorate holder from the University of Pennsylvania, Dr. Keating's own transformation is a powerful testament to the life-changing impact of learning. His four academic degrees are more than achievements—they symbolize what's possible when curiosity meets opportunity.

Driven by a calling to champion the learning profession, Dr. Keating believes L&D is the engine of professional growth and organizational excellence. He is a passionate advocate for repositioning L&D practitioners as strategic value creators and trusted advisors. When he's not teaching, writing, or leading enterprise learning strategies, he's helping others recognize—and realize—their own human potential through the power of lifelong learning.

ACKNOWLEDGMENTS

Writing a book is never a solo journey, and *Hidden Value* would not have been possible without the encouragement, support, and belief of so many people along the way. I am deeply grateful.

To my pre-readers—**Dan Pontefract, Ilona Ovas, Jim Krahn, Dr. Kate Hixon,** and **Gwen Mdinaradze**—thank you for your time, insights, and thoughtful feedback. Your perspectives challenged and strengthened this book in ways I could not have achieved alone.

To **Platte Clark**, who supported the original idea and helped bring the seed to life—your initial guidance in this project gave it the foundation it needed to grow.

To **Sean Stowers, Ron Stefanski,** and **Kristy Callahan**—true champions of this work, and even greater champions of me. Your unwavering enthusiasm, support, and encouragement have meant more than I can express. You are the best cheerleaders anyone could ask for.

To **Chris O'Byrne**, who saw the potential in this idea and believed in it enough to publish it—thank you for making this book a reality.

To **Jake Tobin**, whose illustrations brought the book to life in ways words alone never could.

To **Debbie O'Byrne**, whose creativity and vision turned the book cover into something that reflects the heart of this work.

To my partner, **Jorge Steele**, whose patience and encouragement sustained me through the writing process—even as I missed several holidays in what can only be described as a committed affair with my laptop.

To **Adam Stedham**, who believed in me before I did—thank you for seeing what I couldn't yet see in myself.

To my **parents**, whose love and encouragement gave me the foundation to pursue this path.

To my brother, **Rye Keating**—I see you and love you brother. Shine bright.

To the **L&D community**—those who have paved the way before me and those who continue to fight the good fight every day. This work is for those who believe in the power of learning to change lives, who create opportunities for growth, and who dedicate themselves to making an impact. Many of you may feel unseen or hidden in the work you do, but I hope this book helps shine a light on the incredible value you bring to the world.

And to you, the **reader**—thank you for your curiosity, your commitment to growth, and for taking this journey with me. Whether you're here to refine your approach, challenge old ways of thinking, or simply reaffirm what you already know to be true, I appreciate you. My hope is that this book empowers you to amplify your own impact and inspire others along the way.